IMAGINING WAR

PRINCETON STUDIES IN
INTERNATIONAL HISTORY AND POLITICS

SERIES EDITORS

JACK L. SNYDER AND RICHARD H. ULLMAN

A list of titles
in this series appears
at the back of
the book

IMAGINING WAR

FRENCH AND BRITISH MILITARY
DOCTRINE BETWEEN THE WARS

Elizabeth Kier

PRINCETON UNIVERSITY PRESS　　PRINCETON, NEW JERSEY

Library of Congress Cataloging-in-Publication Data

Kier, Elizabeth, 1958—
Imagining war : French and British military doctrine
between the wars / Elizabeth Kier.
p. cm.—(Princeton studies in international history and politics)
Includes bibliographical references and index.
ISBN 0–691–01191–5
1. Military doctrine—France.   2. Military doctrine—
Great Britain.   3. Political stability—France.   4. Political
stability—Great Britain.   5. France—Politics and government—
1914–1940.   6. Great Britain—Politics and government—
1910–1936.   I. Title   II. Series.
UA700.K54   1997   96–46302
355'.033544—dc21   CIP

To my parents, Mary and Porter

Contents

Acknowledgments

MANY FRIENDS and colleagues made this book possible. Above all, I am grateful to Peter Katzenstein, Richard Ned Lebow, and Judith Reppy at Cornell University. Their criticism, support, insight, and sound judgment were invaluable at every stage.

Lynn Eden, Thomas Risse-Kappen, Scott Sagan, Jack Snyder, and Steve Walt read every sentence and commented on most. Their incisive reading forced me to tighten the manuscript, strengthen its substance, and sharpen its argument. And as valuable as Lynn and Thomas were as readers, I am even more indebted to them as friends. Numerous other people have been similarly generous in their help. Deborah Avant, Aaron Belkin, Thomas Christensen, Renée de Nevers, David Dessler, Ted Hopf, Michael Desch, Colin Elman, Marty Finnemore, Michael Howard, Iain Johnston, Peter Liberman, Susan Peterson, Paul Pierson, Janice Thomson, and Pascal Vennesson read with care and insight. Many colleagues at Berkeley also provided advice and encouragement. I would especially like to thank Chris Ansell, Ernie Haas, Ken Waltz, and Steve Weber. Jason Davidson, Brian Lee, Denise Kim, and John Perosio were excellent research assistants.

Samuel Huntington and Stephen P. Rosen at the John M. Olin Institute for Strategic Studies at Harvard University provided the ideal environment in which to translate field work into a manuscript. I profited immensely from my two years at their institute; the intense intellectual interaction improved my arguments and broadened my understanding of international relations theory. The benefits continue. Sam and Steve have created a community among past and present fellows that extends far beyond Cambridge. I am equally grateful to David Holloway and Michael May for the year that I spent as a postdoctoral fellow at the Center for International Security and Arms Control (CISAC) at Stanford University. The mix of scholars from the physical and social sciences produces an exciting environment conducive to research and intellectual growth. Lynn Eden's Social Science Seminar and Scott Sagan's colloquia on organizational theory and national security enriched my understanding of interdisciplinary work and provided a challenging forum for the discussion of my research. One of the advantages of living in the Bay Area is the opportunity to continue to participate in CISAC's activities. For inviting me to present some of these ideas in their colloquia, I would also like to thank Christine Ingebritsen at the University of Washington,

David Lake at UC San Diego, and Richard Rosecrance at UCLA. I thank
those who attended the presentations for their criticism and suggestions.

Financial support from the Western Societies Program and the
MacArthur Foundation Graduate Fellowship in Peace Studies and
International Security at Cornell helped get this project off the ground.
Fellowships from the Council of European Studies; the Social Science
Research Council, Western Europe; and the Institute for the Study of
World Politics supported my research in France and England. The
Abigail R. Hodgen Publication Fund and the Center for German and
European Studies at UC Berkeley also provided financial support.

I would like to thank the following libraries for the use of their col-
lections: the Bibliothèque nationale and the Centre de documentation,
Ecole supérieure de guerre in Paris; the Service historique de l'armée de
l'air and the Service historique de l'armée de terre at Vincennes; and the
British Library and the Imperial War Museum in London. I am also
grateful to Jean Paul Thomas and Georges Tanengbok at the Centre de
sociologie de la défense nationale in Paris for the use of their library and
office space. Special thanks to Len Argue and Francis Pellenc for enrich-
ing my stays in London and Paris, and to Alice Crane, David Gibson,
Klaus-Peter Sick, Gianvittorio Signorotto, and Kris Waldman for their
laughter and support.

As the manuscript reached its final stages, I benefited from the advice
of Malcolm Litchfield at Princeton University Press and from the keen
editorial skills of Janet Mowery. Portions of this book appeared in
"Culture, Politics, and Change in Military Doctrine," in *The Culture of
National Security*, edited by Peter Katzenstein and "Culture and Military
Doctrine: France between the Wars" (*International Security* 19, no. 4,
1996). I thank the publishers for permission to use the material here.

My debt to Jonathan Mercer is the greatest and most difficult to describe. Jon's sharp editorial eye and dogged insistence on rigor within
richness improved this book enormously. He also made it a lot more fun
to write; I thank Jon for everything. I dedicate this book to my parents,
Mary and Porter, who are important reminders that scholarly achievement is built on passion.

IMAGINING WAR

Introduction

CHOICES between offensive and defensive military doctrines affect both the likelihood that wars will break out and the outcome of wars that have already begun. World War I illustrates tragically how offensive military postures can help transform crises into wars, and the French army's rapid and devastating defeat in the opening battles of World War II exemplifies all that can go wrong on the battlefield.[1] Neither the destabilizing consequences of offensive doctrines nor the dangers of poorly designed military doctrines disappeared with the end of the cold war. Defensive doctrines do not erase ethnic hostilities or suspend territorial appetites, but their adoption could help remove one of the structural impediments to cooperation in the post–cold war world. The conduct of wars continues to be vital to state security.

Although we understand the importance of military doctrine, we are less certain why a state chooses to adopt either an offensive or a defensive doctrine. Contrary to conventional wisdom, I argue that doctrinal developments are best understood from a cultural perspective. My focus on ideational factors is the first important theme in this book: there are not definitive meanings attached to an objective empirical reality. As important as material factors may be, they can be interpreted in numerous ways. This view has important implications for understanding much of our political world.[2] We should not assume that interests are self-evident or that political actors from the same socioeconomic groups prefer the same policies across national boundaries. Making sense of how structure matters or what incentives it provides often requires understanding the meanings that actors attach to their material world.

In addition, although civilian decisions are important in developing doctrine, the intervention of civilian policymakers is rarely a carefully calculated response to the external environment. Instead, civilian choices between different military policies often reflect their concerns about the *domestic* balance of power. This is the second principal theme in this book. International relations scholars should not view civilian choices about military policy exclusively in terms of the foreign policy or the strategic requirements of the state. Few issues within the state are more politicized than questions about who has the support and control of the most important component of a state's material power.

Warfare and the army are tied inextricably to the state-building process. Given the latent power of the armed services, state actors seek to ensure that the military's potential strength corresponds to the desired division of power in the state and society. The British Parliament, worried that a strong standing army would once again threaten English liberties, refused to allow the military to become independent of legislative control. The critical divide in France was not between the Parliament and the Crown, as it was in England, but instead reflected class divisions. The conservative, industrial, and landowning classes felt that only a professional army could ensure social stability and the preservation of the status quo, while labor and center-left parties stressed that only a conscript army could guarantee republican liberties.

Civilian decisions about the military may neglect the structure of the international system, but civilians are not oblivious to issues of power. The domestic implications of military policy are especially important in states that have not reached a consensus about the role of the armed services in the domestic arena. If there is controversy, civilians address their concerns about the domestic distribution of power before they consider the structure of the international system. However, if civilians agree about the domestic role of the armed services, their intervention is more likely to reflect systemic imperatives. Either way, civilian preferences are not given; understanding their cultural beliefs about the role of the armed forces in the domestic arena explains why similar actors choose different military policies in different national settings.

But a cultural approach applies to military organizations as well as to civilian policymakers. Decisions within organizations are framed by their perception of the world, and this is particularly true of military organizations. Required to work as a cohesive group and perform what are often selfless tasks, military organizations develop strong collective understandings about the nature of their work and the conduct of their mission, and these organizational cultures influence their choices between offensive and defensive military doctrines.

However, not all military organizations have the same culture. For example, in the early cold war years the German army's view of warfare as a creative activity contrasted sharply with the American army's more managerial approach: a group of German officers criticized American army manuals for what they saw as a dangerous tendency to try to foresee all possible scenarios.[3] Similarly, the ideal officer can range from the modern-day business manager to the warrior or heroic leader.[4] After the War of Independence, for example, the Israeli army avoided the British emphasis on parade ground drills and instead stressed combat skills and the "paratroop spirit," requiring each of its officers to undergo jump training.[5] In other words, militaries' cultures can differ, and these differences often account for their doctrinal preferences. In particular, the military's culture shapes how the organization responds to constraints set by civilian policymakers. The organizational culture alone does not explain doctrinal change; the military's culture intervenes between civilian decisions and military doctrine.

In short, the interaction between constraints set in the domestic political arena and a military's organizational culture determines choices between offensive and defensive military doctrines. Fearful about domestic threats and instability, civilians endorse military options that they think will ensure the preferred distribution of power at the domestic level. These civilian views about the organizational form of the army then constrain a military's choice between an offensive and a defensive doctrine. Other militaries would neither see the same cause-and-effect relationships nor judge the same factors to be important, but constrained within an organization with powerful assimilating mechanisms, the officer corps imagines only certain alternatives.

In arguing that culture significantly affects choices between offensive and defensive military doctrines, this book challenges much of the previous work on the origins of military doctrine. Scholars working within a rationalist perspective credit civilian policymakers with formulating military doctrines that are well suited to the state's strategic environment, yet blame the armed services for adopting offensive doctrines tailored to their organizational interests.[6] This is an inaccurate portrait of the role of the military and of civilians in the development of a state's military doctrine. It exaggerates the wisdom of civilian intervention and the myopia of military organizations. Balance-of-power theory may help us understand some aspects of the choice between an offensive and a defensive doctrine, but the argument that civilian intervention brings doctrine in line with systemic imperatives misses what civilian policymakers often care most about. Similarly, the argument that military organizations— for reasons of size, autonomy, and prestige—inherently prefer offensive doctrines suffers from many of the problems that often limit functional arguments. A functional view of the military fails to capture the variety in organizational preferences that a cultural analysis reveals.

In using a cultural approach to examine the origins of choices between offensive and defensive doctrines, I hope to insert this book into the debate in the social sciences between cultural, constructivist, and sociological analyses and the more conventional structural, functional, and rationalist approaches. Unlike most rationalists, who take preferences as given and interests as self-evident, I show how actors' cultures help define their interests. Independent exigencies such as technology, geography, and the distribution of power are important, but culture is not simply derivative of functional demands or structural imperatives. Culture has an independent causal role in the formation of preferences.

This is especially true in choices between offensive and defensive military doctrines. Understanding military choices requires moving away from functional analyses and toward an analysis of how the culture of a military organization affects its choices. Similarly, civilians do not conceive of the military needs of their state exclusively according to material or structural incentives, but also, and perhaps more important, according to how certain military policies will affect the domestic distribution of power. By adopting a cultural approach, we can better understand the origins of military doctrine, and in doing so, move one step closer to controlling a potential source of international instability.

Plan of the Book

The first two chapters provide the theoretical foundations for my argument about the origins of offensive and defensive military doctrines. Chapter 1 introduces the question of doctrinal change by focusing on Barry Posen's and Jack Snyder's pathbreaking studies on military doctrine. Their work provides powerful explanations for doctrinal change and provoked many of the questions addressed in this book. Nevertheless, Chapter 1 challenges their two central propositions. I first question balance-of-power theory's ability to explain choices between offensive and defensive doctrines and then raise doubts about whether military organizations inherently prefer offensive doctrines.

Chapter 2 presents my argument about the cultural sources of military doctrine. First, I discuss why civilian decisions often respond to concerns about the domestic balance of power and how culture frames these civilian decisions. I explain why the degree of consensus among civilian policymakers about the role of the armed forces in the domestic arena affects both civilian responsiveness to systemic constraints and culture's causal role. Second, Chapter 2 discusses what a military's organizational culture is, why we should expect military organizations to have particularly strong cultures, and how these cultures influence the development of military doctrine.

The empirical chapters will show culture's causal power, but they also illustrate how easily we can confuse cultural factors that have causal autonomy with cultural beliefs that entrepreneurs manipulate for political purposes. Because of this danger, as well as the potential problem that culture may reflect situational factors (and so have no independent causal weight), it is important to design research projects that isolate culture's causal role. Viewing world politics from the perspective of actors—that is, from the inside—does not mean that rigor must be abandoned. Chapter 2 discusses how this study provides a persuasive test of culture's explanatory power. I draw lessons from previous work on political culture and explain the benefits of testing this cultural argument in case studies of doctrinal developments in Britain and France during the interwar period. The chapter closes with a brief discussion of several questions that must be addressed before assigning causal weight to cultural factors.

Chapters 3 and 4 examine doctrinal developments in the French army during the 1920s and 1930s. Chapter 3 begins with a description of the French army's doctrine and then critiques the two most important alternative explanations for the French army's adoption of a defensive doctrine in the 1930s. First, it is wrong to believe that the French army mindlessly reapplied the defensive lessons of the Great War; its preference for a defensive doctrine cannot be explained away as an overreaction to the bloody defensive stalemate of World War I. Throughout the 1920s, the French officer corps adopted offensive war plans, planned for the offensive use of fortifications, and debated the offensive potential of mechanized warfare. Second, despite compelling and well-understood international constraints, French civilians did not behave as expected by balance-of-power theory. When deciding on the army's organizational form, French civilians responded to domestic, not international, threats.

Chapter 4 explains why the sources of French doctrine are found in the interaction between domestic politics and the French army's organizational culture. Two competing groups in French politics had highly developed beliefs about which type of army best suited the desired domestic political arrangements. The Right worried that a conscript army would not guarantee social stability and the preservation of law and order, while the Left feared that a professional army would do the bidding of the conservative and antirepublican forces in society. Driven by this concern, the center and left-wing parties reduced the length of conscription to one year.

This civilian decision to rely on a conscript army did not, however, determine French army doctrine. Civilians established the organizational form of the army, but it was the French army's organizational culture that sealed France's fate. Another military organization could have responded differently to a constraint that, in the French army's eyes, left it with only one option. Despite its experiences with the German army, the French officer corps could not imagine executing an offensive doctrine with short-term conscripts and reserve forces. As a result, after the parliamentary decision to reduce the length of conscription to one year, the French army adopted a defensive doctrine.

Chapters 5 and 6 analyze doctrinal developments in Britain during the same period. Chapter 5 describes British army and air force doctrines and discusses why the conventional explanations for their development are inadequate. British civilians did not ignore systemic imperatives, but balance-of-power theory cannot explain much of their behavior: British civilians did not try to reform their antiquated army to bring it up to continental standards, and by refusing to make a military commitment on the European continent until 1939, civilians did not give the army the one role that would have encouraged it to prepare to meet a German assault. British civilians made these decisions even though they saw Germany as Britain's greatest threat. Similarly, with the exception of Royal Air Force (RAF) support for strategic bombing, few of the British armed services' choices fit the pattern expected by a functional analysis of military organizations. The RAF also developed and adopted a defensive doctrine; the British army stubbornly refused to adopt an offensive doctrine that would have served its parochial interests; and all three services showed startling budgetary restraint.

Chapter 6 presents my argument about the cultural origins of British army doctrine during the 1920s and 1930s. Because British civilians agreed about which types of military organizations best suited Britain's democratic institutions, civilian decisions were more likely to correspond with systemic pressures and constraints. British civilians sought to ensure the strength of Britain's "fourth arm of defense"—the British economy. Fearful that a weak economy would invite aggressive action in peacetime and cripple Britain's mobilization capacity during war, British civilians kept British defense expenditures to a minimum. Tight civilian control of military expenditures also reflected domestic concerns: in the government's eyes, British domestic stability could ill afford rampant inflation and labor unrest. When it came to choosing strategic policies, British civilians invariably chose the cheapest alternative.

Fears about disrupting the domestic distribution of power also shaped civilian decisions about the basic form of the military, and those decisions later constrained doctrinal developments. British civilians feared that a professional military caste might threaten English liberties; London was content to retain an amateur army befitting an imperial outpost. This reluctance to bring the army up to continental standards meant that the British army had an organizational culture reminiscent of nineteenth-century warfare. Although not a threat to parliamentary sovereignty, the basic assumptions, values, norms, beliefs, and formal knowledge in the British army's culture made it unable to make sense of the revolutionary changes taking place on the modern battlefield. Faced with what it perceived as few options, the British army adopted a defensive doctrine.

Chapter 7 reviews my argument and returns to the evidence of culture's explanatory power. We see that the cultural variables presented are not epiphenomenal or used instrumentally by political actors. We can have confidence that culture affects choices between offensive and defensive doctrines. What we do not know and what this book does not address are the sources of the military's culture itself. I discuss some of the possible sources of a military's culture and why lessons learned from research on organizations in the private sector may not be appropriate for understanding the origins of a military's culture. This chapter closes with a discussion of how to change a military's culture.

1

Structure, Function, and Military Doctrine

MANY SCHOLARS have sought to understand the origins of, and more frequently, the barriers to doctrinal change in the military.[1] These analysts usually examine a specific example of military doctrine and explore the role that technology, defeat in war, and civilian intervention play in doctrinal change.[2] However, the publication of Barry Posen's and Jack Snyder's studies focused attention on the sources of military doctrine.[3]

Posen and Snyder's books have become classic studies of the origins of offensive and defensive military doctrines. Although they disagree on the role of domestic politics and the explanatory weight of organizational factors, Posen and Snyder agree on two major points: (1) that civilian intervention is good because it corresponds to the objective strategic interests of the state, and (2) that military organizations, for reasons of autonomy, resources, certainty, and prestige, inherently prefer offensive doctrines. Civilians are trumpeted as the champions of the national interest and the principal architects of well-integrated military plans. The military is portrayed as pursuing its organizational interests and adopting offensive doctrines that may be poorly integrated with the state's grand strategy.

This chapter challenges both propositions. Although realism and a functional view of military organizations contribute to an understanding of the sources of military doctrine, neither adequately accounts for choices between offensive and defensive doctrines. Both provide explanations that are indeterminate of choices between offensive and defensive military doctrines and fail to capture the sources of civilian and military interests in doctrinal developments. By focusing on the theoretical limitations of realist and functional explanations, this chapter sets up the empirical critiques in the case study chapters.

Civilians and the International System

Realism expects systemic constraints and opportunities to shape civilian understandings of state goals and civilian intervention in the development of doctrine.[4] The parochial interests of the military may govern doctrinal decisions in low-threat environments, but as the international system becomes more threatening, balance-of-power theorists expect civilians to intervene in doctrinal developments, overrule the military's self-interested choices, and realign military doctrine in accordance with systemic imperatives. For example, Posen argues that civilian intervention in doctrinal developments best explains the Royal Air Force's adoption of an air defense system in the 1930s. According to Posen, although the air force championed strategic bombing (an offensive doctrine) as the key to British security, British civilians responded to the growing German threat in the 1930s by forcing the RAF to develop the innovative defensive doctrine that later won the Battle of Britain.[5] Similarly, Snyder argues that the absence of civilian intervention allows the military to adopt self-serving doctrines poorly suited to the state's strategic environment. Snyder claims, for example, that the lack of civilian control in the early 1900s allowed two regional commanders in Russia to adopt an overly ambitious and ill-conceived offensive war plan.[6]

Both Posen and Snyder believe that the international system provides accurate cues for civilian intervention in the development of doctrine.[7] Posen argues that civilians actively respond to systemic constraints, and Snyder, although more cautious, agrees that certain doctrinal responses correspond to particular systemic conditions. Snyder argues that military biases shape doctrinal choices, but he also maintains that the more ambiguous the strategic incentives, the greater the impact of institutional biases.[8] If systemic directives are transparent, then a rational doctrine—one that is well attuned to international considerations—results.

This argument about the role of civilians and the international system exaggerates the power of systemic imperatives and misses what civilian policymakers often care most about. First, as many realists recognize, the structure of the international system is indeterminate of choices between offensive and defensive doctrines. Second, even during periods of international threat, civilians rarely intervene in doctrinal developments, and when they do, their decisions are often damaging to the state's strategic objectives. Third, as discussed in Chapter 2, civilian intervention is often a response to domestic political concerns, not to the distribution of power in the international system.

The International System Is Indeterminate

Although revisionist states require offensive doctrines, both offensive and defensive doctrines can defend the status quo. Even the prospect of fighting a two-front war provides several alternatives. The Schlieffen Plan's double offensive is one possibility, but as Jack Snyder pointed out, Germany could also have chosen "a positional defense of the short frontier in the west, combined with either a counteroffensive or a positional defense in the east."[9] Some military analysts claim that even Israel is not compelled to adopt an offensive doctrine. For example, Ariel Levite argues that the assertion that Israel's geostrategic position demands an offensive doctrine is "flawed principally because it fails to distinguish between choice and compulsion."[10] The Israeli army did adopt an offensive doctrine, but Israel's position in the international system did not require this choice.

A state's position in the international system is indeterminate of choices between offensive and defensive military doctrines. For example, France's relative weakness during the interwar period led to the endorsement of an offensive orientation during the 1920s and a defensive orientation in the 1930s. Neither option was wrong-headed or ignorant of systemic constraints: both were rational responses to relative weakness. In the 1920s, the French sought to avoid a long war by striking offensively and quickly terminating the war before Germany could mobilize its superior economic strength. In the 1930s, the French responded to Germany's relative strength with a defensive doctrine. Their reasoning again makes sense: hold off the German assault long enough to allow for the injection of allied support. In other words, both offensive and defensive doctrines may correspond to the systemic imperatives of a relatively weak state.[11]

The indeterminacy of the international system makes clear why dramatic doctrinal shifts can occur in the absence of systemic variation, or why changes in the international system do not necessarily lead to shifts in states' doctrinal orientations. Although both the French and the British armies shifted from offensive to defensive doctrines between 1914 and 1939, conditions in the international system remained relatively static from one period to the next. Similarly, the U.S. Army's official endorsement of Airland Battle in 1982 changed American doctrine from a defensive to an offensive orientation, despite the lack of significant transformation in the international system.[12] Conversely, although India's strategic position changed dramatically upon independence in 1947, the Indian army did not begin to shed the doctrinal orientation of its British predecessor until the early 1980s.[13]

Civilian Intervention Is Unusual and Can Hinder the Development of Doctrine

During the interwar period, French and British civilians were not active participants in the formation of military doctrine. Their decisions were important, but they did not directly choose the doctrinal orientation of the military. The French Parliament's decision in 1928 to reduce the length of conscription to one year affected doctrinal developments, but even after Hitler's rise to power French civilians did not directly choose the army's doctrine. Similarly, the British Cabinet and the parliament did not concern themselves with army doctrine. In his study of French, German, and Russian military doctrine before World War I, Snyder also found that civilians played only an indirect role in military planning.[14]

In addition, civilian intervention can be counterproductive.[15] Given the antagonistic relations between civilians and the military in France during the 1930s, civilian intervention in doctrinal development was probably the best way to guarantee that a change would *not* occur. In 1936, Charles de Gaulle, then a colonel in the French army, sought the aid of a parliamentarian, Paul Reynaud, in his quest for the adoption of an offensive doctrine. As a result, de Gaulle's reputation within the army plummeted: as Edward Pognon explains, "Rare, very rare are those among [de Gaulle's] comrades who were not scandalized by his appeal to a politician."[16] The following year the high command dropped de Gaulle from the promotion list in part to demonstrate its displeasure with his ideas and his appeal for civilian support.[17] Far from fostering doctrinal innovation, civilian intervention frustrated de Gaulle's efforts.

Whereas balance-of-power theory anticipates that civilian intervention will promote doctrine well attuned to systemic imperatives, civilian choices disrupted the French air force's fledgling development. During the 1920s and early 1930s, the French air force focused on ground support and especially reconnaissance for the army. It debated the value of strategic bombing, but not until the civilian Pierre Cot became the minister of air in 1936 did its emphasis shift decisively from cooperation with the army to strategic bombing missions. Yet civilian support for strategic bombing did not last; the next year Cot shifted the air force's priority back to ground support, and his successor in 1938, Guy La Chambre, reinforced Cot's new position.[18] This inconsistency and instability in the air force's development, caused largely by civilian intervention, contributed to disarray in the French air force. When World War II began, the French air force's primary mission was ground support, but it did not have a well-developed doctrine or tactics, and it lacked the appropriate materiel.[19]

Hitler's Germany: An Easy Case for Realism

Doctrinal development in Germany before World War II should be an easy case for a realist analysis. Hitler actively participated in military affairs, and his foreign policy objectives provide a determinant prediction: revisionist states need offensive doctrines.[20] In fact, during the 1960s, several English historians argued that Hitler and the army high command recognized that Germany could not fight a long war and, as a result, developed a special strategy designed to gain quick, decisive victories.[21] This coordination between social and economic constraints and military doctrine is evidence, Posen argues, of the wisdom of civilian intervention. Recognizing the constraints facing Germany, Hitler imposed the blitz-krieg doctrine on a reluctant army.

But this conclusion exaggerates Hitler's strategic vision. Hitler sup-ported the army's efforts, and as John Mearsheimer has detailed, Hitler's decision to adopt the blitzkrieg battle plan in 1940 was decisive, but civilian intervention did not cause the German army to adopt an offen-sive doctrine.[22] As Robert O'Neill and Williamson Murray argue, the German army supported the development of offensive armored warfare, and Hitler remained in the background of doctrinal developments until January 1938. The German high command financed the development of armored forces and allowed the advocates of mechanized warfare to de-velop their ideas and train forces largely free of outside interference.[23] As early as 1929, tank warfare dominated the modernization of the German army. A historian of the German army, Michael Geyer, explained that "the general staff, led by the 'Young Turks' around Stülpnagel and Blomberg and supported by specialists like Bockelbert (procurement, weapons development) as well as Heinz Guderian (weapons inspec-torate) wholeheartedly embraced the concept of decision-oriented, oper-ationally independent tank warfare." In addition, recent research by British, American, and German scholars questions the degree of coordi-nation between German political, economic, and military strategy. Mur-ray explains that "in reality, almost no connection existed between Ger-many's economic problems and the development of *blitzkrieg* warfare." Indeed, research on German economic conditions before the outbreak of war suggests that Hitler had little understanding of the potential rela-tionship between economics and military doctrine.[24]

I am not arguing that civilian decisions are unimportant in the devel-opment of doctrine. However, as Chapter 2 explains, civilian decisions on military policy often respond to concerns about the balance of power in the *domestic* arena, not in the international system. For example, the French Parliament's decision in 1928 to reduce the term of conscription to one year constrained subsequent doctrinal developments in the French army, yet this decision responded to domestic concerns, not to France's weak position, a resurgent Germany, or the needs of alliance diplomacy.

The Military and Offensive Doctrines

Posen and Snyder expect civilians to wisely adjust military doctrine to conform with national objectives, but they see military organizations choosing doctrines that serve the military's parochial interests. In particular, they argue that offensive doctrines are powerful tools in a military organization's pursuit of greater autonomy, resources, certainty, and prestige.[25] For example, Posen argues that the greater complexity involved in the execution of offensive doctrines justifies increased expenditures, and Snyder claims that quick, decisive, and offensive campaigns enhance the army's prestige and self-image. According to a functional logic, these beneficial consequences are the essential cause of that behavior. Militaries prefer offensive doctrines because they expect to benefit from their adoption. Stephen Van Evera concludes that militaries "may adopt defensive strategies if civilians demand them, but without civilian direction they almost invariably purvey offensive ideas, and develop offensive solutions."[26]

The argument that military organizations inherently prefer offensive doctrines is surprisingly weak. Offensive doctrines often serve the interests of military organizations, but we cannot conclude from this that military organizations choose offensive doctrines because they have this effect. Many of the goals that are posited as leading to the choice of offensive doctrines can be satisfied with either an offensive or a defensive doctrine. Even if these goals were not indeterminate, military organizations sometimes forfeit their attainment. This has happened even when choosing a particular doctrine would have increased a service's budget. Both the British and French cases provide illustrations of military organizations rejecting doctrinal options that could have brought them greater resources. Finally, without civilian prompting, military organizations sometimes ostracize officers who advocate a more *offensive* orientation, and instead willingly and dogmatically endorse *defensive* doctrines.

The Indeterminacy of Functional Logic

Both offensive and defensive doctrines can satisfy many of the goals held by military organizations.[27] Posen and Snyder argue that the military's desire to reduce uncertainty encourages the adoption of offensive doctrines, but defensive doctrines can also structure the battlefield and reduce the need to improvise. Before World War II, an integral aspect of the French army's defensive doctrine was what the French termed *la bataille conduite*—the "methodical battle." Instead of allowing for initiative and flexibility, *la bataille conduite* was tightly controlled and all units adhered to strictly scheduled timetables. As a German officer explained, "French tactics are essentially characterized by a systematization which seeks to anticipate and account for any eventuality in the smallest detail."[28] The French army's *defensive* doctrine maximized the centralization of command and reduced spontaneity to a minimum. During the same period, the British army's defensive doctrine also stressed tight control over the battlefield. Similarly, military organizations can use defensive doctrines to maximize their autonomy—in particular their freedom from civilian interference. For example, the French army's endorsement of a defensive doctrine after 1929 is partly attributable to its being part of larger package that allowed the army to retain what it most treasured, a small (and relatively autonomous) professional force.

Air forces have exploited strategic bombing (an offensive doctrine) to ensure their independence. During the 1920s and 1930s, the RAF manipulated the quest for an offensive doctrine in its crusade for independent status, and the French air force used the call for strategic bombing to deflect attacks from the army and the admiralty on its organizational autonomy. The desire for autonomy cannot, however, account for the extent to which each air force embraced strategic bombing. While the French air force fought bitterly and unsuccessfully for its independence, French airmen only half-heartedly endorsed the offensive doctrine that, according to a functional argument, could have furthered their quest for autonomy. In contrast, the RAF gained institutional autonomy relatively easily but remained enamored of strategic bombing long after it had cemented its independent status as the third service. The desire for autonomy (and thus an offensive doctrine) also cannot explain why the RAF, attached as it was to strategic bombing, was willing to develop a defensive doctrine.

In short, because both offensive and defensive doctrines can have beneficial consequences for a military organization's aggregate autonomy, resources, certainty, and prestige, functional reasoning can shed little light on why a particular doctrine is chosen. To argue that the consequence of a behavior is the principal cause of that behavior leads one to expect that if one behavior does not have the desired consequences then the actor will try another behavior. In other words, the argument that the military's desire for autonomy causes the adoption of an offensive doctrine leads to the expectation that the military will also adopt a defensive doctrine if it can bring the organization greater autonomy. This indeterminacy is inherent in functional logic: it is the presence of similar consequences, but different actions leading to those consequences, that suggests a functional explanation.[29]

Forfeited (Functional) Goals

Even if the desire for greater autonomy, resources, certainty, and prestige were not indeterminate of doctrinal choice, many questions would remain unanswered. For example, when military organizations could gain greater resources or autonomy by adopting offensive doctrines, they do not always do so. Throughout the 1930s the French army had access to the ideas of offensive mechanized warfare and freedom from civilian interference. They also wanted autonomy from civilians: with the recurrent instability of the Third Republic, the rise of the Left, and the outbreak of the Spanish Civil War, the army became increasingly fearful of the republic. If military organizations seek autonomy by adopting an offensive doctrine, the French army should have done so then. Instead, it became increasingly committed to a defensive doctrine.

Still more surprising from a functional perspective is the budgetary behavior of the British army. Throughout the 1920s and 1930s, the British army was the lowest (financial) priority among the British armed services. The army command was familiar with the concepts of offensive mechanized warfare and had even led its development during the 1920s. Moreover, British civilians did not intervene in doctrinal decisions or advocate the adoption of a defensive doctrine. Although it is hard to imagine a military organization better positioned to behave as hypothesized by a functional analysis, the British army ignored this opportunity and adopted a defensive doctrine.[30]

The Desire for Greater Resources

The proposition that the desire for greater autonomy, resources, certainty, and prestige drives doctrinal developments would also leave us unable to explain why militaries sometimes seem unconcerned about enhancing their autonomy, structuring the battle, or, surprisingly, increasing their size and resources. Although the pursuit of the latter goal favors offensive doctrines (most military analysts claim that successful execution of an offensive strike requires at least a three-to-one advantage), military organizations sometimes ignore this goal. Even in times of financial stringency, military organizations may be less concerned about increasing their budget than is commonly thought.

We already saw that the British army ignored the financial benefits that adopting an offensive doctrine could have brought. The British air force also placed other goals above the attainment of more resources. When leading military and civilian decision makers met in the mid-1930s to plan British rearmament, the RAF submitted modest budget requests, arousing the ire of the Foreign Office, which believed that the RAF was underestimating the strength of the Luftwaffe. The RAF did not think that they should, or that the Germans would, expand at a rate that would jeopardize efficiency. The RAF placed a higher premium on efficiency than on increasing its resources, and it assumed that the German air force would do likewise. In fact, the Air Staff argued that the Foreign

Office was placing altogether too much emphasis on the threat of a German air attack, and the programs eventually adopted exceeded what the services themselves considered necessary.[31] This reluctance to submit excessive, or in the Foreign Office's mind, adequate, budget requests, was equally true of the Royal Navy, leading one participant to comment that he found it "curious how, all through, the Chiefs of Staff have been the moderating influence."[32]

We see a similar pattern in Britain in the early part of the twentieth century and in France during the 1930s. As first sea lord from 1904 to 1910, Admiral John Fisher *initiated* reductions in the navy's budget by cutting back the number of small cruisers and destroyers in the Royal Navy. These reforms aroused controversy and led Fisher to comment to the king, "If everybody had everything that was desirable, the Navy Estimates would be a hundred millions!"[33] Similarly, in 1936 the Popular Front government concluded that the chief of the French General Staff's budget request for 9 billion francs was insufficient; Prime Minister Léon Blum and Minister of War Edouard Daladier allocated 5 billion francs more than General Maurice Gamelin asked for.[34] In those instances, civilians, not the military, requested larger defense budgets.

The proposition that military organizations inherently prefer offensive doctrines also has difficulty explaining the RAF's development of both an offensive *and* a defensive doctrine. If strategic bombing would bring autonomy and prestige to this new service, why would the air force also support the development of a defensive doctrine, especially given civilian support for strategic bombing? Laying the groundwork for the air defense system did not give the air force a powerful justification for greater resources.

Militaries Choose Defensive Doctrines

Finally, the generalization that military organizations prefer offensive doctrines cannot explain why some military organizations adopt, and at times dogmatically embrace, defensive doctrines. They do this on their own initiative, without civilian prodding, and despite adequate knowledge of and resources for the development of an offensive doctrine. Although Posen explains the French army's adoption of a defensive doctrine in the 1930s as partly the result of the army's awareness of civilian preferences for a defensive doctrine, civilians did not intervene in doctrinal developments to force a defensive doctrine upon a reluctant high command. Indeed, from the mid-1930s, civilians voiced support for a more offensive orientation. For example, in 1936 Blum and Daladier encouraged Gamelin to develop some armored divisions with offensive capabilities.[35] Nevertheless, the French army ignored these calls and instead became committed to a defensive doctrine. Similarly, although Posen argues that during the postwar period "British military organizations were allowed to pursue whatever parochial doctrine they wanted,"[36] the British army adopted a defensive doctrine and marginalized those officers who advocated the offensive use of massed tanks.

The British navy in the early twentieth century provides another example of a military organization preferring a defensive doctrine. Although some within the navy disagreed, Admiral Fisher adopted the defensive naval doctrine first outlined in the *Green Pamphlet* in 1906: the navy would no longer strike out offensively and destroy the adversary's fleet but would instead engage in combat only if the enemy threatened British communications. One of the authors of the *Green Pamphlet* explained that it was "an amateurish notion that defence is always stupid or pusillanimous, leading always to defeat, and that what is called the 'military spirit' means nothing but taking the offensive."[37] Indeed, British civilians often argued that navy doctrine was too passive. As first lord of the Admiralty in 1916, Winston Churchill supported a more aggressive posture, and in the House of Lords in 1916, Lord Sydenham called for a change in navy doctrine, arguing that "a defensive naval policy" was "the absolute negation of all the finest traditions of the British Navy."[38] Yet the Royal Navy had chosen just that—a defensive doctrine.

These examples do not indicate that military organizations prefer defensive doctrines or that organizational goals do not influence military choices. Offensive doctrines can benefit military organizations (as can defensive doctrines), but this does not mean that the beneficial consequences determine the outcome. Even if the desire for greater autonomy, resources, certainty, and prestige were determinate of doctrinal choice, we could not argue that these goals cause the adoption of offensive doctrines without documenting how the pursuit of these goals initiates the adoption of such a doctrine.[39] Otherwise we cannot know that the doctrine was not adopted for another reason (perhaps even a dysfunctional one), but nevertheless brings benefits with it. In fact, the presence of functional equivalents that can also aid the military's attainment of its goals points to the possibility that culturally derived preferences infuse the exercise of choice between organizational alternatives.

Organizations differ—in their culture and in their relation to their external environment—and failure to differentiate among them leads to an inability to account for differences in their behavior. *We cannot deduce military organizations' interests from their functional needs.* In other words, we cannot explain a military's choice of an offensive or a defensive doctrine based on a posited goal of greater autonomy, resources, certainty, and prestige. As Chapter 2 argues, the military's organizational culture shapes what it perceives to be in its interest.

What has often emerged from earlier studies of the determinants of military doctrine is a black-and-white portrait of the role of the military and civilians: military organizations pursue parochial interests; civilians promote the national interest. But this depiction is inaccurate and misleading. Military organizations do not inherently prefer offensive doctrines; their preferences vary and are a function of their organizational cultures. Similarly, making sense of civilian intervention in doctrinal development requires going beyond a consideration of the structure of the international system; we must also understand how concerns about domestic power influence civilian policymakers.

My argument that conditions in the international system do not determine doctrinal developments may strike some readers as counterintuitive. If military doctrine, designed to defeat an adversary's armed forces, is not shaped by the international system, one might reasonably ask what would be. I argue that it is counterintuitive to assume that military policy would respond to the objective conditions in the international arena. Military doctrine is about state survival, but it is also about the allocation of power *within* society. After all, what could be more politicized than questions about who within the state has the support and control of the armed services? Designing military policy requires that civilians address their concerns about the distribution of power at the domestic level.

My argument that military organizations, constrained by their own culture, ignore international imperatives may seem more intuitive. Many analysts argue that military organizations pursue their parochial interests. If we are to categorize a military's interests in a way that leads to accurate explanations of its doctrinal choices, we must recognize that different militaries view the world differently. Deducing organizational interests from functional needs is too general and too imprecise. Understanding the variation in organizational behavior requires an analysis of cultural characteristics and how these constrain and shape the choice between an offensive and a defensive doctrine.

Civilians and the military do not respond to structural or functional demands. While civilians interpret military policy according to how it influences power politics at the domestic level, the military reacts to civilian decisions through the means available in its culture; understanding the interests that civilians and the military bring to doctrinal decisions requires taking into account the cultural dimension of domestic politics and organizational life.

2

Culture and Military Doctrine

THE CHOICE between an offensive and a defensive military doctrine is best understood from a cultural perspective. Systemic imperatives are important to the development of doctrine, but conditions in the international system are not the sole or even the primary factor guiding civilian intervention. Instead, civilians' cultural understanding of the role of military force in the domestic arena governs their participation in developing doctrine. And because the military plays a pivotal role in building and maintaining the state, the domestic implications of military policy often shape civilian decisions. In designing military policy, civilians address their concerns about domestic threats and stability, such as whether the proposed military policy will threaten civilian control or the army's ability to execute its domestic responsibilities. However, once civilians reach a consensus about these issues, their decisions are more likely to correspond with systemic imperatives.

Although civilian decisions set the framework for doctrinal developments, they rarely determine doctrine. Instead, the interaction between the constraints set in the domestic political arena and the military's organizational culture shapes the choice between offensive and defensive military doctrines. Understanding why military organizations behave differently requires an analysis of the organizations' cultures and how their basic assumptions, values, norms, beliefs, and formal knowledge shape the collective understandings of the organizations' members. We cannot assume that most military organizations, most of the time, prefer offensive military doctrines; what the military perceives to be in its interest is a function of its culture. However, the military's culture alone does not explain changes in military doctrine; the military's culture intervenes between civilian decisions and doctrinal choices.

Civilians and the Domestic Balance of Power

> The true objective of troops is to give the king
> power that is independent of the people.
>   (Madame de Stael)

Whereas military doctrine is about state survival, military policy is also about the allocation of power within the state. One does not have to be a Marxist to recognize the truth in Mao's statement that "political power grows out of the barrel of a gun." Political liberals are intensely aware of the tension between building an army as an instrument of foreign policy and ensuring that the army does not usurp the state's power. Civilians want a military establishment that reflects and upholds their desired polity. The U.S. Constitution ensured that the individual states would retain control of their militias and Congress control over defense expenditures.[1] Even after the establishment of a state, the domestic implications of military policy continue to haunt policymakers. At the beginning of the cold war, Congress' fear of a "Prussian-style" general staff helped block Truman's efforts to create a tightly unified defense establishment.[2]

In designing military policy, civilians' concerns about power politics are often at the domestic level. In the first half of the nineteenth century, for example, many European states maintained military institutions that answered their concerns about domestic instability, not external threats. In the 1890s, the relatively poor state of the Austrian army corresponded with the Magyars' fears about the domestic repercussions of a strong army, and not to the requirements of Austria's position in the international system.[3] Similarly, in 1888 the Stanhope memorandum ranked the British army's missions: aid to the civil power came first, before home defense or defense of the empire.[4] This concern about the domestic repercussions of military policy has not disappeared from Europe, where contemporary debate about the elimination of conscript armies often focuses on the latent domestic power of a professional army, not the requirements of national defense.[5]

At the founding of the United States, James Madison declared that "a standing military force, with an overgrown Executive will not long be safe companions to liberty. The means of defense against foreign danger have been always the instruments of tyranny at home." Samuel Adams concurred: "It is a very improbable supposition, that any people can long remain free, with a strong military power in the very heart of their country."[6] These concerns persisted. After the Spanish-American War, many Americans resisted attempts to create a general staff modeled after the Prussian system because they worried that the system, though militarily efficient, was inimical to American democratic values.[7] In 1894, when Congress defeated an attempt to increase the size of the U.S. Army, a congressman remarked that the bill, "never had a chance of becoming law. There seems to be a deep-seated conviction that 30,000 men, enlisted from citizens of the Republic, would be a menace to 70,000,000 of their fellow citizens."[8]

Concerns about the domestic ramifications of military policy also drive civilian decisions in the developing world. Why, for example, would Algeria, a country that won independence through a protracted guerrilla struggle, develop a professional, modern, high-technology army and weed out the very military leaders who had successfully fought the French army while retaining many of the soldiers who had once served with the French army? Why didn't Algeria develop a people's army similar to that adopted in Yugoslavia, especially given government rhetoric that the Algerian army was a "popular army" and government advice to other Arab countries to use a "people's war" against Israel?[9]

The answer lies in domestic political battles, not foreign threats. In the years immediately following independence in 1962, the future president of Algeria, Houari Boumedienne, used the development of a professional army to challenge the power of then President Ben Bella and the Wilaya commanders (the leaders of guerrilla forces in Algeria). In response, Ben Bella attempted to create popular militias staffed by former guerrillas that could balance Boumedienne's rising power, but those efforts ultimately failed.[10] In June 1965, Boumedienne ousted Ben Bella, subordinated the militias to the regular army and consolidated the development of a professional modern army.

The same pattern is repeated in Latin America. Civilian governments' desire to create a military force capable of counterbalancing the military's power, not external threats, drove the widespread development of popular militias—as it had in England four hundred years previously.[11] Similarly, after the social revolution in Bolivia in 1952, the government initially reduced the size of the army, but fear of the power of the still-armed tin miners triggered the reconstruction of the military. Finally, while many armed services keep division-size forces together for training purposes, the Brazilian army is often divided into regiments and battalions and spread throughout the country to better control the population.[12] In all these cases, domestic political considerations trumped strategic ones.

Even something as seemingly innocuous (but militarily important) as the color of army uniforms can become a political issue if it is seen as favoring some domestic actors over others. French soldiers did not charge forward to their slaughter in World War I dressed in bright, colorful uniforms because the French army was ignorant of the advantages of camouflage khaki or green; the French army had been studying the need to shift to more subtle colors since 1899 and had already outfitted three regiments in 1911 with green uniforms. However, right-wing politicians did not support this reform, whatever its value for military efficiency. The conservative newspaper *L'écho de Paris* argued that the less targetworthy colors were part of a masonic plot against the army: "The camouflaged uniform . . . seems calculated to diminish [the army's] already compromised prestige." By 1912 the camouflaged uniforms had been discarded.[13] In short, individual states, or different groups within the state, often tailor military policy to their preferred domestic situation.

The Cultural Context of Military Policy

Questions about the distribution of domestic power are not about interests in the way that is commonly understood. A structural analysis would not accurately predict which groups in society would prefer which types of military policy. Actors believe that the meanings they attach to certain policies directly reflect reality, but their interpretation is often not the only way to see the world or their interests. We cannot just assume that all left-wing parties prefer the same policies and that all right-wing factions have similar interests; policy preferences are not reducible to material conditions. They must be understood within their cultural context.

For example, on the basis of a study of the development of railroads in the United States, Britain, and France, Frank Dobbin argues that a country's beliefs about rationality and self-interest influence how different social actors define their interests. Although we might expect all railroad companies to welcome public financing of any sort, the railroads in France, Britain, and the United States had very different reactions to the offer. Most American railroad companies preferred state and local financing to federal support. The French, however, viewed the American choice as inefficient and irrational. Instead, they opted for public support from Paris, not regional or local financing. The British believed that any type of public financing would be inefficient. Dobbin concludes, "At most points in railroad history, in fact, we could have predicted a person's policy preferences much better by knowing his nationality than by knowing his relationship to the means of production."[14]

Margaret Weir makes a similar argument to explain the relative success of Keynesian ideas in Britain and the United States in the 1930s and 1940s. Documenting the political power of certain socioeconomic groups would not, she argues, explain the adoption of Keynesian policies. In Britain, business and financial groups accepted Keynesian policies relatively quickly; to them, Keynesianism denoted freedom from excessive intervention. However, in the United States business and financial interests zealously opposed these new economic policies because they saw them as opening the door to excessive government intervention. Weir says, "If we want to make sense of the roles that social interests played in accepting or rejecting Keynesian policies, we must study more closely the meaning of these policies in each national setting, not simply assume policy preferences on the basis of 'objective' economic interests."[15]

What is true for many industrial or economic issues is equally true for military policy. A structural analysis would not lead to accurate predictions about which actors would prefer which types of military policy. For example, the French and the Americans attached different meanings to the battleship. While the U.S. electorate saw battleships as the "guardians of liberty," the French Left saw them as tools of the business elite and symbols of the capitalists' monopolistic control of the steel industry.[16]

Similarly, while both the British Left and Right supported the development of the Royal Air Force in the 1920s and 1930s, the French Right and many military officers viewed the air force with suspicion. The French Left welcomed this new service and the French air force developed a reputation for being the most republican of the French armed services. While the French Right worried that this symbol of Marianne, this "revolutionary" organization, would give the Left a powerful counterweight to the army's power, the French Left actively promoted its development during the 1930s and in the post–World War II period. For example, in 1946 the Socialist Party's blueprint for the future of the French military establishment endorsed universal military service, reserve forces, and a weak general staff; it also gave priority to the air force.[17] These sentiments have not disappeared. As late as 1990, an army officer could be overheard saying to another, "Between you and me, the air force is the Popular Front's air force. That says it all."[18]

In addition, the British and French cases in this book illustrate that conscription can have very different meanings in different national contexts. While the French Left viewed conscription as an expression of community spirit and equality, and most important as insurance against the growth of a praetorian guard that could threaten the French republic, the British Labour Party and Trade Union Congress feared that a conscript army would militarize society and serve as an instrument for domestic repression. In fact, the very social forces that opposed a conscript army in France mobilized to support it in both England and the United States in the early twentieth century. Contrary to their French counterparts, wealthy social and political conservatives in Britain and the United States advocated conscription as a way to control the emerging politicized masses.[19] These contrasting preferences despite similar economic and social positions can be understood only within the cultural context.

Political Culture

To explain the role of domestic politics in choices between offensive and defensive military doctrine, I focus on civilian policymakers' beliefs about the role of the armed forces in the domestic arena. The composition of this aspect of political culture varies from state to state, and among political actors in a state; at its heart are a number of questions about the military's power within the state. For example, what is the perception of the role of the military in society? Do domestic political actors fear the latent force inherent in military organizations? Is military service seen as an honor, or merely accepted as an obligation of the citizenry? Should the armed services reflect the society at large, or are they viewed as separate and insular organizations? Many of the answers originate in each state's experience with the military in the state-building process.

Over time, concerns about the distribution of power within the state become institutionalized and shape decision makers' opinions about military policy. When civilians make decisions about military policy their choices often reflect their country's experience with the armed services and the role that the military played in securing a particular distribution of power within the state. Although not completely static, political cultures show remarkable endurance once institutionalized. Contemporary French debates about military policy attest to the importance of the contending political cultures that date from before the turn of the century.[20]

Competing versus Consensual Cultures

In some countries, all important political actors share the same view of the military. In Britain in the 1920s and 1930s, there was general agreement across the political spectrum about the role of the armed forces in the domestic arena. In other countries there are competing views of the military, as there were in France during the same period. The presence of one or several cultures affects the causal role of cultural factors.

Where only one culture exists, these ideas and values can best be understood as approaching common sense. As the sociologist Ann Swidler explains, a *culture* is "the set of assumptions so unselfconscious as to seem a natural, transparent, undeniable part of the structure of the world."[21] Culture consists of many assumptions that are rarely debated and seem so basic that it appears impossible to imagine that things could be different. Thus, when there is consensus about the role of the armed services, the independent role of culture is more difficult to determine and appears to have a weaker, less direct control over action. But in fact, it shapes behavior by establishing what is "natural" and making other patterns of behavior inconceivable.

In contrast, when there are several competing cultures, each culture more closely approximates an *ideology*, which Swidler defines as "a highly articulated, self-conscious belief and ritual system, aspiring to offer a unified answer to problems of social action." Ideologies are powerful because they tell actors what their goals are and how to achieve them; ideological goals are explicit, openly debated, and exhibit much greater internal coherence and consistency than cultural precepts. According to Swidler, because ideologies (or competing cultures) call for actions that do not "come naturally," they have a direct control over action.[22] Where there are competing cultures about the role of the armed forces in the domestic arena, ideological factors play a more visible and direct role in determining military policy.

The existence of one or several cultures also affects the extent to which civilian intervention in doctrinal developments corresponds with systemic imperatives. When there is more than one culture, civilian decisions are more likely to respond to domestic considerations because civilians worry about securing the preferred domestic distribution of power. However, if there is consensus among civilian policymakers about the role of the military in the domestic arena, the external environment is more likely to shape civilian participation in doctrinal developments. Civilians will not be preoccupied with domestic battles over military policy and, as a result, their decisions are more likely to correspond with systemic imperatives.[23]

Although civilians often view the details of military doctrine as the responsibility of the armed services, civilian decisions about military policy often affect doctrinal developments. If civilians agree on the nature of the military and its role in the domestic arena, their decisions are likely to respond to international conditions. If, however, civilians disagree about the domestic role of the armed services, civilian choices in military policy are more likely to correspond with domestic threats and opportunities. In either case, civilian decisions rarely determine doctrine. Instead, the military's organizational culture works within the constraints set by civilians; the military's culture intervenes between civilian choices and military doctrine.

The Military's Organizational Culture

> The military spirit separates a man from his
> family and makes him adopt another.
> (Alfred de Vigny, French officer, 1815–1825)

Disillusioned by studies that emphasized the structural and objective features of organizations, organizational theorists began studying how the *culture of an organization* affects organizational behavior and decisions.[24] Organizational cultures are the conventional wisdom within organizations. They include collective standards of relevance about the critical aspects of the organization's work or goals and often provide a special language. Analysts have taken many different approaches to studying organizational culture and have adopted different definitions; I define organizational culture as the set of basic assumptions, values, norms, beliefs, and formal knowledge that shape collective understandings.[25]

The culture of an organization shapes its members' perceptions and affects what they notice and how they interpret it: it screens out some parts of "reality" while magnifying others. Organizational cultures define what is a problem and what is possible by focusing its members' attention on certain features of events, institutions, and behaviors; how a problem is defined determines the range of possible solutions and strategies appropriate for solving it. For example, one study illustrated that different organizations' worldviews about racial integration led to vastly different operations-research models for achieving integration.[26] Another found that the best predictor of a hospital's response to an external shock was the organization's culture, not structural variables or available resources.[27]

While most of the research on organizational culture has been applied to private companies, it is particularly well suited to studying the military. Although they do not use the concept of organizational culture, many military analysts have already shown the value of this type of analysis. Morton Halperin discussed how the armed services' "essence" affects policy decisions, and Carl Builder argued that military institutions have "distinct and enduring personalities of their own that govern much of their behavior." Jack Snyder examined military "ideologies," and Richard Head and Edward Katzenbach implicitly discussed the role of organizational culture in doctrinal developments. More recently, Jeffrey Legro used organizational culture to explain why some restraints are respected in warfare, and Deborah Avant examined how organizational "bias" influences the degree of political-military integration.[28]

Even organizations with frequent and complete turnovers in membership, such as sororities and fraternities, are able to maintain their organizational culture. It is not surprising that military organizations, with long-term membership and powerful assimilation mechanisms, develop strong cultures.[29] After spending several months aboard U.S. Navy carriers, a team of researchers explained, "We have been struck by the degree to which a set of highly unusual formal and informal rules and relationships are taken for granted, implicitly and almost unconsciously incorporated into the organizational structure of the operational Navy."[30] While some organizations refer to the assimilation of their members as "orientation" or "mentoring," the military does not hesitate to call it what it is: indoctrination. Corporations hoping to develop strong organizational cultures often imitate some of the more familiar aspects of military training. Andersen Consulting, for example, sends its new employees to the company's 150-acre training center for three weeks to be "indoctrinated in a rigid corporate culture and a strict methodology."[31]

Like other "total" institutions such as prisons, monasteries, and mental hospitals, military institutions are well equipped to inculcate a common culture.[32] Contact with outsiders is relatively limited, and members work, play, and often sleep in the same place. The organization defines its members' status, identity, and interactions with others.

Military organizations may be the most "complete" societies of any "total" organization. Unlike most civilian organizations, militaries do not hire people with experience outside the military to become part of the core organization. Potential members must first pass a selection process designed by the organization and are then both trained and educated by the organization itself.[33] A principal goal of the training process is to replace the inductee's individual or civilian identity with a corporate spirit, or esprit de corps. Members of the military use terms and phrases that have limited application outside the military environment. Thousands of slang words in the navy have little if any meaning to outsiders. Who, for example, could define a "barber's cat," "barrack mould," or "monkey's breakfast"?[34] The army base at Fort Benning, Georgia, has even published a guide entitled *Military Language for Army Wives*.

Part of the effectiveness of any organization stems from its development of an organizational culture. Organizational life would be unmanageable if specific actions did not call for specific responses, if members had no expectations about others' actions, or if they had no understanding of the effects of their own actions on others. Some predictability is necessary. And what is true of organizations in general is particularly true of the military. In contrast to many professions in which individuals perform specific tasks (e.g., a professor gives a lecture; a nurse takes a patient's blood pressure), fighting a war is a group task. Decisions must be made and implemented automatically in order to ensure the integration of diverse units; the fog of war further intensifies the need for coordination and efficient implementation of group tasks.

Soldiers in combat must know automatically what to do, and they must be fully willing to do it: soldiers must risk their own lives to kill others. As the military analyst Martin van Creveld explained, "To reach the troops' souls, to influence them, to make them move in the desired direction—that is the supreme challenge facing every commander."[35] The combat value of a sense of solidarity partially explains why armies maintain a division or regiment's legal identity (its name, number, and history) even when it would seem more efficient to disband or replace the unit. As Thomas Schelling explained, "The tradition that goes with the legal identity of the group is an asset worth preserving for a future buildup."[36] In short, the military's effectiveness depends on the assimilation of its members.

Three points about the organizational culture of the military are particularly important. First, the military's culture is not equivalent to "national character." It may reflect some aspects of its society's culture, but the military's powerful assimilation processes can displace the influence of the civilian society. Second, organizational culture is not another word for strategic culture. Organizational culture refers to the collectively held beliefs of a particular military organization, not to the beliefs of civilian policymakers.[37] Third, military culture does not mean "military mind"; it does not refer to a general set of values and attitudes that all militaries share.[38] The armed services may be more authoritarian or conservative than the civilian sector, but there are still important differences between different military organizations. For example, the relationship between the officers and the rank can range from extremely hierarchical to paternalistic to almost egalitarian. During World War II the German army minimized distinctions between officers and enlisted men: it used a comprehensive term, "soldiers," for both the officers and the rank, encouraged contact between the enlistees and officers, and required German soldiers to salute each other as well as their officers. In contrast, the American army had no term for all members of the military, and American officers were discouraged from fraternizing with enlisted men. An official War Department publication during World War II expressed surprise that the German army encouraged its officers to sing "Happy Birthday" with their men.[39] In sum, military culture refers to the organizational culture of particular militaries; it does not refer to the organizational culture of the military in general.

Determining a Military's Organizational Culture

While some organizational theorists use content analyses and quantitative methods to document an organization's culture, most analysts use an interpretive or ethnographic approach. Investigators typically participate in the daily life of the organization over a period of several months to a year.[40] In this book I use an interpretive approach based on archival, historical, and other public documents. I examine curriculum at military academies, training manuals, personal histories of officers, internal communications in the armed services, and the leading military journals. Since we can often learn more about a culture from those who reject its assumptions than from those who accept them, I also look for who or what is considered deviant or taboo in the culture. Comparisons with other organizations also help illuminate what is assumed or implicit within an organization.[41] Effectively using an interpretative approach requires reading a large body of literature produced and used by the organizations in question. A culture expresses the same basic assumptions, values, norms, beliefs, and formal knowledge in many different arenas. It demonstrates consistency despite changes in leadership and regardless of audience. I focus on documents that the military produces for its internal consumption rather than on those designed to communicate with outsiders (especially policymakers) because of the difficulty in distinguishing political expediency from genuine beliefs.

Culture as a Means, Not an End

Traditional cultural approaches assume that culture shapes action by supplying the ultimate ends or values. Culture provides preferred ends, and individuals and organizations change their behavior to achieve those ends. This is end-guided action: the means vary, but the goal (provided by the culture) remains constant. Swidler argues for a different explanatory role for culture. She views culture as providing generally accepted ways of accomplishing tasks, not as defining goals; every culture contains "tool kits" or a "repertoire" of ways of organizing behavior. In Swidler's words, "A culture has enduring effects on those who hold it, not by shaping the ends they pursue, but by providing the characteristic repertoire from which they build lines of action."[42]

In adopting Swidler's framework, I view the military's culture as providing limited means to the organization, not as providing the values that guide action. A military's culture includes approaches to issues that provide each military organization with a finite number of ways of ordering their behavior. For example, the British and German armies have different command structures. While the German army has a decentralized command that leaves considerable initiative to subordinates, the British army has a more centralized command structure in which subordinates have very little freedom of action.[43]

This view of culture's explanatory role allows for change in the dependent variable, doctrine, despite continuity in the intervening variable, culture. Even though constraints set outside the organization may vary, the culture remains relatively static. The organization continues to operate according to guidelines set by its culture and integrates exogenous changes into its established way of doing things. As Swidler explains, people "value ends for which their cultural equipment is well-suited."[44] The outcomes (doctrine) may change, but the means for getting there stay the same.

   Examining the military's organizational culture also helps explain why
some militaries become dogmatically committed to their doctrinal orientation. Organizational theorists argue that hostility in the external environment strengthens the organization's culture. Managers who encounter a hazardous business environment react by "pulling in the reins"
in hopes of gaining a sense of control over the situation; mid-level employees become more willing to rely on managers and executives.[45] These
responses strengthen the organization's culture (measured by consistency
among members of the organization) at the same time that they reduce
the organization's adaptability. As the culture tightens, established methods and ideas become further entrenched and the organization becomes
increasingly unable to consider alternatives. Research on organizations
and disasters, for example, has concluded that strong cultures inhibit
timely and innovative reactions.[46] In short, the greater the hostility in
the organization's external environment, the greater the potential for organizational dogmatism. Applying this to military organizations, I expect that as civil-military relations deteriorate, doctrinal dogmatism will
increase.[47]

   Focusing exclusively on domestic politics or military organizations
provides neither a necessary nor a sufficient explanation of choices between offensive and defensive doctrines. Political decisions set constraints, but rarely do they determine outcomes. Likewise, the organizational culture alone does not explain a change in doctrine. There must be
some change in the external environment of the organization—primarily
the domestic political environment—to which the military organization
reacts.

Research Design and Execution

But how can we be confident that culture has causal power? This question is important not only because culture can be more of a consequence
than a cause but also because culture can be used instrumentally; political entrepreneurs can use culture as well as be unknowingly constrained
by it. David Laitin refers to this as culture's second "face." While arguing that culture affects political behavior, Laitin also stresses that cultural
analysts often miss culture's other face—that individuals and groups
often choose their cultural identity for instrumental reasons. For example, in his study of the Yoruba community in Nigeria, Laitin shows that
British colonial administrators deliberately engineered the dominance of
the ancestral city culture in order to ease British political control.[48]

   Although my argument challenges the rationalist tradition that as-
sumes that the social environment minimally affects rational, self-inter-

ested behavior, it is important to avoid taking an "oversocialized" view of human behavior. Actors are the products *and* the producers of their cultural environment; we need to watch out for what I call "manipulated myths." Both the British and the French cases show the power of cultural factors, but they also provide examples of cultural products that are used instrumentally or are all consequence, not cause.

The potential for the instrumental use of culture highlights the importance of carefully crafting research designs when testing culture's causal autonomy.[49] Even if beliefs or ideas are collective and taken for granted, there are still ways to provide persuasive arguments and evidence that culture has causal weight. I stress this point because some of the recent work adopting a constructivist approach argues that certain epistemologies are inappropriate for examining the role of intersubjective factors.[50] Although perhaps true for some research questions, there is nothing inherent in using culture that requires a fundamentally different method: many of the pioneering studies of political culture used quantitative methods, while other scholars have taken a more interpretivist route.

Explanatory Variables

One of the lessons for designing cultural analyses provided by the initial work on political culture is the importance of avoiding abstract and unobservable cultural variables. By focusing on political culture, Gabriel Almond, Sidney Verba, and Lucien Pye overcame many of the problems otherwise encountered in studies of national character, but the concept often remained too broad to support a causal argument.[51] National political culture may affect political outcomes, but we are more likely to be able to isolate the role of cultural factors the more we focus on clearly defined and easily identified explanatory variables. For example, Judith Hellman analyzed whether local social and political traditions shaped the development of feminist organizations in five Italian cities.[52] Instead of subsuming ethnic, occupational, social, religious, and regional divisions under a "national" political culture, Hellman used the more restrictive and more easily tested *local* political tradition, or culture, as the explanatory variable.

In restricting this analysis to the set of values, attitudes, and beliefs held by civilians about the role of the armed forces in the domestic arena, I adopt a similar tactic. Just as Hellman's examination of the role of culture benefited from a geographic restriction, mine profits from a substantive limitation. Focusing on the military's organizational culture has similar advantages.

By using specific and observable cultural variables, I am able to overcome three problems common to cultural explanations. First, this design avoids describing the explanatory variable (culture) on the basis of the outcome (doctrine). Both the political culture and the military's organizational culture can be described independently from the choice of military doctrine. Second, my use of political culture recognizes the possibile existence of different and competing cultures. Cultural analyses often assume a societal consensus or a national political culture, yet this view ignores the presence of cultural conflicts in society and constrains culture's explanatory power. Third, narrower explanatory cultural variables also facilitate process-tracing. Although it is difficult, if not impossible, to trace the process whereby a "civic culture" leads to a stable democracy, this task is much easier with a restricted cultural variable like organizational culture. To paraphrase Alexander George, I can examine the ways in which officers' beliefs and values (their organizational culture) influence their assessment of incoming information, their definition of the situation, and their identification and evaluation of options, as well as their choice of a course of action.[53] In short, it becomes easier to connect the phases of the policy process and to identify the reasons a particular doctrine was adopted.

Dependent Variable

Although some scholars argue that the presence of a civic culture leads to stable democratic politics, it is difficult to establish culture's causal role when explaining broad, long-term political behavior. It is just as likely that stable democratic politics lead to the attitudes that are, according to the early theorists, conducive to stable democratic regimes. With concurrent data it is difficult to establish the direction of causality (if one exists). The remoteness of the connection between cultural values and political behavior limits any assignment of causal weight to cultural values.

Cultural analyses are more likely to provide persuasive tests of the role of cultural factors if they focus on narrow outcomes. For example, cross-cultural studies in organizational theory use cultural differences to explain specific firm or industry behavior and structure.[54] Other studies show how cultural antecedents influence the development of sectors of governmental activity.[55] In testing the role of cultural factors in choices between offensive and defensive doctrines, this book adopts a similar tactic. Not only is the dependent variable specific and easy to identify (both at the time and in hindsight, civilians and the military agree on the offensive or defensive nature of any particular doctrine), but it also exists during a specific and distinguishable time period.[56] This makes both process-tracing and moving from correlation to causation more likely. Simply put, the more that both the explanatory and dependent variables are specific and identifiable, the more we are likely to be able to test for culture's causal autonomy.

Case Selection

I selected the cases of doctrinal developments in the French and British armies and air forces during the interwar period for four reasons. First, these cases provide variation in the explanatory variables—both the political culture and the military's organizational culture. During the 1920s and 1930s, there was a consensus in Britain about the role of the armed forces in the domestic arena; during the same period in France, two competing political cultures dominated French policymaking. The British case also provides a hard test of the importance of domestic politics. Although many analysts might not be surprised to find that domestic politics affected military policy in France, this outcome is less expected in Britain, where civil-military relations were relatively harmonious.

These cases also make it possible to test the argument that the greater the hostility in an organization's external environment, the stronger the organizational culture. Whereas the British case provides an example of low threat perception, the French army had a much more antagonistic relationship with civilians. In addition, there is variation in the French case between the 1920s and 1930s. These differing circumstances in France and between France and Britain make possible several tests of the hypothesis about the relationship between adversity in the external environment and doctrinal dogmatism.

The British case provides a particularly good test for the effect of variation in the military's organizational culture when most other factors are held constant. Because of its regimental system, the British army had several cultures. This variation in organizational cultures allows one to test whether actors with different cultures, but facing similar domestic and international constraints, prefer the same doctrine. Analyzing both the army and the air force in France and Britain during the interwar period also allows for a comparison between old, tradition-laden military organizations and those just beginning to forge their organizational identity. Organizational culture should be more important in the former case.

My second reason for selecting these cases was to confront the most powerful alternative explanations on their own turf. Not only do the cases have to provide adequate tests for my argument, but they should also be relatively easy cases for realist and functional explanations. Realism should have little difficulty explaining doctrinal developments in France in the years preceding the outbreak of World War II. France had identified its main adversary, devoted enormous resources to meeting a German assault, and knew the German army's doctrine. Since France did not misperceive or fail to respond to the imperatives in the international system, we have every reason to believe that systemic constraints shaped French doctrine. The British case is more difficult for balance-of-power theory. As a declining power with competing demands from the continent and its empire, Britain faced a more ambiguous strategic environment.

Although only the French case provides an easy test for a realist explanation, a functional analysis should have little difficulty explaining both the French and the British cases. The British army knew about offensive options, was free from civilian intervention, and most important for a functional argument, had a pressing need for greater resources. The French army also had access to new offensive concepts, freedom from civilian intervention, and the desire for greater autonomy from civilian policymakers. In both cases, the pursuit of an offensive doctrine was possible and would have satisfied important organizational needs.

My third reason for selecting these cases has more to do with accurately depicting each military's organizational culture than with testing the different explanations of doctrinal choice. Describing the cultural variable is one of the greatest challenges of cultural analysis. In some cases, survey research may be adequate, but because surveys often look for variation in opinion, they may miss what culture is all about: that which is taken for granted.[57] Because looking at an organization raises similar difficulties, comparative research is important. Ideally, an investigator might bring out what is taken for granted by, for example, exposing British officers to the French army with the aim of recording the French officers' reactions to events, beliefs, or habits that seem "natural" to the British.[58] Some memoirs and reports of military exchanges provide this type of evidence, but it is insufficient. By comparing the French and British armies' organizational cultures (and to a lesser extent, the air force and army cultures), I can begin to see what appears natural and taken for granted in each organization.

Fourth, these cases provide for the possibility of a full range of variation in the dependent variable; during the 1920s and 1930s both offensive and defensive doctrines were possible in both the air force and the army. The British air force adopted an offensive doctrine (strategic bombing), but it also endorsed a defensive doctrine. The French air force could have acted similarly. Although both the French and British armies eventually developed defensive doctrines, offensive doctrines were possible.

Culture's Causal Autonomy

Having set forth some of the strategies for designing projects to test culture's explanatory power, here I briefly review three questions that should be answered in each case study before claiming that culture has causal autonomy. First, can it be established that the outcome is not readily explained by other factors? In both the French and British cases, claims about the explanatory power of the military's organizational culture must be preceded by evidence that if the organizational culture had been otherwise or did not exist, the outcome could have been different. In other words, before claiming that the army's organizational culture shaped the adoption of a defensive doctrine, it is important to show that an offensive doctrine was "objectively" possible. There is little point in arguing that the military's organizational culture shaped the adoption of a defensive doctrine if, for example, civilians did not allow the military to adopt an offensive doctrine or if the available technology or resources precluded the adoption of an offensive doctrine.

Second, is the culture simply a reflection of the underlying social relations or material conditions, or can it be shown that individuals and groups that share similar structural positions also possess different orientations? For example, it must be shown that the positions taken by civilians representing similar socioeconomic categories differ across national boundaries. This issue also influenced my selection of the British and French cases. If organizations' beliefs and values merely reflect situational constraints, we should expect the British and French armies to have had similar organizational cultures. Not only did both fight modern armies in the trench warfare of World War I and have responsibilities for colonial warfare, but they also served advanced industrial democracies with a similar industrial and technological base. If, despite these similarities, the militaries had different cultures, we can begin to be confident that the culture was not merely a consequence of those factors.

But this is not enough to show culture's causal autonomy. The third question is: Are actors using the so-called cultural belief to achieve other goals? If they are, the culture might still be part of the explanation, but it would have little causal autonomy. In order to make a stronger claim about culture's explanatory power, it is important to show that the belief was genuine, and not invoked just to serve other interests. One of the ways of doing this is to show that the actors' beliefs persist despite the fact that continuing to hold those beliefs keeps them from achieving other important goals.

Stressing the importance of the sincerity of cultural beliefs should not let us lose sight of this book's central argument, or fall into the trap of treating interests and culture as separate factors. To argue that culture matters is not to argue that interests do not. Culture and interests are not distinct, discrete, competing factors. Actors' definitions of their interests are often a function of their culture. Artificially dividing interests and culture into separate categories obscures culture's explanatory role; it leads theorists wedded to interest-driven or political-power approaches to discount cultural analyses as naive. But discounting culture is itself naive. Actors do not put lofty cultural aspirations above their organizational needs or the defense of their country. How they define their interest is a function of their culture. In other words, rationality is culturally conditioned.

Cultural explanations are not about explaining dysfunctional behavior. The French army's rapid and humiliating defeat in 1940 makes it easy to lose sight of this point, but unlike much of the early work on misperception in international relations, I do not use ideational factors to explain why the wrong or irrational decision was made. I do not, for example, argue that the basic assumptions, values, norms, beliefs, and formal knowledge in the French army's organizational culture were right or wrong. Instead of assuming that there are definitive meanings attached to particular policies, I am interested in understanding why actors see some means as possible and certain ends as desirable. Military officers in different countries take different "realities" for granted, and these differences affect their choices between offensive and defensive doctrines. In short, instead of taking preferences as given and interests as self-evident, this study shows how actors' cultures help define their interests.

3

Explaining French Doctrine

FRANCE had used the interwar period to bolster its military and was prepared to fight a war against Germany—but only if Hitler fought the war on French terms. When war broke out in May 1940, the French army had a defensive doctrine that was incapable of breaking the German assault. As a result, few defeats were as rapid or as devastating as the May–June campaign in Western Europe.

The initial reaction of the French to its army's collapse in 1940 was to blame others. Deputy Paul Reynaud criticized the king of Belgium, and after the armistice Philippe Pétain accused the British of undermining French security. During the Riom Trial in 1942 (initiated by Pétain's Vichy regime in February 1942 in an attempt to discredit the republican regime it had replaced) the Vichy regime blamed the politicians, the republic, and in particular the leaders of the Popular Front. Capturing the spirit of this critique, John Fuller described the French army as having been "rotted by the corruption and communistic ideas of the Front Populaire government, created in 1936 by M. Léon Blum."[1] After the war, the Fourth Republic held its own inquiry and used this forum to blame Pétain and the Vichy regime.[2]

Many analysts argue that the French state or weaknesses in French society were responsible for the French defeat.[3] Others blame the French army, both for developing an inappropriate doctrine and for its conduct of the military campaign.[4] The French army in turn often deflected these charges by claiming that the Third Republic had failed to provide it with the necessary means of preparing for its continental adversary.[5] Many of these explanations for France's collapse dovetail with arguments about the origins of the French army's defensive doctrine. Is French military doctrine best understood as the product of the parochial interests of the French army, or were the French civilians, as expected by balance-of-power theory, carefully calculating the French response to the rising German threat?

France's Defensive Doctrine: Firepower and Control

The Maginot Line has come to symbolize the highly defensive nature of the French army's doctrine.[6] Firepower and a centralized command structure took precedence over mobility and initiative. The French army

had motorized its units in the 1920s and 1930s, but tanks were to operate as support for the infantry, not independently in breakthrough operations. The French anticipated successive series of methodical battles
that would eventually wear down and destroy the enemy's ability to
fight.

The French army's force structure and mobilization requirements further crippled any offensive possibilities. There was a small core of professionals, but their role was essentially to train recruits, man the frontier
fortifications, and provide a framework in which to absorb the conscript
army. After 1928 the army was valuable only in the context of a total
war; no significant operation could be carried out without recalling at
least some part of the reserves.[7]

The French army knew that the tank was one of the most important
weapons introduced during World War I, but it did not recognize the potential striking power of massed armor; the French army dispersed the
majority of its tanks among the infantry units. Even after forming an independent tank unit, the French army anticipated that this armored formation would plug breaches, not create breakthroughs. Only reluctantly
did French doctrine allow the tank to act on a mission not involving
close support of the artillery and subordination to infantry units.[8]

Two concepts—firepower and the methodical battle—dominated
French thinking about the conduct of war. The French army believed
that the new weapons and greater firepower made the battlefield even
more lethal; Pétain's famous dictum *"le feu tue"* (firepower kills) captured this sentiment. Rather than immediate fire in support of smaller
units, French doctrine called for the use of artillery to provide massive
fire support for the infantry. Because of the difficulty of massing and controlling large forces, subtle and rapid maneuvers were unlikely; attacking
units could not go beyond the effective range of their artillery.[9]

This emphasis on highly centralized control over large-scale artillery
barrages reinforced the need for the *bataille conduite* (methodical battle).
In contrast to a decentralized battle in which officers at all levels are expected to show initiative and flexibility, the French army preferred rigid
centralization and strict obedience. The methodical battle called for
tightly controlled operations in which all units and weapons were carefully marshalled and adhered to strict timetables. French doctrine left little room for mobility or the possibility that one continuous battle could
lead to the rupture and defeat of enemy forces.[10]

Although it had adopted new technologies, the French army entered
World War II with a defensive doctrine that ignored the offensive mobility of tracked vehicles and air power. However, this defensive orientation
did not typify the entire interwar period. Until 1929, the French would
have begun a war with an offensive into Germany, and in general, the

French army's orientation in the 1920s did not mirror the trench warfare of World War I. Only in the 1930s did the doctrine assume the highly defensive characteristics outlined above.

The Legacy of Verdun

The lessons of World War I seem to explain why a functional explanation cannot account for French doctrine. According to this argument, the 1920s and 1930s are an exceptional period: emerging from the carnage of the Great War, perceptions of the offense-defense balance were so skewed that an otherwise accurate generalization—that military organizations prefer offensive doctrines—does not apply.[11] Given the French army's doctrine in 1939, it seems plausible that the leadership of the French army, marked by the bloody experiences of World War I, had prepared for a rematch of the previous war. Devastated by the disastrous results of the *offense à outrance*, and influenced in particular by the battle for Verdun, the French officer corps had learned its lesson and prepared to fight the next war behind the reinforced concrete of the Maginot Line.[12]

Although the legacy of Verdun is the most popular explanation of the origins of French doctrine, the French army did not immediately adopt a defensive doctrine. In the 1920s, the decade following the signing of the Versailles Treaty, the French army actively debated the offensive value of fortification and massed tanks and adopted offensive war plans.

Within months of the signing of the armistice, the French military elite began discussing the future use of fortifications to ensure the inviolability of the frontier. This evidence appears to confirm the defensive legacy of World War I, especially given the operational form that the Maginot Line came to assume. Throughout the 1920s, however, the General Staff debated the potential use of prepared positions, and in particular whether the fortifications would serve offensive or defensive functions.[13] Not until the late 1920s did the advocates of a continuous line of fortifications dominate the debate; until then, a more offensive conception for the use of fortified regions held sway.[14]

Generals Berthelot, Debeney, Fillomeau, Mangin, and Guillaumat, and Marshals Foch and Joffre were the primary partisans of an offensive use of fortifications. Concerned that too great an emphasis on fortifications might cripple the French army, they argued that fortified regions should serve as centers of resistance to facilitate offensive actions.[15] These French officers rejected the notion of a continuous frontier and instead placed a premium on mobility and the ability to conduct offensive strikes into Germany.[16] General Weygand, the director of the Center for Advanced Military Studies and later the chief of staff, argued that fortifications should be used to economize forces so that a greater portion of the French troops could strike offensively into Germany.[17] In contrast, Marshal Pétain, General Buat, and others argued that fortifications were primarily defensive. These officers were unwilling to sanction surrendering a part of French territory to maneuver.[18] They advocated a continuous line of fortifications close to the frontier.

The controversy between these two schools of thought continued throughout the 1920s.[19] In a meeting of the Superior Council of War in 1926, Generals Guillaumat, Berthelot, and Fillomeau attacked Pétain's proposals. Supported by Joffre and Debeney, Guillaumat insisted that it would be dangerous to place greater importance on fortifications than on the equipment that would allow the prepared positions to be used as points of maneuver.[20] Foch agreed: "If we don't have the tool, it will not be the umbrella that will protect the country."[21] General Guillaumat also spoke out strongly against Pétain's defensive conceptions: "The Wall of France is a dream financially speaking, and from the military point of view can be a danger. It could lead us to subordinate all war plans. . . . It would be better to build a strong army capable of going on the offensive. Whatever money is remaining—if any does remain—could be used to construct fortifications that would serve as a base of departure."[22] Both Guillaumat and Debeney argued that fortifications should be used to facilitate offensive actions in order to avoid repeating the static defense of World War I.[23]

The debate continued for almost a decade, and this prolongation, a leading historian of the Maginot Line explained, is indicative of the "markedly offensive spirit of the French high command."[24] When the high command decided in 1925 to form a commission to study the use of fortifications, the proposal establishing the Commission of the Defense of the Frontier specified that the prepared positions would be used to enhance offensive operations. The commission's report in 1927 outlined a system of fortified regions that would reinforce the covering force and strengthen the possibilities for offensive maneuvers. The project specified that the fortified regions would serve as a base to allow the French army to begin operations with a bolt into German territory.[25] However, as the decade closed and it became increasingly clear that the Parliament would again shorten the term of conscription, support for the offensive use of fortifications began to wane.[26] In 1929, Pétain's conception of a continuous frontier triumphed.

In sum, there was a fundamental difference between the eventual form that the Maginot Line took, and the initial projects proposed by the commission and the conceptions shared by many of the leading French officers.[27] In 1932, General Gamelin explained that France's fortifications were initially part of an offensive orientation:

> [The project proposed in 1927] did not consist of the organization of a defensive front, but instead was to prepare, at the edge of the frontier, a mobile force and to ensure its rapid transfer into Belgium. According to the file submitted to the Superior Council of War today, everything has changed. It is no longer a question of mobile equipment, but instead, the organization of a barrier.[28]

The debate had been lively and official proposals had endorsed an offensive role for fortifications, but the conception of fortified regions and strong points around which the French army could maneuver slowly ceded place to the plan for a continuous, prepared battlefield close to the frontier. Ironically, the French politician after whom the concrete fortifications were named had argued passionately in the 1920s for the maintenance of forces capable of taking the offensive.[29]

The debate within the officer corps about mechanized warfare is additional evidence of the French army's openness to offensive operations in the aftermath of World War I. Just as there was no consensus among the military leaders over how best to use fortifications, there was also disagreement in the 1920s about the optimum use of armor.[30] While some officers advocated the development of independent tank units that could take advantage of the speed and maneuverability of the new technology, other officers argued that tanks should be assigned to fill traditional roles of support for the infantry in defensive operations.

Encouraged by the chief of staff, General Edmond Buat, the French army actively debated the use of tanks.[31] In 1919, General Buat wrote, "The future battle will no longer be fought against the enemy foot soldier, but against the armored infantryman. . . . The appearance of the motor on the battlefield once again gives mobility and movement its full importance."[32] A study by general headquarters in 1919 endorsed the independent use of massed armor, and a report by the chiefs of staff in 1923 spoke of the speed and mobility of modern warfare.[33] The 1920 army manual outlining the use of tanks stated that tanks were essentially offensive weapons and were most effectively employed "in mass."[34]

In the early 1920s the military journals and academies were alive with debate over the potential of massed armor.[35] One author estimated that in the early 1920s, two-thirds of the articles in professional military journals endorsed mechanized warfare.[36] The French army also experimented with mechanized units, and the tank inspectorate, General Jean Baptiste-Estienne, advocated the creation of autonomous mechanized units capable of extreme mobility and with the striking power necessary for offensive operations. Numerous other young officers like Colonels Jean Perré and Joseph Molinié seconded Estienne's proposals.[37] Colonels Velpry, Chedeville, and Romain also argued for the creation of autonomous tank units.[38]

The debate over the potential use of armor should not obscure the fact that on the whole the French army adopted a more traditional role for tanks. The infantry was successful in organizationally subordinating armor to the older branch, and this hindered the development of independent tank units. A 1919 study on the peacetime reorganization of the army did not give tanks a role independent of the infantry, and the tank manual published in 1920 stated that "tanks are not able to conquer or occupy terrain by themselves alone. They are only a strong aid placed at the disposition of the infantry."[39] However, the lessons of World War I and the subordination of armor had not created a consensus about the appropriate role for tanks. Throughout the 1920s, the French officer corps actively debated the offensive use of massed armor.

The war plans of the 1920s raise further doubts that the lessons of Verdun led to the French army's defensive doctrine: these plans officially endorsed offensive operations. If a conflict with Germany occurred, the French intended to bring the battle to Germany and divide the country in two.[40] Defensive plans later superseded these offensive ones, but the initial reaction to the threat of a resurgent Germany was to once again plan offensive strikes beyond the French frontier.[41]

The first war plans drawn up after World War I were unequivocally offensive. Plan T and Plan P, in service from May 1920 to March 1923, called for an offensive action into German territory: either a limited land grab or a large-scale maneuver toward the Ruhr. In operation from 1924 to June 1926, Plan A integrated mobilization requirements, but endorsed the intentions of the previous plan: a mass of twenty-four to thirty divisions would strike out with great rapidity, occupying and dividing the industrial regions of Germany in order to disrupt German mobilization and precipitate a rapid collapse of the German forces.[42] A letter by Marshal Fayolle to the minister of defense in 1925 reiterates these offensive designs: "We must therefore and at any price have at our disposal at the beginning of a conflict offensive forces capable of decisive strikes into Germany such that Germany will be required to maintain the mass of her forces in face of us and to fight on her territory."[43] These plans show little resemblance to the intentions of an army overwhelmed by the defensive lessons of World War I.

However, with the reduction in the military service to eighteen months in 1923 and the military's recognition that it would be further reduced to one year, the plans shifted and became increasingly defensive. Plan A/a (June 1926 to April 1929) moved away from an immediate offensive, but it was not until the adoption of Plan B in May 1929 that the French

army—for the first time since the end of World War I—adopted an un-
ambiguously defensive war plan.[44] Plan B marked the beginning of more
than a decade of defensive plans.

One of the first and principal army manuals of the interwar period,
published just three years after the end of World War I, adopted a pru-
dent tone, showing no preference for either the offense or the defense.[45]
Indeed, the 1920s was a period of debate and diversity. Many important
and influential officers advocated an offensive orientation. The initial
projects for the fortification of the French frontier endorsed an offensive
conception, many French officers saw mechanization as a way to break
out of the defensive stalemate that dominated the last war, and French
war plans called for offensive strikes into Germany.

In short, contrary to what is often assumed, the French army did not
single-mindedly endorse a defensive doctrine after World War I.[46] The
French army eventually adopted a doctrine that in many ways reflected
the defensive stalemate in World War I, but "the lesson" of the trench
warfare was far from universally endorsed in the first decade after World
War I. It was only later, in the late 1920s and especially the 1930s that
the lesson of World War I became dominant. Although the memory of
World War I was etched in France's collective memory, the French army
did not leave World War I convinced that the only possible doctrinal orientation was a defensive one reminiscent of the trench warfare in northern France.

World War I, and in particular the Battle of Verdun, did take on legendary proportions for the country at large and the army in particular.
The myth of Verdun became indelibly marked in the memory of the
French army. For example, Pétain's famous maxim during the battle for
Verdun, "*Ils ne passeront pas*" (they [the Germans] will not get through),
came to symbolize the fortitude, courage, and determination of the
French forces despite their enormous suffering. Twenty years later, the
troops who manned the Maginot Line wrote across their hats, "Ils ne
passeront pas."[47] During the fall of Dien Bien Phu in 1954, the cries "Ils
ne passeront pas" reemerged.[48]

The French Right and Left have also used variations on Pétain's phrase
to express determined resistance. During the negotiations for the end of
the Algerian War, the unofficial French terrorist organization that sought
to keep Algeria French declared, "De Gaulle ne passera pas."[49] Similarly,
during May 1968 a political cartoon attacking the Communist trade
union (CGT) for supporting the government depicted the CGT locked
arm in arm with the police forces, with a banner across the top reading
"La révolution ne passera pas."[50] The myth of Verdun became a powerful symbol of modern France.

Although Verdun—or the power of the defensive—became the lesson of World War I, other lessons and interpretations were available, especially if the French army had looked beyond its own experiences in 1914–18. Moreover, the offensive potential of armored units was evident even if the French officer corps relied exclusively on its own experiences.[51] For example, in arguing for the adoption of an offensive doctrine in the 1930s, de Gaulle pointed to several examples of the offensive use of this new technology during the previous war.[52] The offensive lessons of World War I were available to the French army, and important and influential sectors of the French army endorsed offensive war plans and the offensive use of massed tanks and fortifications in the 1920s. However, as the myth of Verdun grew to heroic proportions, it became increasingly difficult to grasp that World War I's defensive lessons were not the only ones available or supported. The German army also fought at Verdun, and it was not spared the tremendous bloodletting that occurred throughout the ten long months of battle. Alistair Horne argues that the German and French experiences were similar: "The German soldier of World War I—the *Reichsarchives* admit—was more deeply affected by Verdun than by any other campaign of the war. Each post-war year the German survivors also trekked to Verdun by the hundred, trying to find the positions where they had fought so long and so desperately, or merely visiting the innumerable cemeteries."[53] Although veterans of World War I also dominated the German officer corps, the German army developed an offensive doctrine.

The lessons of history are multiple and often inform policymaking after a particular policy has been chosen. They are often not the origin of the policy itself. In other words, the French army adopted a defensive doctrine in the interwar years for reasons other than those provided by the lesson of Verdun and the trench warfare of World War I. Once it selected a defensive orientation, history began to be read and used in a particular way to justify or bolster the chosen policy or institution. As Jack Snyder argues in his study of the myths of empire, "Statesmen and societies actively shape the lessons of the past in ways they find convenient, [more than they] are shaped by them."[54]

Systemic Imperatives

Doctrinal developments in France during the interwar period should be an easy case for balance-of-power theory. French civilians understood the German threat and devoted extensive resources to ensuring France's security. The French case is not an example of objective international requirements' being misperceived or not addressed. France had spent twenty years preparing for the German assault.

Germany's defeat in 1918 had not tempered French fears; French policymakers were acutely aware of the threat of a resurgent Germany. The French General Staff was convinced that Germany would not accept its defeat, and the French attempted to use the negotiations at Versailles to devise mechanisms to harness German power. French policymakers worried about Italian intentions in the Mediterranean, but they were convinced that Germany was the primary threat to French security. Overseas possessions, including French interests in North Africa, remained secondary in France's strategic priorities.[55] As early as the 1920s, the French had also identified the nature of the German threat, and in particular, knew that German doctrine was offensively oriented.[56] Paris became preoccupied with the threat of an *attaque brusquée*—a sudden attack of extreme intensity by small and powerful German units. Both the popular and the military press warned against the dangers of this type of fierce surprise attack, and the Superior Council of War repeatedly discussed measures to parry the threat.[57]

As the decade continued, French intelligence about the form of a German attack became increasingly specific. In November 1934 a report from the army intelligence office discussed German combined air and army tactics, and in 1935 a German publication on the offensive use of tanks generated considerable attention in the French infantry journal.[58] In March 1935 the war minister, General Louis Maurin, spoke to the French Parliament in strikingly prescient terms about the nature of a German attack: "We should suffer a rapid . . . breakthrough by armoured and motorized units moving through the breach at hitherto unknown speed and dislocating our mobilization centres whilst the enemy air forces . . . sealed off the battle zone to prevent the arrival of our reserves."[59] The French knew that German air power would work in conjunction with the ground attack, not in independent strategic bombing missions.[60]

The French army had also translated and distributed General Heinz Guderian's *Achtung Panzer*, and French intelligence had compiled an extensive file describing the organization of German armored units.[61] The Spanish Civil War further revealed German operational art, and the Polish campaign in September 1939 again demonstrated the Reichswehr's capabilities. The French military attaché in Poland accurately reported the German attack, and Gamelin, then chief of staff, dispatched this information to the major garrisons of the French army.[62] In short, translations of German military literature and reports of German military exercises and operations in Spain and Poland gave the leadership of the French army an accurate portrait of German armored warfare and its emphasis on mobility, surprise, and combined arms operations.

Cognizant of the threat of a powerful Germany, France responded vigorously—even when rearmament strained France's limited budget and resources. As Robert Doughty points out, between 1918 and 1935 France spent a greater percentage of its gross national product on defense than any other major power.[63] The Depression reduced defense expenditures to their 1927 level, but the reduction was less than the budgetary figures indicate because of the creation of special funds.[64] France spent over 7 billion francs from 1930 to 1937 for the Maginot Line alone and allocated 14 billion francs for a rearmament program in 1936.[65] This pace continued until the outbreak of war: army allocations for weapons and other equipment (in constant 1938 francs) were nearly two and one-half times greater in 1937 than in 1935 and over three and one-half times greater in 1939 than in 1937.[66] Not surprisingly, French national defense absorbed more resources than it had before World War I: by 1938 defense expenditures were 2.6 times as much in real terms as in 1913.[67] And in 1939 France was still devoting proportionally greater resources to its defense than Britain or Germany.[68]

Immediately after its defeat, the Vichy regime blamed the Popular Front, and especially the leader of the Socialist Party, Léon Blum, for failing to support French national defense. The Right also argued that the Popular Front's nationalization of the French aviation industry had undermined French security.[69] Historical research has shown those charges to be false; the balance of forces was not in Germany's favor, and the left-wing government generously supported national defense. As a percentage of both the general budget and the national revenue, the amount allocated to national defense during the Popular Front period surpassed that of the preceding sixteen years.[70] No previous conservative government had allocated as much to national defense.

The Popular Front not only increased defense expenditures; this left-wing government also allocated funding over and beyond that requested by the chiefs of staff. In September 1936 the Council of Ministers adopted a four-year plan calling for 14 billion francs for national defense; the military chiefs had requested 9 billion francs.[71] Throughout the interwar period, the Parliament never refused the credits that the armed services requested, and for several years during the 1930s the military was unable to spend all the money that it had been allocated.[72]

The Vichy regime and the French staff also claimed that Hitler's army overran French forces because the German units had such crushing quantitative superiority—during the war, the French staff declared that the Germans were attacking with over 7,500 tanks.[73] This charge is also unfounded. The Third Reich's propaganda machine created the impression of overwhelming power, but the balance of forces did not favor Germany.[74] There were differences in quality and design, but the allied forces and Germany's were roughly equivalent. For example, by 1940 Germany

did not have more tanks than France; each had about 2,500 modern vehicles.[75] Similarly, the French army deployed 2,240,000 troops (of the
3,740,000 allied forces) and the Germans 2,760,000; the allies and the
Germans each fielded about 140 divisions.[76] The allies enjoyed a three-
to-one superiority in artillery pieces. However, the German Luftwaffe
significantly outnumbered the French air force.[77]

Even before Hitler seized power, the French never wavered in their insistence on maintaining strong forces. While the British called for a reduction in armaments during disarmament negotiations in the interwar
period, the French sought to avoid any practical attempts to disarm.
French negotiators hid behind technical objections in order to subordinate arms control to traditional means of guaranteeing a state's security.[78]
In addition, the French did little more than flirt with the popular notion
of collective security. As Michael Mandelbaum argues, the French relied
on self-help mechanisms of national defense.[79]

During the interwar period the demands of the international system
were transparent and compelling to French decision makers: Paris feared
Germany's relative power and the German army's offensive orientation.
Inadequate financial support did not constrain French preparations to
meet this challenge. French policymakers grasped France's standing in
the international system and responded to its security requirements.
However, as explained in Chapter 4, the French army's doctrine did not
correspond to these international imperatives but instead mirrored domestic political conflict and the organizational culture of the army. Even
in this easy case, balance-of-power theory is unable to explain the choice
between an offensive and a defensive doctrine.

FRANCE AND BALANCE-OF-POWER THEORY

Barry Posen argues that France's position in the international system best
explains its almost exclusive reliance on a defensive doctrine, its lack of
innovation, and its poor political-military integration. Owing to France's
relative weakness, French policymakers focused on external balancing,
and in particular on gaining British support, which would allow France
to "pass the buck." According to Posen, this strategy required France to
adopt a defensive doctrine in order to avoid appearing bellicose in British
eyes.[80] In addition, because French civilians focused on external balancing, the lack of innovation and poor political-military integration remained uncorrected.

Although logically compelling, this argument is empirically difficult to
sustain. First, the French did seek Britain as an alliance partner, but there
is little evidence that French policymaking focused on reassuring British
anxieties. To the contrary, the French repeatedly antagonized the British.

Second, claiming that external balancing dominated French policymaking ignores the significant *internal* balancing that France conducted and is therefore questionable in and of itself. French alliance formation was highly selective and insufficiently implemented.

French policymakers did not appear to be exclusively, or even primarily, motivated by a desire to avoid antagonizing Britain; in fact, the French were more than willing to court British displeasure. This was evident during a crisis in Anglo-Turkish relations in 1922, but French preparations for the occupation of the Ruhr most aroused British censure. Britain strove to prevent French action, and even after it was a fait accompli, Britain maintained its strong opposition. Relations between the two countries so soured that the French prime minister, Raymond Poincaré, in search of a new ally, opened negotiations with Japan. The French also came into direct conflict with the British over financial issues. As Jonathan Kirshner has shown, from January 1927 to August 1931 the French attempted to exploit their ability to undermine the existing international monetary regime and to weaken the position of its leader—Great Britain. Hoping to extract concessions from the British on other issues, France manipulated the flow of gold between the two states.[81] These efforts ultimately failed, but Paris's attempt to disrupt London's management of the monetary system is not the action of one state seeking another's approval.

Furthermore, French military policy, and especially its war plans, could not help but antagonize the British. Preventing Germany from controlling the Low Countries was vital to British security, yet French plans were explicitly designed to draw Germany into Belgium. One cannot claim that France chose a defensive doctrine to avoid appearing bellicose to Britain and at the same time elected to deploy its forces in a way certain to threaten British interests. In fact, Posen acknowledges that encouraging the Germans to attack via Belgium "had the unavoidable consequence of poisoning relations with Britain."[82]

Depicting France as following the dictates of its "English governess" was a convenient way to blame the British and so deflect responsibility, but it is not an accurate representation of the sources of French policy, especially in regard to army doctrine. As both Anthony Adamthwaite and Martin Alexander argue, French policymakers acted independently—not in response to British pressures—until the late 1930s.[83] In other words, French policy was much more independent than commonly depicted, and most important, was independent of British desires when the French army adopted a defensive doctrine in 1929.

The French may have tailored certain policies to conform with British desires, but these actions do not indicate that French decision makers chose a defensive doctrine because they worried about appearing aggres-

sive to the British. Posen provides no evidence that the political repercussions of an offensive doctrine concerned French or British statesmen.
In fact, France seemed unconcerned about potential British reactions to
an offensive strategy: French war plans were offensive throughout the
1920s. And in the late 1930s, British policymakers were alarmed that the
French *did not* have an offensive doctrine: London reacted with disbelief
to the news that if a war over Czechoslovakia broke out, the French
army did not have the capability or the intention to strike offensively
into Germany or the Italian Alps.[84]

It is also difficult to sustain the argument that France focused on external balancing because of its relative weakness. If alliance formation
took precedence and French statesmen were preoccupied with securing
allied support, how could Paris so flagrantly ignore its treaty obligations
to its eastern allies? Balance-of-power theory would also expect France
to have the capability to assist its allies in Central Europe. After 1929
France no longer had that capability. The French high command believed
that cooperation with France's eastern allies was important, but the planning never got beyond the theoretical stage. The French never shared
their mobilization plans or asked their allies what assistance they would
need if war broke out. Military assistance was so limited that General
Weygand complained, "Our policy is of a meanness that is prejudicial to
our highest interests. What are some dozens of millions of francs if they
could help us eliminate the risk of war?"[85] France had an alliance with
Czechoslovakia, but the French army had no plans to go to its assistance
if Germany attacked. In response to British demands in 1938 for clarifi-
cation of how France would aid its Czech ally, the French Permanent
Committee for National Defense reported that France could offer little
assistance.[86] Although the French were willing to spend money for their
own defense, these efforts were concentrated on internal, not external
balancing.

France's failure to conclude a military alliance with the Soviet Union
is further evidence that external balancing did not dominate French security policy. Throughout the interwar period, the Soviets sought to foster closer ties with France, but French policymakers repeatedly scorned
Soviet advances.[87] If external balancing had been the primary motivation
behind French security policy, French recognition of British reluctance to
make a continental commitment should have encouraged France to seek
alternative sources of assistance. French policymakers could have ensured that France form a military alliance with the Soviet Union or that
it have the military capabilities to honor alliance commitments in Eastern Europe. France did neither. Such selective balancing, especially by a
country acutely aware of its relative weakness, speaks poorly of the
power of systemic imperatives.

There is also little evidence to support the argument that French policy-makers sought to pass the buck. To the contrary, there is evidence that French civilians fervently objected to such an idea. During a meeting of the Superior Council of War in December 1927, one of the military officers remarked that France could only aid herself with the help of allies. The (civilian) minister of defense quickly responded that such a remark was extremely serious, useless, and dangerous.[88] And as discussed above, France devoted enormous resources to *internal* balancing. France did of course seek allied support, but to accuse French policymakers of buck-passing does not take into account the substantial financial resources that French defense spending consumed throughout the interwar period—even during economic crises and left-wing governments.

Posen acknowledges that balance-of-power theory does not adequately explain French doctrinal decisions, and he points to two major decisions in the late 1920s that contributed to the defensive nature of French military doctrine that were not, he argues, the result of systemic imperatives. Posen explains that the reduction in the term of conscription and the creation of the Maginot Line resulted from the "technological lessons" of World War I.[89] The shadow of World War I cannot be ignored, but the timing of these decisions and the endorsement of offensive action immediately after World War I shows that the technological lessons of trench warfare did not drive these choices. If this were the case, why was this lesson submerged during the intervening decade? As discussed above, in the 1920s the French army did not adopt a defensive doctrine. More important, the reduction in the term of conscription was not in response to the previous international conflict but was part of a long-standing battle between the Left and Right in French domestic politics (see discussion in Chapter 4).

THE INDETERMINACY OF THE DISTRIBUTION OF POWER

The distribution of power in the international system is one of the most important considerations in realist analyses. Variations in power, it is argued, are the key to the operation of international politics. French policymakers and international relations theorists concur that during the interwar period France was weaker than Germany. The unequal distribution of power between France and its main adversary does not, however, tell us much about the military posture that the French army did or should have assumed. Relative weakness is indeterminate of choices between offensive and defensive military doctrine.

Both Barry Posen and Michael Mandelbaum argue that France's relative weakness required the adoption of a defensive doctrine.[90] During the 1930s, French statesmen also argued that French security required a defensive doctrine. According to this reasoning, France could only buy time against a German assault and would have to wait for allied reinforcements before conducting a counteroffensive.[91] The structure of the international system seems to explain French doctrine: France was relatively weak in the 1930s and adopted a defensive doctrine to ensure allied support.

Yet in the 1920s the French argued just the opposite—that the only war France could win was a quick and decisive offensive. France needed to defeat Germany before it could marshal its superior manpower and industrial resources.[92] An official French report in the early 1920s argued that a French offensive was necessary because speed and the advantages of preparations were France's most important assets. The report explained, "An offensive conception is the only one that would permit us to compensate for the inescapable causes of our weakness, which result from the inferiority of our population and industrial strength."[93]

In the 1920s, French policymakers supported an offensive doctrine because war with Germany had to end before Germany could exploit its relative power and mobilization potential. In the 1930s, only a defensive doctrine and thus a long war held the prospect of a French victory because, they argued, France needed the added power of its allies. In other words, because of France's relatively weak position in the international system France needed to fight offensively in the 1920s and defensively in the 1930s.

These contrasting policies do not mean that the logic behind either orientation is unfounded, only that relative weakness says little about the offensive or defensive orientation that a state should assume. Both responses make sense and at one time or another were adopted by French policymakers. In a study of the impact of the distribution of power on states' security policy, Mandelbaum acknowledges that France's position in the international system did not determine strategic policymaking:

> Because their position in the international system is less constraining than are those of the strong and weak, states that fall into the intermediate category have a wider range of choice than the other two types. Here, too, French policy between the two world wars was representative. France adopted each of the basic approaches to security available to sovereign states: collective policies, alliances, conciliation and the use of force.[94]

Once a particular doctrine has been chosen, it can be justified (and explained) in terms of the distribution of power, regardless of whether an offensive or defensive orientation was adopted.

Realists might respond that France's position in the international system changed from the 1920s to the 1930s and that the shift in the distribution of power, especially after 1933, explains its doctrinal development. After all, Germany had virtually no army in the 1920s. And there does seem to be a powerful correlation between German power and French doctrine. When Germany was relatively weak in the 1920s, the French army had an offensive orientation; when Germany was strong in the 1930s, the French army had a defensive doctrine.

But this argument cannot be sustained. It did not take German rearmament for the French to respond to German power. The French used the Versailles negotiations to weaken Germany, and the series of alliances that Paris concluded with Eastern Europe belies any notion that it took Hitler's rise to power to wake up the French to the potential threat on their doorstep. More important, France switched to a defensive doctrine in 1929—five years before Hitler's seizure of power, seven years before the reinstatement of conscription, and eight years before the remilitarization of the Rhineland. There is not a correlation between French doctrine and German power: the French army switched to a defensive doctrine *long before* Germany began to rearm. Nor is the correlation supported by process-tracing. When France switched to a defensive doctrine in the late 1920s, the French army repeatedly and explicitly linked this change to the government's decision to reduce the length of conscription. In other words, the French army did not connect the rise of German power with the adoption of a defensive doctrine. There is neither correlation nor causation between German power and French doctrine.

A comparison of French military policy before both world wars underscores the indeterminacy of the structure of the international system. From 1914 to 1939, France's position in the international system remained static: a stronger Germany was the greatest threat, England a key ally, and France a status quo power.[95] Nevertheless, the French army's doctrine underwent a radical reorientation—from an *offense à outrance* in 1914 to a highly defensive doctrine in 1939. Such dramatic doctrinal change unaccompanied by significant variation in the external environment casts doubt on the extent to which military doctrine responds to conditions in the international system.

Contrary to what one would expect from balance-of-power theory, much of civilian behavior in France during the 1930s seemed immune to the quickening pace of international events. Many of Hitler's policies compromised France's security system, but French civilians did little to realign French army doctrine with the new strategic realities. In 1936, after sixteen years of a close military alliance with France, Belgium declared its neutrality. All ties between the French and Belgian General Staffs were officially severed; the French army could no longer prepare positions in Belgium and thereafter had to wait for a Belgian request before moving forward to repulse a German attack. To compensate for the reduction in French security, France could have organized a mobile force or extended the Maginot Line along the Belgian frontier, but it did neither.[96] In the same year, French paralysis in the face of the German re-militarization of the Rhineland underscored what French civilians had long since been told: that the French army could not take decisive action against Germany without a full mobilization.[97] Yet again, little was done to adapt the French army to new strategic demands.

After the German invasion of Poland in September 1939, and in an attempt to maintain morale during the "phony war," the French command took the dramatic action of instructing the troops to plant rose bushes around the Maginot Line.[98] The rose bushes were planted, but de Gaulle's calls for the creation of an armored force capable of offensive strikes against Germany were ignored.[99] In all three of these cases—the Belgian declaration of neutrality, the remilitarization of the Rhineland, and the German offensive against Poland—French civilians recognized that France's strategic position had been weakened, but each time, they took little action to reorient French army doctrine.[100]

This does not mean that the distribution of power is unimportant or that French civilians foolishly disregarded their state's national interests. However, as compelling as the international system may be, it does not determine a nation's choice between offensive and defensive military doctrines. Throughout the interwar period, French civilians did not behave as hypothesized by balance-of-power theory. As I argue in Chapter 4, when designing military policy, French civilians were often more concerned about the balance of power in *domestic* politics than about the distribution of power in the international arena.

Nor can the French army's adoption of a defensive doctrine be explained as resulting from the powerful defensive lessons of World War I. To the contrary, in the decade following the armistice that ended the bloody carnage of the Great War, the French army showed a preference for offensive operations. But this orientation did not last. Eventually, the French army adopted—without civilian direction—a defensive doctrine. This outcome challenges the functional proposition that military organizations inherently prefer offensive doctrines. What the French army thought was in its interest was a function of its culture.

4

Culture and French Doctrine

An army organized by politicians stops being a
military force against outside enemies; it becomes
a political weapon against internal adversaries.
  (Etienne Lamy)

THOUGH ill suited to defeating France's continental adversary, the French army's defensive doctrine made sense given domestic political battles and the French army's organizational culture. In 1928 the French Parliament voted to reduce the term of conscription to one year. This decision was based not on a calculation of the threat posed by a resurgent Germany or the needs of alliance diplomacy. Instead, domestic political conflict motivated civilian intervention in French military policy; reducing the term of conscription was part of a long-standing battle between the Left and Right in French domestic politics.

Since the mid-nineteenth century the Left and Right had fought over the organizational form of the army. While the Right demanded a professional army, which in its view was the only army that could ensure domestic order and stability, the Left believed that the retention of a professional army threatened French democracy. To the Left, only a militia or conscript army could guarantee the survival of the French republic against reactionary forces in society. In 1928, after more than fifty years of fighting against the Right's preference for professional soldiers and a long term of conscription, the center and left parties adopted a one-year term of conscription.

Once French policymakers reduced the term of conscription to one year, the army had to work with this decision. How an army will react to such a change cannot be deduced from the functional requirements of all military organizations. In the case of the French army, it is necessary to understand the attitude of officers socialized within the army toward short-term conscripts. Unlike German officers, French officers believed that short-term conscripts could fight only defensive battles and that an offensive doctrine required a professional army. In other words, once the Parliament reduced the term of conscription to one year, the French army could imagine only one possibility. Although a functional analysis would suggest that the French army would prefer an offensive doctrine, a cultural approach explains why it adopted a defensive doctrine. The French army's culture is the intervening variable between the civilian decision to reduce the length of conscription and the army's choice of a defensive doctrine.

Competing Political Cultures

Much has been written about the instability of the Third Republic. It is a dreary picture of one Cabinet after another giving way to another equally powerless coalition. Yet it was not the fragility of the French governments that established the framework for French doctrine but the strength of the competition between contending political forces with conflicting political cultures about the role of the armed forces in the domestic arena. Within months of the signing of the armistice, the old political struggle over the organizational form of the army reemerged.

Since the French Revolution, and especially in the second half of the nineteenth century, two major divisions in French politics had fought over the army's organizational structure. The Right wanted a professional (volunteer) army consisting of long-serving soldiers; the Left advocated a national army founded on militia principles or based on short-term conscripts.[1] The Right wanted a professional army as protection against domestic instability and the rising power of the Left; the Left feared the repressive power of a professional army. For the Left, only militia, reserve, or conscript forces could guarantee the preservation of republican liberties.[2] Domestic politics determined these positions, not France's international ambitions, its adversary, or its position in the international system.

The presence of two cultures was very different from the situation in Great Britain, where there was a consensus about the role of the armed forces in the domestic arena. In circumstances where there is only one culture, the elements of the culture seem like common sense or tradition. The elements of a consensual political culture are ideas and assumptions so unself-conscious that they seem natural. This was not the situation in France during the interwar period. Constantly in conflict with each other, the competing cultures became highly articulated and self-conscious belief systems. They more closely approximated ideologies than common sense. Whereas a consensual culture affects choices by establishing what is "natural" or by making other patterns of behavior inconceivable, competing cultures have a more direct effect on policy. In France, each culture held a consistent set of assumptions about, and prescriptions for, military policy.

The Left and Short-Term Conscripts

> Permanent armies, if they sometimes appear to
> be instruments of war, are singularly dangerous
> instruments that break in the hands of those
> who use them, often mortally wounding them.
>   *(Bernard Nardain)*

The French left wanted an army based on short-term conscripts.[3] In the Left's view, it was imperative that the army not be a separate caste, isolated from society, and imbued with military values. If the army were able to retain its conscripts for several years, it would be able to elicit passive obedience and to use this force for domestic repression. The Left believed that the elimination of the professional army would diminish a threat to French democracy.

Seeking to avoid the development of a state within a state, the Left wanted to create, in its words, an osmosis between the army and society.[4] Léon Blum, the leader of the Socialist Party, argued that "military service is not the exercise of a profession, but a civic responsibility. Every citizen is a soldier, every soldier a citizen."[5] The Left proposed numerous policies that would prevent the insulation of the officer corps from the wider society and their development as a separate caste. After the Franco-Prussian War, for example, the Left called for regional recruitment and permanent garrisons as safeguards against the development of a praetorian guard with few links to the nation.[6] Before World War I, the renowned socialist Jean Jaurès recommended that officers receive their education in the universities and not in the isolation of the war colleges.[7] Similarly, during the interwar years, Edouard Daladier argued that all officer cadets should spend twelve months at the university before their second year at St. Cyr, the French military academy. The Left also championed the development of physical education and military preparatory classes for French youth.[8] Appearing as right-wing or even fascistic to the Anglo-Saxon mind, these policies were specifically designed to reduce the time in the barracks to a strict minimum so that the young men would acquire a more civic, as opposed to military education.

The Left feared that if the conscript spent several years within the grasp of a total institution like the army, the officer corps would be able to mold what were once citizens into pliable instruments of the reactionary factions within society. For the Left, the soldier must always be first and foremost a member of society and not owe primary allegiance to a corporate entity. In early 1934, Blum expressed this sentiment:

History teaches very clearly that collective feelings develop in professional armies. They are . . . waiting to become the army of a leader. Isolated from the surrounding life, compressed and focused on itself by training, customs and discipline, the army establishes within the nation an enclosed enclave. . . . Public duty is replaced by hierarchical obedience. National solidarity is replaced by professional solidarity.[9]

The Left sought to retain the individuality of the conscript and to avoid losing the citizen-soldier to the collectivity of a professional and potentially reactionary army.[10]

For the Left, the less time spent in the barracks the better; the conscript needed to be under the colors just long enough to learn the requisite military skills. To stay longer would allow *l'esprit militaire* to develop and with it, passive obedience.[11] As Etienne Lamy explained, "*L'esprit militaire* is the voluntary death of a personality of which the only thing surviving is obedience."[12] For the Left, long service instilled the passive obedience that allowed the Right to use the army to repress domestic unrest. To motivate a Frenchman to fire on his fellow countrymen required draining all individuality from the citizen-soldier until nothing remained but blind obedience. The Left maintained that if protection against the external adversary was the army's primary role, passive obedience would be unnecessary. Patriotism alone would motivate and discipline the citizen-soldier.[13]

Only by avoiding a divorce between society and the army could it be possible to create an army that would defend the country as a whole and not one particular political class. During parliamentary debates over the length of conscription in the early 1920s, a member of the Radical Party declared, "It is necessary that France have the army of its policies; but I don't want France to carry out the policies of her army."[14] Similarly, at a Communist Party rally immediately after World War II, Laurent Casanova expressed this long-held ideal: "The army of tomorrow must be an instrument of democratic politics and of the independence of France. It must be a conscript army, national and republican . . . it must be an army in which the career officers keep in contact with the nation and will be nourished on the same ideals as the nation. . . . It will not be the army of a faction or of a party."[15] The Left demanded that the army be of the people, not of a particular class.

The Left's rejection of a professional army should not be mistaken for a renunciation of military force. Unlike some Left or Socialist Parties in Europe, the French Left, born in and inspired by revolution, has never been antimilitaristic or pacifistic. Armed masses had succeeded in overthrowing the Old Regime, the Restoration in 1830, and the July Monarchy in 1848. The National Guard and the mass army resisted foreign invasion and occupation during the revolutionary years and in the after-math of the Franco-Prussian War.[16] As a commentator on the French army explained, "The revolution transformed subjects into citizens and citizens into soldiers."[17] The first Bastille Day celebrations after the elec-tion of a Socialist government in 1981 symbolized the Socialist Party's continued support for a strong national defense. The parade included in-fantry units from throughout the country, intervention forces, and as-pects of the nuclear deterrent. For the first time, military parades were also held in seven large provincial cities.[18]

Far from rejecting the use of force, the French Left understood that it was vital to control the ultimate source of power. Some of the most prominent French Socialists devoted considerable attention to designing an army that met the needs of the French republic. In 1910, Jean Jaurès published his celebrated study, *L'armée nouvelle*, which outlined the basic principles of the Left's military agenda.[19] Whether a militia force or a mixed army heavily dependent on the mobilization of reserves, the leftist ideal required a short term of service that would, in the Left's view, harness the repressive designs of the reactionary part of French society.[20]

The Left's fear of the army's domestic power was long-standing. Since the mid-nineteenth century the Left had sought to reduce the length of conscription, and Jaurès's ideas culminated in a legislative proposal in 1910. The Left scrutinized many military proposals for their political ramifications, and in particular for their effect on the domestic strength and orientation of the army. For example, in 1924 the Left objected to various mobilization plans out of fear that partial mobilizations would be used as strikebreakers.[21] A similar rationale was behind the Left's ob-jection to a unified command and a ministry of national defense. Though repeatedly proposed by the Right and army officers, the Left opposed these proposals because they feared the potential domestic power of a highly centralized and effective general staff.[22]

This fear of the latent domestic force of a professional army had dom-inated leftist rhetoric and its legislative agenda since the Franco-Prussian War. Political tracts, books, and newspaper articles denounced profes-sional armies as a threat to domestic order. The leader of the Socialist Party asked rhetorically, "If there are political problems, what will be the attitude of a professional army that has been taught contempt for civil-ians, and which is controlled by officers of whom the most loyal would only resign themselves to the Republic?" In Blum's view, "it is always the professional armies that conduct coups d'état and *pronunciamentos*."[23] Only soldiers who remained members of society could be entrusted with the preservation of the French republic. To the Left, a permanent army would serve the needs of a monarchic state or become a reactionary force in a democratic state. For some, the primary reason to have a permanent army was to ensure the maintenance of a capitalist society.[24] As a writer in *L'humanité* explained in 1934: "The fear of a popular army tied to the masses haunts the chief of staff. As class warfare worsens, the army leaders increasingly attempt to recruit soldiers whom they hope to make into docile instruments by . . . the long separation from their home."[25] The Left feared that a professional army would serve the Right's domestic agenda.[26]

For the Left, a professional army threatened domestic liberty and would be incapable of defending France. A professional army might be appropriate for wars between princes, or for short foreign expeditions, but in their view, it was poorly suited to defend France in an age of total war.[27] This belief is an important reminder that the Left's insistence on a conscript army did not mean that it was unconcerned about French security or unwilling to protect French national integrity. The rise in German power and Hitler's ascent alarmed the French Left. In response to the deteriorating international conditions, the Popular Front initiated rearmament programs in 1936 that far surpassed the programs of the previous, more conservative governments. In fact, the Popular Front's rearmament program cut into social programs: while military expenditures accelerated after 1936, money for social programs decreased.[28] But the Left did not want a professional army.

The Left was so convinced of the connection between a conscript army and the protection of democratic liberties that it applied this link regardless of the context. During the Versailles negotiations on the future of the German army, the leftist press denounced the British proposals for a professional army. An article in *Les débats* exclaimed, "The creation of a professional army in Germany risks putting between the hands of the Prussian military caste a remarkable means of political action."[29] For democracy to survive in defeated Germany, the creation of a permanent army had to be avoided. In the Left's view, the Weimar Republic needed an army that would preserve republican virtues. Similarly, in those regions where the French Left did not worry about democratic principles, it did not care about the length of conscription or the presence of a professional army. Long-serving soldiers comprised the French colonial armies, but no leftist government during the interwar period tried to apply the same republican principle of conscription to those French forces.[30]

For the Left, the battlefield for which a professional army prepared was internal. The headlines across the left-wing papers during the debate about reinstating the two-year service in 1935 declared: "The threat of two years."[31] "Mobilize public opinion against the two years."[32] Two weeks later, the paper declared, "TWO YEARS, IT'S WAR."[33] The reason for the Left's rejection of the longer service had nothing to do with Germany, Britain, or France's eastern allies. As Blum put it, "It will be a danger for republican liberties, that is to say for domestic peace."[34]

The Right and Professional Soldiers

I do not want obligatory military service that will
enflame passions and put a rifle on the shoulder
of all the socialists; I want a professional army,
solid, disciplined, and capable of eliciting respect
at home and abroad.
  (Louis-Adolphe Thiers)

Like the Left, the Right believed that the number of years the soldier spent in the ranks determined whether the army could be relied upon to maintain the status quo. In a domestic crisis, only soldiers toughened by many years of strict discipline could be depended upon to guarantee social stability and the preservation of law and order. For the Right, one of the army's chief tasks was to preserve peace at home.[35]

Whereas the Left sought to avoid a deep divide between the army and society by minimizing the length of conscription, the Right wanted to keep the conscript under arms for at least two years. The Right agreed that a shorter military service would be sufficient to train soldiers in the technical aspects of the trade, but believed more time was needed to create the necessary passive obedience.[36] A parliamentarian explained this process: "A soldier who has served for one year has learned without doubt to use his weapons, but he has not learned to obey; his character has not been subjugated, his will has not been broken; he has not yet become what makes an army strong: passive obedience."[37] Developed in the eighteenth century to fight against insubordination and to ensure obedience whoever the adversary, this autocratic conception of command also ensured that orders would be followed "literally, without a murmur or hesitation."[38] Although the Right and especially military officers spoke of the need to instill passive obedience, they more often emphasized the importance of developing cohesion:[39] "The improvised soldier—half taught—will certainly lose his head without the support that solidarity gives. These qualities are the result of military education, very different from training and it demands a lot more time. . . . Training is relatively easy to teach. Education is an altogether different thing. It is the latter that gives a man his genuine value."[40] The solidarity that a long term of service produced would guarantee that the "spirit of the collective being" would replace the soldier's individuality.[41]

For the Right, a long term of service would allow the officer corps to instill an esprit de corps in the troops and thus detach the allegiance of the men from the society at large; in their new collective identity they would follow orders unquestioningly. While the Right argued that long-serving conscripts were the most effective soldiers for international conflicts, it readily admitted that a long-serving army was also necessary in order to ensure domestic stability.[42] For example, during a strike wave in 1936, the leader of the conservative wing of the Radical Party, Camille Chautemps, invited Charles de Gaulle to a secret meeting. In commenting on their discussion, de Gaulle said that Chautemps "seemed very favorably disposed . . . even greatly stressing . . . the importance that my specialized corps [of professional soldiers] would assume in current and future public order problems in both France and North Africa."[43]

Discussions in the right-wing press during the Versailles negotiations repeated the Right's desire for an army that could be used to enforce domestic stability. In discussing proposals for the German army, L'écho de Paris questioned whether Germany would retain a military force capable of guaranteeing domestic order.[44] A columnist in Le temps emphasized the army's dual role: "We find ourselves facing a dilemma: we allow the Reich to retain its army and we can be almost certain that this army will become an instrument of aggression, or we reduce the German armed services to almost nothing and we run the risk that anarchy will be installed at our doors: instability, insolvency, contagion."[45] When discussing the future army of France's main adversary, the Right, like the Left, examined the domestic repercussions of each proposal.

A diverse group of clergy, aristocrats, and politicians on the right in French politics advocated the maintenance of a permanent army composed of long-serving soldiers. To the most conservative, a strong standing army was one of the last remaining bulwarks against the rise of the Left and social instability. Remembering the lessons of the workers' revolt in 1848 and hardened by the experience with the Paris Commune in 1871, the Right believed that one of the army's chief tasks was to preserve peace at home. In a domestic crisis, only soldiers toughened by many years of strict discipline could be depended on to guarantee the preservation of law and order.

The Adoption of a One-Year Term of Conscription

The creation of the Garde Nationale in 1789 and a mass army in 1793 had originally drawn the battle lines between the Left and the Right on the organizational structure of the French army.[46] In the early 1800s, the royalist Chateaubriand denounced the "republican principle of conscription" and claimed that it was incompatible with the monarchy: "How can we permit under a monarchy a recruitment system whose egalitarian principles smack of democracy."[47] The French government abolished conscription in 1814, increased the length of military service to six years in 1818 and to eight years in 1824, and then reduced it to seven years in 1832. Legislation in 1855 further reinforced the professional character of the army. By mid-century, a professional army had supplanted the revolutionary and Jacobin heritage of the French army. This army fired on the revolutionaries in 1830 and supported the conservative forces in 1848. Louis Napoleon's Second Empire repeatedly used the professional army to suppress domestic unrest.

In 1870, the Franco-Prussian War confirmed the quantitative superiority of the Prussian military system, which was based on universal military service. At the same time, the experience with the Paris Commune strengthened the Right's conviction that only a professional army could be trusted in times of domestic peril. Led by Adolphe Thiers, the Right instituted a five-year term of service in 1872. Although conscription was theoretically in existence, it was only intermittently and partially enforced; this legislation in effect reestablished the dominance of the professional army. The lesson of the Commune had triumphed over the lessons of the war itself: domestic order came before national defense.

The Left majority in the Chamber of Deputies in 1876 failed to reduce the dominance of the professional army, and it was another twelve years before the Left was able to reduce the term of service from five to three years. Just as the Commune had reinforced the Right's fears, the threat of Boulangism in 1887 and 1889, and the Dreyfus Affair at the turn of the century, became potent reminders to the Left of the need to curtail the domestic strength of the professional army.[48] The Left grew in electoral strength at the end of the nineteenth century, captured the Senate in 1902, and two years later reduced the term of conscription. Not surprisingly, the return of the Right to power in 1913 brought in its wake a return to a three-year military service. In response, Jaurès proposed the creation of a militia force and, using rhetoric that would sound strikingly familiar fifteen years later, declared that the prolongation of the military service was "a crime against the republic and against France."[49]

After the initial defeat of the professional army in the opening battles of World War I and the eventual victory of the nation-in-arms, the Right could no longer question the principle of universal military service.[50] For example, in 1925 Jean Fabry, a former officer and a leading member of the Army Commission in the Chamber of Deputies, defended the maintenance of a professional core of the army. He was, however, careful to reassure his audience that he was not questioning the value of the nation-in-arms.[51] Unlike the moderate Right, however, the extreme Right did not hesitate to express its continued support for a large professional force.[52]

The Right and the army could no longer dismiss the value of a conscript army, but they would not relinquish their demand for the retention of a significant professional component of the army. The battle between the Left and Right shifted from a conflict over a choice between a professional army and a nation-in-arms to a question of the size of the professional component of the conscript army and the length of conscription.[53] The Left had gained considerable ground with the acceptance of the nation-in-arms, but the old political battle had not disappeared. Within months after the conclusion of World War I, the Left and Right again began to fight about the structure of the French army.

This debate continued throughout the 1920s and was concentrated during three periods: immediately after World War I, from 1921 to 1923, and in the late 1920s. The Parliament reduced the length of conscription to three years in 1921, to eighteen months in 1923, and finally to one year in 1928.[54] So important was this choice that in just two months in 1919 French deputies proposed no fewer than eight ways to reorganize the army. In the spring of 1922, the Parliament again debated this issue. As one would expect, the proposals developed by the Right sought to maintain a core of active soldiers ready at all times. The Right repeatedly stressed that the inviolability of the French frontier required a permanent army that would be capable of meeting a sudden attack without resorting to a general mobilization. The Left's proposals ranged from establishing a purely militia force reminiscent of Jaurès's designs to creating an army with a small professional core, but composed primarily of reserves. Integral to each position was a short term of conscription and either the abolition or subordination of the professional component of the army.

A collection of center and left-wing parties captured the Parliament in the elections in 1924, and within three years the Chamber of Deputies adopted legislation that outlined the organizational structure of the army. These new laws endorsed the Left's views about the role of the armed forces in the domestic arena and established the framework of the army that France took to war in 1939. Based on a one-year term of conscription, the legislation also called for the maintenance of a professional core that would train the citizen-soldier during peacetime and, upon mobilization, absorb the mass of reserves. The Left's agenda had triumphed; the army was transformed from an active force to a potential force.

The Retention of a Professional Component

The Left achieved what it had sought since the Franco-Prussian War—a short term of conscription—but the legislation in 1928 is best viewed as a compromise that also responded to the Right's desire to maintain a professional core.[55] By agreeing to "prior conditions" that would increase the professional component of the army, the minister of defense, Paul Painlevé, obtained the Superior Council of War's support for the one-year term of conscription: Articles 103 and 104 of the recruitment law specifically mandated the retention of 106,000 professional soldiers and civilian replacements for noncombat roles in the army in order to free up more professionals for active combat roles.

This compromise, or the coupling of the "prior conditions" with the reduction in the length of conscription, did not pass unnoticed by leading figures of the center-left government. Much of the subsequent debate focused on the mandate for the retention of professional soldiers, and both the Radicals and the Socialists drafted proposals specifically designed to exclude these conditions. However, Painlevé prevailed on their inclusion.[56] In exchange for a one-year term of conscription, the professional component of the army would be enlarged.

A professional army had become politically untenable in the interwar period, but the Right did not relax its demands.[57] The Right used two tactics to protect the professional army: the prior conditions and the supposed requirement to avoid any loss of French territory during a war. Painlevé's inclusion of the prior conditions in the military legislation in 1928 was the culmination of the Right's long-standing attempt to tie any reduction in the terms of conscription to an augmentation of the army's professional core.[58] This tactic began with the earlier reduction in the length of service and dominated many of the discussions in the Superior Council of War in the 1920s. For example, in April 1925 the council unanimously rejected the reduction in the terms of conscription if it were not accompanied by the fulfillment of the prior conditions.[59] Jean Fabry made a similar demand in the Chamber of Deputies in March 1922 and the right-wing press seconded the motion.[60] The irony of this stipulation was not lost on Bertrand de Jouvenel: "In this way, the more we organize an army based on short-term conscripts, the more professional soldiers become necessary. The result of the Boncour bill—which is supposed to give us a militia army—will be to give us 106,000 professional soldiers!"[61]

The Right's insistence on the principle of the "inviolability of the frontier" was the second tactic that it used to protect the professional army. Defending a country does not require that the battle begin at the frontier with the aim of avoiding any territorial loss. The French plan of 1895 called for a defense in depth: French divisions would be deployed deep in French territory in order to reveal the enemy's intentions and to blunt its initial attacks. Once the enemy had advanced on a field of France's choosing, the French army would concentrate against the enemy's flanks in a powerful counteroffensive.

In the interwar period a defense in depth was no longer politically feasible for the French army. During the opening battles in 1914, France's professional army had failed to protect the rich iron ore fields in northern France. After the war, the Parliament criticized the army's inability to protect France's industrial base, and in order to deflect this criticism the army tied itself to the principle of avoiding any territorial loss. This principle would not only reassure the Parliament that the army would never again lose part of French territory, but it also justified the maintenance of a strong professional corps ready at all times to protect French territorial integrity. Not coincidentally, the principle of the inviolability of the frontier also undermined calls for exclusive reliance on a conscript army.[62]

Throughout the 1920s, the Right used the principle of the inviolability of the frontier to justify maintaining a professional army that could act as a permanent covering force.[63] In 1925, Deputy Jean Fabry argued that the potential reduction in the term of conscription would threaten the viability of the covering force and require a reorganization of the army to ensure that military professionals could defend the frontiers of France. Fabry explained: "The principle is admitted that no part of French territory should be undefended against invasion. . . . Another principle is that only well-instructed and homogeneous units [professional soldiers] can be immediately brought together, transported, and used. In a word, the units ready to undertake action are capable of furnishing an efficient covering force."[64] Throughout the mid-1920s, members of the Superior Council of War, including Weygand, Debeney, and Franchet d'Esperey, reiterated the "inevitable" link between a strong covering force and a professional army.[65] Ten years later, General de Castelnau, former president of the Army Commission of the Chamber of Deputies, repeated this link in an article in *L'écho de Paris*.[66] Similarly, a partisan of *Action française* argued that only a professional army could adequately man the covering force, and de Gaulle agreed that there could be "no covering force without a professional army."[67]

This was not the first time that the Right and the army had advocated this particular strategic design—the inviolability of the frontier and the consequent need for a permanent army ready at all times—to protect the professional army. The Right had used this tactic in the 1870s, and again during the debate in 1913, to increase the term of conscription.[68] In reference to the conflict during the nineteenth century, Monteilhet explained that "the theory of the covering force, which is not derived from any sound principle, is therefore a new manifestation of the secular conflict between the professional and national army."[69]

The tactic was successful. During the interwar period few politicians would argue against the protection of France's territorial integrity; the military legislation of the late 1920s incorporated the principle of the inviolability of the frontier.[70] What had begun as a political maneuver became one of the fundamental tenets of French military policy.[71] The army was able to save a professional cadre, but it also became committed to a military policy based on a forward defense. The first step toward the creation of the Maginot Line had been taken, not out of fear of a resurgent Germany, but from the determined effort of the French Right and military officers to defeat the leftist challenge to the regular army.

During the nineteenth century, the domestic role of the French army had so dominated its development that the French forces were ill equipped to withstand the Prussian army in 1870.[72] This preoccupation with domestic questions did not disappear in the twentieth century. As a French commentator explained, "The recruitment laws have a political aspect which in the Parliament dominates all other considerations. . . . The governments were always more worried about the domestic political role of the army than its military role against an external enemy."[73]

The Meaning of Conscription

I call these civilian choices "cultural" rather than just labeling them "interests" because there is such underlying meaning—or cultural connotation—attached to them. Similar social and economic positions do not translate into similar policy positions across national boundaries. We cannot assume that all left-wing parties, like the French Left in the 1920s, fear a professional army, or that all right-wing or conservative parties do not want a conscript army. There is nothing inherent in reserves or a conscript or militia army that makes them a force for the Left.

The types of armies that the British and French Left imagined to be in their interest were opposites.[74] For the French Left, conscription expressed community spirit, equality, and most important, it prevented the growth of a praetorian guard. In contrast, the British Left, as well as most British politicians, have historically rejected conscription and mass armies as attacks on individual liberty and instruments of continental imperialism. And in contrast to their French counterparts, the British Left did not view a standing army as a threat to British democracy. The very social forces (the Right) that opposed reliance on reserves, or a conscript or militia army in France, supported this system in England and the

United States. In Great Britain, the militia (or auxiliary forces) were traditionally tools of the propertied classes to maintain public order. In the nineteenth century, for example, the government repeatedly used those forces to control industrial disputes and political reform movements. Not surprisingly, it was military officers and conservative politicians who supported universal military service in Britain.[75]

Just as British conservatives advocated conscription (and the French Right did not), the representatives of the most elite sector of American society (corporation managers, financiers, Wall Street lawyers, railroad magnates, and major publishers) led the campaign for conscription in the early twentieth century. For these men, educated in the most prestigious prep schools and universities and representing the Eastern business-oriented wing of the Republican Party, conscription responded to a number of America's needs. They believed military service would help protect the United States and its access to markets in Latin America and the Far East, as well as help tame class, ethnic, and regional divisions.[76]

Worried that the traditional institutions of social control would be unable to assimilate millions of immigrants and members of the working class, American advocates of conscription argued that mandatory military service would spread the military values of duty, discipline, and respect. An article in the *Yale Review* in 1916 extolled the adoption of military conscription and explained that "the spectacle in democratic England of hundreds of thousands of coal miners utilizing the extremity of their country's agony as a means of extorting from society a selfish pecuniary advantage for themselves, bring before us vividly enough the workman's understanding of his 'democratic ideal.'"[77] Universal military service could help replace class consciousness with national loyalty and "Americanize" immigrants. It could also help produce disciplined workers. "We have everything . . . except discipline," an advocate of conscription said. "We have initiative, we have imagination, we have capacity, but one thing we have not got is capacity to steadily, day in and day out, for a period of months, stick to a definite job and do it under any conditions." Military conscription, in the view of the American Right, would transform the masses into "far more desirable citizens and far more productive laborers."[78]

While the French Left thought their interests best protected by militia forces, the American Left feared militia forces, and with good reason. After the American Revolution, militias were used repeatedly for social control: militias controlled slave populations in the South and suppressed Shay's Rebellion in Massachusetts in 1786 and the Whiskey Rebellion in Pennsylvania in 1794. American militias declined after the 1820s, but then underwent a dramatic revival in the late 1870s, especially after the great railroad strike of 1877. States with large working-class populations took the lead in the militia's revival, and strikebreaking

became the militia's main function; from 30 to 50 percent of National
Guard activity was connected with strikes.[79] In 1892, Samuel Gompers,
the president of the American Federation of Labor, declared, "Membership in a labor organization and the militia at one and the same time is
inconsistent and incompatible."[80]

In the early part of the twentieth century, the American Left bitterly attacked proposals for national service. Anarchists, socialists, the United
Mine Workers, many local and city labor councils, and more radical
working-class organizations such as the Industrial Workers of the World
attacked universal military service.[81] The publisher of *The Nation* explained, "We have always valued the American's self assertiveness—yes,
his refusal to recognize masters, his independence of thought and action. . . . We hated the servile obedience of the foreigner. Universal conscription . . . drives men into intellectual slavery."[82] The reformer Amos
Pinchot accused the Wall Street interests behind the campaign for compulsory service of wanting meek and disciplined workers that would be
"obedient slaves of a ruling money class." Conscription, he stressed,
would destroy America's democracy: "The moment you find the American citizen disciplined to authority and trained to look for leadership to
a superior class, at that moment you have lost democracy."[83]

Instead of universal conscription (which the French Left supported),
the American Left advocated the creation of a well-equipped and volunteer professional force. Pinchot, for example, claimed that a professional
army of 250,000 would best serve U.S. national interests, and the *New
Republic* advocated reliance on a professional army. In their view, only
"doctrinaire militarists" supported universal military training.[84] What
the American Left supported the French Left opposed (and the French
Right supported). To make sense of these choices, we must understand
the meanings actors attach to different policies; that is, we must examine the actors' cultures.

The Army's Culture and the Meaning of Conscription

> A direct, essential and inevitable connection exists
> between the conduct of war, strategy, tactics, and
> the morale of the soldier.
>   (*Charles de Gaulle*)

After World War I and the election of a left-wing coalition in 1924, the
republican ideal finally triumphed: the French Parliament reduced the
length of conscription to one year. The army resisted the decision, but
once it was made the high command had to design a doctrine within this

constraint. However, the leeway that the French army had cannot be determined objectively; all military organizations would not respond similarly to the need to work with short-term conscripts. The shorter length of service did not require the adoption of a defensive doctrine. Yet the French army's organizational culture prevented it from continuing its offensive orientation after 1928 and the introduction of short-term conscripts. The French army had been offensively oriented in the 1920s, and, with a different organizational culture, that posture could have continued.

The Offensive Option

An offensive doctrine was "objectively" possible after 1928. The French army had the money and the ideas. Throughout the interwar period French policymakers were much more willing to support large expenditures than their British counterparts. The French army was not quantitatively inferior to the German army, and it could have acquired the requisite materiel for armored warfare.[85] The French officer corps was also aware of offensive alternatives; the French army was well versed on doctrinal developments in Germany and had its own advocates of mechanized warfare. De Gaulle's campaign in the 1930s is the most renowned, but de Gaulle was not the only French officer to support the offensive use of massed tanks. General Jean-Baptiste Estienne, often considered the father of French armor, organized the first French tank units during World War I and in the 1920s became head of the Tank Inspectorate.[86] A collection of other officers, including Colonels Emile Alléhaut, Charles Chedeville, Joseph Doumenc, Jean Perré, Joseph Molinié, and Pol-Maurice Velpry, joined Estienne in calling for the creation of an independent tank force. During the early 1920s the chief of staff, General Edmond Buat, encouraged innovative uses of tanks, and articles advocating the independent use of tank units filled the military journals.[87]

The French army had direct evidence of the potential of massed and highly mobile tank units. In 1925 it used independent and highly mobile tank companies to quell rebellions in Morocco, and in the 1930s it conducted several exercises to test mechanized warfare.[88] The French high command used the Spanish civil war to reinforce existing doctrinal tendencies, but other lessons were readily available from the successful German combined arms assaults in Aragon and Catalonia in 1938.[89] Finally, the German campaigns in Czechoslovakia and Poland provided all the evidence necessary for a reevaluation of existing doctrine. Ignorance of offensive alternatives cannot explain the French army's endorsement of a defensive doctrine in the 1930s.

In addition, French civilians did not demand a defensive doctrine or actively participate in the formation of military doctrine. Operational decisions were left to the military. For example, in the spring of 1932 there was controversy within the officer corps over the fortification of the French-Belgian border. Theoretically, French civilians could have resolved the disagreement and imposed a decision on the divided staff, but civilian intervention was not considered an option. "It was not within the purview of French civilian defense authorities to make military strategy—still less to arbitrate between different operational plans," a historian explained. "It was the task of the politicians to determine the grand strategic objectives of national policy. It was the task of the military leaders to identify the optimal means of attaining them."[90] Indeed, when the high command's indecision about the fortification of the French border became apparent, the civilian ministers present at the meeting fell into a "painful silence."[91]

French civilians were no more active in the formation of military doctrine. The parliamentary decision to reduce the term of conscription was important, but civilian input went no further. French civilians believed that doctrinal questions were beyond their purview.[92] A historian of French civil military relations, Philip Bankwitz, commented on "governmental passivity in questions of doctrinal and organizational reform."An investigatory commission after World War II also commented on the relative autonomy of the French army, describing the General Staff as a "real State within a State."[93]

Even if civilians had believed it was their role and responsibility to decide the doctrinal orientation of the army, their preferences were mixed. The overwhelming support for the Maginot Line speaks to civilian support for a defensive orientation, but civilians also supported a more offensive orientation. During the 1920s, the Chamber of Deputies agreed that France should have the capability to undertake coercive actions against Germany, and French Rhineland policy was predicated on the ability to launch an offensive into Germany.[94] After Germany's remilitarization of the Rhineland in 1936, Prime Minister Blum and Minister of War Daladier advocated the formation of an armored force capable of offensive action.[95]

Many analysts argue that French public opinion was largely defensive during the 1920s and 1930s and that this sentiment forced the government and army into a defensive posture. But there is a difference between a state's intentions and its army's doctrine. As Joseph Paul-Boncour declared in the Chamber of Deputies: "I am speaking of defensive policies; I am not speaking of a technique or even a defensive strategy."[96] Nevertheless, the preferences of civilian policymakers or the public for an offensive or defensive doctrine were largely irrelevant; French policymakers deferred to the military on questions of doctrine. The French army could have adopted an offensive doctrine if it had wanted to.

Even construction of the Maginot Line left open offensive possibilities. As discussed in Chapter 3, the fortifications were initially conceived to support offensive operations. Shielded by concrete, the French army could have lightened its defending forces and assembled a powerful striking force to hit Germany where it least expected. Thus, despite adequate funding, knowledge of offensive alternatives, and freedom from civilian interference, the French army did not integrate offensive concepts into its doctrine, and instead, after the reduction in the term of conscription to one year in 1928, became increasingly committed to a defensive doctrine. Its organizational culture would not allow otherwise.

The French Army's Organizational Culture

The French army could not imagine short-term conscripts executing an offensive doctrine.[97] For the French officer, one-year conscripts were good for only one thing—implementing a defensive war plan. In the army's view "young troops" could only be engaged methodically; they could not handle sophisticated technology, new methods of warfare, or demonstrate the élan necessary for offensive actions.

For the French officer, a short term of conscription would not allow the necessary cohesion to develop within the units. In discussing the annual intake of conscripts, General Debeney explained, "[These] men are far from having the solidity of professional soldiers since they have only done six to eleven months of service. . . . In effect, this mass of reservists will only be good for the second echelon."[98] Likewise, General de Castelnau spoke of the cohesion that develops within units consisting of professional soldiers: "Permanent units have a soul that vibrates, a heart that palpitates, a spirit that has penetrated diverse levels. . . . The leader, subordinates, and comrades have learned to know one another; they are bound together by lines of mutual confidence, and by the imponderable but very real force of cohesion."[99] The French officer did not think a one-year conscript would be able to develop the collective spirit necessary for difficult operations.

Short-term conscripts were also not thought capable of manipulating new technology. Several years before World War II, a war that was dominated by mass armies and new technologies, General Mordacq questioned one-year conscripts' ability to use modern equipment: "With the service of one year, it was absolutely impossible to give to our contingents an instruction responding to the demands of modern warfare."[100] For de

Gaulle, even two years would not be enough. Taking advantage of the new technology of modern warfare required a professional army. In de Gaulle's words, "Modern warfare demands that the warrior have ever increasing technical skills. . . . The time has come for elite soldiers."[101]

General Weygand, the inspector general of the army, shared de Gaulle's disdain for the technical capabilities of short-term conscripts: "The professional army is capable of using certain materiel. . . . A militia, to the contrary, will be incapable of manipulating modern materiel."[102] This lack of faith in a conscript army's ability to take advantage of new technology was not new to the French army. In 1898 a French officer spoke of the technical ineptitude of short-term conscripts: "Patriotic enthusiasm, bellicose fervor, and all the morale factors do not suffice to ensure success in this age of mechanization. . . . Militia will always be wanting, and their chivalrous efforts will easily shatter when confronted with well-trained troops . . . With the creation of a militia—France will be open, France will be lost."[103] The French officer held out little hope for the short-term conscript in an age of technological warfare.[104]

QUANTITY VERSUS QUALITY

The dichotomy between quantity and quality, a contrast noted repeatedly in the writings of French military officers, captures the stark distinction in the French army's culture between the capabilities of short-term conscripts and professional soldiers. In 1925, General Duval argued, "It is necessary to choose: either sacrifice the value of the officer for the sake of numbers, or sacrifice the numbers for the value of the officer and the equipment."[105] Similarly, in 1930, General Debeney spoke repeatedly of the distinction between quantity and quality.[106] During his parliamentary campaign for the adoption of de Gaulle's ideas on armored warfare, Paul Reynaud again stressed the importance of quality: "Through the lack of numbers [quantity], we should seek advantage by way of quality."[107] For most French officers, a one-year term of conscription reduced the army to marginal value; the priority given to quantity foreclosed quality troops. Just after World War I an officer explained that "short-term conscripts . . . in the end, a myriad of men, are ready for everything, good at nothing, and have an average output that is very low, morose, fussy, and passive."[108] Ten years later, General Weygand seconded this evaluation: "The character and the possibilities of the French army were profoundly modified the day that France adopted military service of less than two years."[109]

The French army also believed that short-term conscripts were only capable of static warfare; only long-serving soldiers would be able to conduct maneuvers. One of the important training manuals of the mid-

1930s noted that success required maneuverability, speed, and mobility, but it nevertheless spoke out against encounter battles because reservists made up the majority of the army.[110] The French army also considered reserve officers inept in mobile warfare. At a meeting of the Superior Council of War in 1927, General Niessel claimed that he had met only three reserve officers during World War I who were really at home at the head of an infantry battalion. He continued, "We must not forget that this was a war of stabilization. One cannot at the beginning of a campaign, especially if it is a war of movement, allow a reserve officer to command an infantry or cavalry battalion."[111]

This view that short-term conscripts were good only for defensive operations was pervasive in the French army. General Targe, a high-ranking French officer, noted in 1930 that "only a professional army could go beyond our frontiers . . . a militia army is apt for the defensive at prepared positions, but is not apt for maneuver."[112] Similarly, General Louis Maurin argued that the shorter length of military service would severely diminish the cavalry's ability to conduct mobile operations.[113] The French officer believed that only years of service could endow a soldier with the necessary aptitude for maneuver warfare; that inexperienced troops could not handle offensive operations; and that young troops lacked the requisite quality. A report submitted by the Superior Council of War after the occupation of Austria was pessimistic about the ability of the army—a conscript army—to seize part of German territory. Because of both its organization and its training, the French army was, according to this report, ill suited for battle with Germany: "Speaking only of the infantry one could very probably count on one's fingers the units which have been trained to fight over ground strewn with shell holes, and crisscrossed with trenches and obstacles."[114] Representing only quantity, short-term conscripts could not be entrusted with offensive operations.

BELIEFS TRANSLATE INTO POLICY

The French army's approach to the Versailles negotiations illustrates this link between an offensive doctrine and a professional army. In 1919, Marshal Ferdinand Foch sought to impose on the defeated German army a one-year term of conscription; the French officer corps argued that the German army should not be allowed to become a professional force. After the negotiations had ended and the British demand for the formation of a professional army had triumphed, a French officer wrote: "[It] would be better to let Germany have a relatively numerous army, without seriously trained officers than a smaller army of well-tried, proven officers that Germany will have and which I fear she will know how to make use of."[115]

French proposals at the disarmament conference in the early 1930s again reveal the desire to impose on Germany what in the army's view would be a less threatening military instrument (one incapable of offensive operations). Whereas some states attempted to ban certain types of weapons as "aggressive" or "offensive," the French delegation focused on the type of army. According to the French delegation, "The intrinsic nature of the weapon, its caliber and tonnage, were important, but still more important was the question of the army that would use it." The French military's proposals called for the replacement of the Reichwehr, a professional army, by a conscript army serving short terms of service. This type of army was not, in its view, "adapted to a sudden offensive."[116] The French high command argued that if Germany were stripped of its professional army and thus its offensive capabilities, France—as a status quo power—could also rely exclusively on a militia force.[117]

The French army's evaluation of the value of short-term conscripts was not mere political rhetoric to be applied to the German army. After the reduction in the term of conscription in 1928, the French army made numerous adjustments in its war plans, the intended use of fortifications, and its training manuals. Each change marked a shift toward a defensively oriented doctrine.

As discussed in Chapter 3, only after the French military elite understood that they would be commanding one-year conscripts did the defensive use of fortifications prevail. The French army had previously endorsed the construction of fortified regions as points of maneuver for offensive operations.[118] Whereas throughout the 1920s an army of thirty-two divisions stood poised to carry the war into German territory while the nation-in-arms mobilized, after 1929 French war plans became unabashedly defensive.

The French army also adjusted its training manuals in response to the reduction in the length of conscription. In order to accommodate these "ill-trained" troops, the high command minimized the complexity of the doctrine and emphasized its defensive elements. The 1928 training manual stated that the result of the army reorganization because of the one-year service "is the necessity to simplify all that can be simplified more, to give a restricted feature to programs of training."[119] The army emphasized the methodical battle because it was the only type of warfare that short-term conscripts could execute. The general directive on the 1935 manual leaves no doubt on this score: "The prepared defensive battle is the form of war that leaves the least to the unexpected and that responds the best to the possibilities of a troop recently mobilized and embarked on a campaign."[120] Both of these movements—toward greater simplicity and an increasingly controlled battlefield—worked against the speed, initiative, and mobility necessary for offensive operations.

The French army's approach to mechanization and motorization is another manifestation of its conceptual link between short-term conscripts and defensive doctrines. The French army had procured at least as much motorized equipment as the Germans, but with the exception of several tardy and unsuccessful attempts to create mechanized units, the increased mobility did not enhance the army's offensive capabilities. Instead, the army parceled out the tanks and mechanized vehicles among the infantry units and expected them to advance at the infantry's pace.

The French army did not, however, reject the new massed-armor concepts under all circumstances. In June 1930, at General Weygand's request and with the approval of Marshal Pétain and other leading French generals, the Superior Council of War adopted a ten-year plan to develop a strong maneuver and mechanized element within the army that would consist of *active or professional units*.[121] These plans were never completely executed, but this example is important because it shows that the French army was much more open to innovative ideas *if* they were to be realized by a professional army. In contrast, if all the French officers had was a conscript army—an army in their view that was devoid of the speed, spirit, and maneuverability necessary for offensive operations—then it rejected the ideas of de Gaulle, Fuller, and other advocates of mechanized warfare. Even Jean Fabry, who strongly favored retaining offensive capabilities, switched course after the term of conscription was reduced to one year and thereafter became preoccupied *not* with how an offensive could be undertaken with active units but with how the French army should be organized to best parry a German attack.[122]

OTHER EVALUATIONS WERE POSSIBLE

The French army had numerous opportunities to see that it could use reserves and short-term conscripts offensively and that other military organizations did not share its evaluation of conscript or reserve forces. For example, after the Prussian defeat of Austria in 1866, Napoleon III supported the adoption of universal short-term military service. However, the minister of war, Marshal Jacques Randon, led the successful opposition to this proposal; Randon commented that reconstituting the Garde Nationale into a force similar to the German Landwehr (citizen militia) would "only give us recruits; what we need are soldiers."[123] Four years later Prussian forces destroyed the French army.

This humiliating defeat within just six weeks by a quantitatively superior army of conscripts should have alerted the French to a potential source of power that they had previously dismissed. In commenting on the French defeat, Brian Bond explained that "the mass Prussian armies of the 1860s proved to be a match for their opponents in marching and fighting and superior to them in education and motivation. The French belief in quality against quantity . . . was proved to be mistaken."[124] But the French did not learn this lesson. They explained away the German victory as the result of the French army's abandonment of Napoleonic offensive concepts and their retention of muzzle-loading rifles.[125]

Far more devastating was the French army's refusal to recognize the value of reserves before World War I. Again, this view contrasted sharply with that of the German army. While Joseph Joffre declared, "Under no circumstances will we absorb the reserve formations in the active units," the German army stated, "Reserve troops will be employed in the same way that the active troops are."[126] But the French army simply did not see what the Germans were doing. In describing the German army, a French officer carefully distinguished between the capabilities of an army of the masses and the professional army: "After 1870 [the German army] sought to create a first-echelon army of superior quality that reduced the proportion of reserves to a strict minimum. . . . The roles of the reserve formations and citizen militia are limited," he explained. "It is quality troops of the first echelon, the professional army, that will hold back the adversary and execute the decisive action that will break or turn the enemy front. . . . The reserve formations constitute the quantity, that is, the mass of soldiers who . . . are only intended to exploit the results that have already been obtained by the quality troops."[127] This French officer could not have been more mistaken about the German army. In August 1914, Germany attacked with thirty-four corps; twelve were reserve units and all of them were used in the front line of the attack.[128]

The French army could have been better prepared to defeat the German offensive during the opening battles of World War I. In 1911 the vice president of the Supreme War Council, General Victor Michel, proposed a radical reorganization of French forces. Michel worried that the Germans would invade through Belgium in a wide sweep west of the river Meuse and proposed that the French army counter this threat by shifting the bulk of French forces to the left toward the Belgian frontier, thereby extending the French front. In order to fill the additional units required for such a deployment, Michel proposed bringing reserves to the front and giving them the same combat duties that the active forces had. Michel was proposing a system very much like the German one of mixing reserve and active units.

The Superior Council of War convened a meeting in July 1911 to consider Michel's proposal. When the question of whether a reserve regiment, when joined to an active regiment, could fight effectively in the front line was first introduced to the meeting, someone muttered aloud, "There is nothing to consider; General Michel has become a looney." The Intelligence Section of the French General Staff supported this conclusion; in one historian's words, this group "had attributed French *prej-*

udices against the reserve to the German High Command."[129] The Superior Council of War unanimously voted down Michel's proposals, French staff officers never seriously studied Michel's proposal, and two days later Michel was dismissed from his position. Interestingly, the British director of military operations, General Henry Wilson (an army officer outside the French army culture), agreed with Michel that the Germans would mix reserve and active forces in the front lines.[130]

The French army's insistence that reserve or conscript forces had little offensive combat power was very costly to French security. If the French army had reorganized its forces in line with Michel's proposal, it would have doubled its total strength and permitted coverage of the entire frontier from Switzerland to the English Channel.[131] Instead, only five or six French reserve divisions participated in the crucial battle of the frontiers; none were used in the front lines.[132]

Furthermore, if the French army had believed that reserves could work directly with active forces they could have correctly evaluated German military potential. But they did not, despite having received accurate intelligence reports on the nature of the potential German attack. As a result, the French army underestimated by between seventeen and twenty corps the forces that Germany would use in attacking France. Given that there were 40,000–44,000 soldiers in a German corps, the French army faced at least 680,000 more soldiers than it anticipated.[133] In fact, more than two weeks after Germany declared war on France and as German forces were sweeping through Belgium, a French officer, General Berthelot, telephoned his commander that "reports on German forces in Belgium are greatly exaggerated. There is no cause for alarm."[134] Because the French officer corps did not think the Germans could use reserve formations in offensive operations, it also did not think the German army would have the numbers to invade through Belgium.

But the German army did invade through Belgium; French offensives by the professional army were a disaster; and the battle for the frontiers was lost and with it some of the richest industrial and iron- and coal-producing regions in France. Though the Battle of the Marne in September 1914 stopped the German offensive, the initial German success meant that the western front of World War I would lie in France's agricultural and industrial heartland. The French army's refusal to recognize the value of reserves had catastrophic consequences.[135] Since it was Napoleon who first took full advantage of conscript forces and in so doing conquered all of Europe, the French army's blindness is all the more surprising.

Despite its experiences with Napoleonic warfare, the Franco-Prussian War, and most salient of all, the opening battles of World War I, the French army continued to believe that only a professional army could endow France with offensive capabilities. In a meeting of the Superior Council of War in 1933, Weygand stated that "a conscript army's value in mobilization, concentration, cohesion, and warfare is severely reduced." And Pétain agreed: "I have gathered a certain number of reports on the attitude of the reserve formations in 1914. . . . These divisions, during the first two months, were incapable of even defensive warfare."[136] French officers even argued that the use of German reserves in the opening battles of World War I *was not* evidence of their value in offensive maneuvers but instead demonstrated once again the importance of professional armies.[137] The French army never recognized that one of the fundamental tenets of its organizational culture—that reserve or short-term conscripts were ill suited for offensive operations—was neither universally endorsed nor empirically validated.

It was not only before World War I that the German army planned to use reserve formations in offensive operations. During the interwar period it treated active and reserve troops alike. War plans in the 1920s called for the creation of divisions with varying proportions of regulars to reserves.[138] Similarly, at the disarmament negotiations in the early 1930s, the Germans disagreed with the French assessment of a short-service army as good only for defensive operations. As a historian of these negotiations explained, "The German delegates expressed pained surprise at the distinction drawn by France between offensive and defensive army organizations."[139]

Like the German army, the Israeli army has a highly offensive doctrine and relies heavily on reserves.[140] The Israeli system was initially greeted with skepticism, but early maneuvers in 1950 and 1951 showed that "reserve formations performed as well as active force units."[141] Even the armored units are primarily reserve formations.[142] Although the French reserve units were low-quality troops, that was due more to problems with their equipment and training than to any inherent limitation. The French army gave them little training and used them as the "dumping ground of the active army:" those officers judged poorly qualified were assigned to train and command reserves units.[143] Haphazardly assembled units with little systematic training will be of poor quality, but as the Israeli and German armies have shown, permanently organized and well-trained reserve companies can successfully take the offensive.

De Gaulle's Proposal for a Professional Army

In the early 1930s, Charles de Gaulle, then a colonel in the French army, lobbied actively for the adoption of an offensive doctrine. De Gaulle's campaign failed, but its occurrence appears to cast doubt on my argument about the French army's organizational culture. Here was a French officer, assimilated into the organizational culture of the French army, calling for the adoption of an offensive doctrine in the 1930s. However, a closer look at de Gaulle's actions illustrates both the strength of the French army's culture and the importance of domestic politics.

In *Vers l'armée de métier*, de Gaulle called for the creation of a professional army and the adoption of an offensive doctrine. Intended as an addition to and not a substitute for the mass-conscript army, de Gaulle advocated the establishment of seven armored divisions comprising 100,000 soldiers serving a six-year tour of duty. De Gaulle envisioned that these highly mobile divisions would be capable of immediate action into enemy territory and would return the offensive to the battlefield.[144]

De Gaulle was convinced that the defense and ultimate *grandeur* of France depended on the adoption of a new offensive doctrine, yet he endorsed these offensive operations only if they were coupled to a force of professional soldiers serving *six years* of military service. As a product of the organizational culture of the French army, de Gaulle could not imagine entrusting young, unseasoned troops with the tasks involved in offensive mechanized warfare. Only professional soldiers, he believed, possessed the skill and training to implement lightning-speed armored attacks. De Gaulle persisted in this belief even though he knew there would be considerable parliamentary resistance to the creation of a professional force of long-serving soldiers.

The reception that de Gaulle's ideas received in the French army again reveals the link between a professional army and an offensive doctrine in the French army's organizational culture. The high command was not persuaded. Because de Gaulle's plan did not call for the army to receive additional professional soldiers, the officer corps feared that creating a specialized corps from the existing troops would cut the army in two.[145] The officers could not imagine a conscript army implementing an offensive doctrine, so adopting de Gaulle's proposal would require taking the army's professionals from the conscript army, and the latter, stripped of its professional officers, would have little if any combat value. The French officer corps could only accept de Gaulle's ideas as a package; separating the offensive doctrine from the professional army was inconceivable. Either these concepts were to be implemented by a professional army, or not at all.

De Gaulle's campaign also reveals the impact of domestic politics. The Left was not pleased with de Gaulle's proposal.[146] Commentators in a leftist magazine referred to de Gaulle's proposed force as "hand-hired killers, each of which possesses all the aptitudes of murder and all the extraordinary instruments to kill." They asked, "When will this army then march on Paris?"[147] This fear of the domestic ramifications—and not whether the proposal was best suited to repel a German attack—emerge time and again in the leftist press and parliamentary debate. In discussing de Gaulle's project for the creation of a professional army, Blum exclaimed, "In order to save the national independence of France, you are risking the loss of her domestic liberty."[148] Similarly, the leader of the Radical Party, Edouard Daladier, worried that a professional army might be "more dangerous than one might believe for the security of our nation."[149] Perhaps the best summary of the Left's reaction to de Gaulle's proposal is the title of a book published by a Communist as a response to de Gaulle's *Vers l'armée de métier*. In *Vers l'armée de la République*, Bernard Nardain attacked the professional army and advocated the creation of a military system based on universal military service.

Whereas the Left mobilized against de Gaulle's proposal, *Vers l'armée de métier* received a different reception from the Right and the extreme Right. In the Parliament, a deputy representing the extreme Right voiced his support for a professional army, and articles in *L'aube*, *L'écho de Paris*, *Le matin*, *L'époque*, and *Le temps* advocated the organization of an elite army of "technicians."[150]

The Left's fear of the political ramifications of de Gaulle's professional army was not unfounded. In a letter to Reynaud in 1935 de Gaulle acknowledged that the creation of a professional army *was not* just a response to the German threat: "Little by little, the economic and morale crises push the question of public order to be of primary importance. . . . Under every regime, the army has had the role and the responsibility of maintaining order." De Gaulle then asked how units composed of citizens could fulfill this role and concluded that "the creation of a specialized corps is not only necessary for today's international conditions, but also for the impending necessities of domestic order."[151] For de Gaulle, both offensive warfare and domestic stability required a professional army.

Even though the international environment had become dramatically more threatening, the domestic political divide persisted. Domestic considerations determined the army's reliance on mass conscription. With this constraint, the French army could imagine only one possibility. De Gaulle and the French army were incapable of decoupling offensive concepts from a professional army, yet insisting on a professional force doomed de Gaulle's effort because such a force was politically impossible. In discussing the failure of de Gaulle's proposals General Gamelin explained: "At root, it was the connection . . . made between the question of large armoured units and the question of the career army which certainly proved detrimental in parliament and in a section of military opinion to the creation of tank divisions."[152] The French were trapped: the Left would not accept a professional army and the army could not envision an offensive doctrine without one.

From Doctrinal Debate in the 1920s to Dogmatism in the 1930s

Given the constraints set by French politicians, the French army's culture explains why the army adopted a defensive doctrine. But it does not explain the extent to which the French army became dogmatically attached to its doctrine. This case illustrates the conditions under which military organizations become increasingly unable to consider alternatives. In particular, the French case highlights how the perception of hostility in the external environment affects the strength of the military's organizational culture.

Organizational theory predicts that, when faced with a threatening external environment, organizations respond dysfunctionally by strengthening the organization's culture: the righteousness of the chosen policy is magnified and the value of alternatives dismissed. This is what appears to have happened in France during the interwar period; the contrast between the 1920s and 1930s is striking. In the decade immediately after World War I, relations between the army and its external, domestic environment were relatively harmonious. The 1920s was also a period of considerable debate and flexibility about the army's doctrine. In the early 1930s, however, this pluralism disappeared. Perceiving itself increasingly under attack by the Left and terrified by the Communist Party's infiltration of its ranks, the French army became even more rigid, applying the rules of its doctrine almost regardless of the circumstances.

During the early 1920s the army extensively debated the use of fortifications and the implications of the mechanization of the battlefield. The military journals conducted a lively discussion of the merits of each position, and the army did not ostracize officers who proposed alternative approaches.[153] This period of doctrinal diversity was also a time of relatively good relations between the army and the state. Despite an increase in the strength of the Socialist Party and the Communist trade union in 1919, the elections of that year brought to power the most right-wing government since 1875. Referred to as the *bleu horizon* after the number of army veterans in the chamber, the National Bloc had campaigned on a stridently anti-Bolshevik, anti-Socialist, and anti-German platform. This government posed little threat to the conservative and right-wing army.[154]

This center-right coalition remained in power until the victory of the *cartel des gauches* in 1924, a weak coalition of Radicals (a center party) and republican Socialists. Although the cartel undertook such symbolic gestures as transferring Jaurès's ashes to the Pantheon, most of its policies were moderate. The old majority of the National Bloc replaced the cartel in 1926. Led by Raymond Poincaré, and representing most of the center and right parties, this new coalition, the *Union Nationale* excluded the working-class parties. The majority was further strengthened in the 1928 elections and the *Union Nationale* remained in power for the remainder of the decade.

In short, throughout the 1920s the army had little to fear in its domestic political environment. The republican forces had succeeded in reducing the term of conscription in 1928, but Painlevé had simultaneously agreed to increase the professional component of the army. The army perceived little hostility in its external (domestic) environment in the 1920s, and its doctrine was correspondingly flexible and open.

In contrast, during the 1930s, French politics became increasingly polarized. From 1929 to 1932, André Tardieu's right-wing government harshly persecuted the extreme Left and the Depression reduced the number of strikes, but this more stable environment did not last. The elections in 1932 returned a Radical and Socialist majority to power, and between December 1932 and February 1934, five governments rapidly succeeded one another. The government's paralysis encouraged antirepublicanism on the right, and the riots of February 1934 inaugurated a period of increasing uncertainty. By highlighting the threat of a fascist coup, these riots paved the way for the Popular Front in 1936 and a dramatic increase in the membership of the Communist Party and its trade union.[155] The election of this left-wing coalition also sparked an unprecedented wave of sit-in strikes. Worst of all for the army, the Popular Front was led by Léon Blum, a man despised by the Right as epitomizing a combination of Jaurès and Dreyfus. Indeed, one of the greatest worries in 1936 was "whether the military would cohabit with the socialists."[156] The outbreak of the Spanish Civil War further fueled the army's fear of the Left's increasing power.

After 1936, contact between the army and the government deteriorated. The institutions for military consultation like the Superior Council of War and the Permanent Committee of National Defense met rarely, and their advice was sought infrequently. Relations also soured between the Radical Socialist war minister and General Weygand.[157] Only General Gamelin maintained a semblance of contact with the government, and he served more to calm civil military relations than to lead a fight for the military's position.[158] Indeed, Jacques Benoist-Méchin's memoirs reveal that many on the Right viewed Gamelin as nothing but a government lackey.[159]

The French army became extremely anxious about domestic instability. In January 1937, the press published a document, supposedly of Spanish origin, that had been circulated to all the army commands and that gave instructions on the methods for carrying out a coup d'état.[160] The fear of breakdown in civil order also led the army to station colonial and North African troops—those that it believed were politically reliable—in the red belt, or leftist suburbs, of Paris.[161] The Bolshevik revolution and the Black Sea mutinies had ignited fear in the French army, which devoted enormous time and effort to uprooting the Communist threat.[162] Memos concerning the circulation of seditious newspapers in the barracks fill box after box in the army archives.[163] However, it was in the 1930s that the French army's reaction to the fear of Communist infiltration took on a more ominous form, revealing the heightened threat perception on the part of the officer corps. Two underground networks of army officers, *La Cagoule* and *Corvignolles*, fought against Communist infiltration of the army. Created after the outbreak of the Spanish Civil War, these two organizations became well organized and active in the French army in the late 1930s. Operating with the knowledge of the high command and the active participation of Marshal Franchet d'Esperey, these antirepublican organizations sought to purge the army of Communist influence, prevent a Communist coup, and bolster military morale.[164]

Describing the climate in the mid-1930s, General Gamelin wrote that "the very idea of rearmament is a victory at a time when no one believes in war, when the army is scorned and held up to ridicule. The rearmament demands a daily battle."[165] A letter to the minister of education in 1936 in which the minister of war complained about the treatment of the army in primary school textbooks further reveals the army's belief that it was misunderstood and held in low esteem.[166] Similarly, Pétain, speaking with General Weygand, warned against coming into conflict with the Parliament about the need to modify the recruitment legislation. He believed the army should express its views privately because to go public would risk causing a genuine revolution and hence derailing its projects before appropriate consideration had been given to their merits.[167]

There were also changes in the general public's view of the military. During the 1920s pacifism had been a minority position, and the antiwar literature, epitomized by the widely popular novel by Henri Barbusse, *Le feu*, focused on the daily horror of war. As the 1930s unfolded, however, support for pacifism increased.[168] In addition, the antiwar literature shifted from attacking the brutality of war to depicting officers as cowards and the military as guilty of crimes against ordinary Frenchmen.[169]

In short, during the 1930s the army felt ignored and dismissed by the government, despised by the wider public, and under threat of Bolshevik

machinations both within the army and in the unstable and polarized domestic political arena. The army had learned to live with republican institutions, but the latter's ability to hold the country together was, in its
view, increasingly questionable.

The French army became more dogmatic during the 1930s. In 1935,
Gamelin tightened the control of military writings, requiring that all
publications receive prior approval. Only the official view could be presented, and as one officer commented, "Everyone got the message and a
profound silence reigned until the awakening of 1940."[170] In 1934, de
Gaulle was refused permission to publish an article in the *Revue militaire
française*, and after his public campaign for armored offensive tactics,
this upstart colonel was taken off the promotion list.[171] Dissidents were
silenced, and one of the more open journals, the *Revue de l'infanterie*,
was suppressed at the end of 1936.[172]

After analyzing more than six hundred articles in five major French
military journals in the interwar period, Faris Kirkland concluded that
the tone of the publications in the late 1920s and 1930s differed dramatically from those of the early 1920s. Endorsement of the official position replaced the lively debate that had characterized the 1920s.[173] The
French army's interest in the Spanish Civil War also shows this rigidity
of thought. While both the Soviet and German military journals devoted
enormous attention to the study of this conflict, the *Revue militaire
française* rarely covered the developments, and when it did, it provided
little analysis.[174]

In conclusion, the army's perception of threat in the domestic political
environment may explain its doctrinal dogmatism in the 1930s. Perceiving itself increasingly under attack by the Left and fearful of the instability and social upheaval of the 1930s, the army closed ranks, shut out
dissenting views, and focused on internal preservation. As a result, the
tightly wound organizational culture of the French army became more
impervious to challenge. Developments in the French army around the
turn of the century also support this hypothesis. As Jack Snyder has
shown, from 1880 to 1898 the French army had a moderately offensive
doctrine and a relatively benign relationship with the French state. After
the Dreyfus Affair, however, the army developed an increasingly antagonistic relationship with the state and became dogmatically committed to
an offensive doctrine.[175]

Neither balance-of-power theory nor a functional analysis of military organizations adequately explains doctrinal developments in the French
army during the interwar period. Although civilians were important to
the development of the French army's doctrine, domestic, not interna-

tional political goals drove their actions. The adversary and the threat were internal. Similarly, little about the French case corresponds with the expectations about military behavior derived from functional arguments. According to these studies, military organizations inherently prefer offensive doctrines. Yet in the 1930s the French army chose a defensive doctrine.

Although realists rightly focus on power, their conception of its role is too narrow. First, they often ignore the impact that military policy can have on power politics at the domestic level. In the French case, the pivotal decision to reduce the length of conscription stemmed from concerns about the domestic distribution of power, not about the structure of the international system. Second, realists neglect the intersubjective dimension of power. There is, for example, nothing about universal military service that makes it objectively appealing to left-wing parties, as it is to the Left in France. In other words, we cannot generalize about how civilians in different countries will view the effect of a particular military policy on the distribution of power in their state. As the French case shows, the instruments of power are culturally defined.

The French case also sheds light on the different ways that cultural factors affect policy decisions. The French army's inability to imagine the use of reserves or conscript forces in offensive operations illustrates the power of an organizational culture. In addition, this case illustrates the role that culture plays in a country where there are competing sets of beliefs about the role of the military in the domestic arena. Constantly in conflict with one another, the competing cultures in France became tightly bound prescriptions for action. Both the Left and the Right had specific policy objectives: the Left wanted short-term conscripts, the Right a professional army. This stark conflict begins to explain the different roles that cultural factors can play.

Chapter 5 examines doctrinal developments in a country where there is a domestic consensus across the political spectrum about the use of force. Comparing a case with a consensual culture with another with competing cultures allows several questions to be addressed that could not be examined using the French case alone. For example, in the absence of controversy about the domestic repercussions of policies that affect doctrinal developments, do policymakers devote more attention to the international requirements of security policy? If so, then realism's concentration on the international determinants of doctrinal developments may not be so misguided. In addition, analyzing a case in which there is only one set of beliefs highlights the different ways in which culture can affect policymaking. In contrast to France where the cultures functioned more like ideologies, the consensual culture in Britain more closely resembled common sense. Does this consensual culture affect military policy, and if so, how does its role differ from that of competing cultures? By comparing the French case with doctrinal developments in the British army, we gain a greater understanding of the role played by cultural factors.

5

Explaining British Doctrine

ON THE EVE of the greatest challenge of their generation, two branches of the British armed forces seemed prepared to fight different adversaries. While the Royal Air Force (RAF) adopted offensive and defensive doctrines tailored to continental warfare, the army seemed nostalgically focused on imperial duties. Relying on a defensive doctrine ill suited to meet a German assault, the British army suffered a series of defeats in May 1940 that culminated in the evacuation at Dunkirk. In contrast, although strategic bombing contributed little to the war effort, the RAF's innovative development of a defensive air doctrine led to the defeat of the German air offensive during the Battle of Britain.

Historians and military analysts offer a variety of explanations for British army and air force doctrine. Some scholars explain the failure to adopt armored warfare as the product of mistaken governmental policy, while others blame the military. The successful development of air defense also receives contrasting reviews: some credit civilian policymakers while others praise Hugh Dowding and Fighter Command. Most analysts agree that strategic bombing was an air force product—developed and honed to correspond with organizational interests. Organizational and balance-of-power theory incorporate many aspects of these explanations, and in particular, the role of civilians and the military in doctrinal change. Did British civilians choose policy options out of sync with British strategic interests? Were the army and air force foolishly pursuing policies that weakened British security but enhanced the services' autonomy, resources, certainty, and prestige?

British Army and Air Force Doctrine

The slaughter in World War I exposed the defensive power of modern firepower, but the Great War also introduced new technologies—manned flight and the tracked vehicle—with the potential to return the offensive to the battlefield. In the 1920s the British army led the development of mechanized warfare but by the 1930s had adopted a more traditional doctrine.[1] The army motorized most of its units and formed

the Mobile Division, but the appearance was misleading: the new vehicles were used in traditional roles.[2] The British army entered World War
II with a defensive doctrine.

The British army's defensive doctrine emphasized painstaking preparation and tight control over the battlefield. A 1926 infantry training
manual stressed, "The above organization is fixed and definite, and, except as laid down in paragraph 4 below, must never be varied. Only
when a force is uniformly organized can every part of it be relied on by
its commander to carry out the same orders in the same way, and to suffer casualties with the least injury to its efficiency. *To maintain the organization, in or out of battle, no matter what the difficulty, is therefore
one of the first duties of every commander.*"[3] The fluid battlefield envisioned by the Germans was far from the British mind. In British eyes,
only firepower could create the possibility for maneuver. Another infantry training manual from the same year explained that the "superiority of fire is essential" and that "to attempt movement, inadequately prepared and insufficiently supported by fire, is to risk a premature check."[4]
Battles would be precisely planned, carefully timed, dominated by firepower, and methodically executed.

British infantry remained the "queen of the battlefield." "The task of
the tank," explained a 1937 training manual, "will be to enable the infantry to advance by silencing the enemy's small arms fire which is hold-
ing it up. In order to do this, each unit of tanks should be responsible for
the advance of a unit of infantry onto a definite objective."[5] British tanks
supported the infantry, heavily armored tanks supplemented the traditional artillery barrage, and motorized cavalry units did little more than
replace one means of locomotion with another. The instructions in the
mechanized cavalry's manual were straightforward: "The principles and
system of training will be as laid down in *Cavalry Training, (Horsed)*
with certain modifications which are suitable for armored car regiments
only and are laid down in this chapter."[6] Only minor changes were
thought necessary; cavalry would fight as it always had.

The British army's Mobile Division was more a reconnaissance unit
than an independent striking force. "The Mobile Division (excluding the
Tank Brigade) has the task of protecting the Main Field Force when on
the move and with reconnaissance at all times," explained the director of
staff duties in 1937. "It would thus find itself between the Main Force
and the Enemy until the battle front was formed at which moment it
would be withdrawn." The Mobile Division's training manual stressed
its traditional missions: "To provide the mechanized mobile component
for the Expeditionary Force in precisely the same way as the old Cavalry Division was the mobile component in the days prior to mechanization. . . . The role of this formation remains, as of old."[7] The creation of

the Mobile Division could have revolutionized army doctrine, but the British army used it to fulfill the traditional roles of mobile troops.

Ironically, the British army had led the early development of mechanization, and some of the most intelligent and persuasive advocates of armored warfare were British. Both John Fuller and Basil Liddell Hart, for example, advocated the use of independent, fast-moving tank formations as a means of restoring strategic mobility and gaining decisive results through deep thrusts into enemy rear areas. The army formed several experimental divisions and conducted exercises with them in the late 1920s and early 1930s. Nevertheless, the British army allowed its lead to slip away and entered World War II with a defensive doctrine poorly adapted to the modern battlefield.

In contrast, the Royal Air Force took advantage of the offensive and defensive potential of manned flight. Under the leadership of Hugh Trenchard the RAF enthusiastically adopted strategic bombing, an offensive doctrine. Unlike the Italian general Giulio Douhet's emphasis on defeating the enemy's air force and gaining command of the air, RAF's Bomber Command sought to strike offensively and paralyze the adversary's industrial capacity. Once World War II began, the RAF's inability to target accurately and penetrate German defenses during the day forced it to resort to nighttime area bombing. After the Allies gained air superiority in autumn 1944, it returned to its policy of targeting war potential. The RAF focused on strategic bombing, but the air staff, and especially Fighter Command and Lord Dowding, also developed an effective air defense system.[8] Working in close cooperation with the scientific community, Fighter Command brought together the critical components of this defensive doctrine. By 1938 the radar system was operative and the air force had incorporated single-seat fighters—the Hurricane and Spitfire—into the integrated air defense system that saved Britain during the lonely months from July to October 1940.

Alternative Explanations

The International System and Civilian Intervention

Whereas doctrinal developments in France were an easy case for balance-of-power theory—France recognized the German threat and prepared for it—Britain faced a more difficult test. During the 1920s and 1930s, Britain was the classic example of an overextended empire. While France had one primary adversary, Britain was torn between balancing in Europe and protecting its far-flung empire; Britain faced competing demands with declining resources.[9] By the 1930s, British fears about Rus-

sian designs on Afghanistan and India lessened, and Britain recognized
Germany as the "ultimate potential enemy."[10] In 1934 a leading government official explained that England had "at her front door the most formidable, dangerous and pugnacious of all countries, namely Germany."
Neville Chamberlain agreed that "our greatest potential danger" remained Germany. British civilians also knew that the rise of air power
put their island nation at risk in a way never before experienced. The
threat of a naval blockade had always worried London, but now Britain
itself could be attacked at the outset of a war. Maintaining control of the
channel ports no longer guaranteed British security; the threat of strategic
bombing shattered Britain's insularity. Britain had to prevent Germany
from controlling the Low Countries (Belgium, Luxembourg, and the
Netherlands). "Since the day of the air," Stanley Baldwin declared, "the
old frontiers are gone. When you think of the defense of England you no
longer think of the chalk cliffs of Dover; you think of the Rhine."[11]

Barry Posen argues that British civilians intervened in doctrinal developments according to systemic imperatives. When Britain faced relatively few threats during the 1920s, London took a hands-off approach
and allowed the military to pursue its organizational interests and so
adopt offensive doctrines. With the rise of German power in the 1930s,
British civilians intervened, corrected the military's ambitions, and
brought British doctrine in line with systemic demands. In Posen's words,
"Ultimately, British leadership got fed up with the RAF offensive bombing doctrine and intervened to change it, at least temporarily."[12]

British civilians considered international objectives, but they did not
bring the military services in line with systemic imperatives as the German threat became imminent. This was particularly true for the army.
British civilians saw Germany as the "ultimate potential enemy," but
they did not reform their antiquated army or give the army the role that
could have allowed it to prepare to meet the German assault: the British
expeditionary force was no match for the German forces and the British
did not adopt a continental commitment until February 1939. Even in
the case of the RAF, civilian and military behavior was often at odds with
what would be predicted by balance-of-power theory.

NO CONTINENTAL COMMITMENT

London's reluctance to make a military commitment on the European
continent weakened British security.[13] Clinging to a policy of limited liability until the last possible moment deprived the army of an incentive to
plan for war against Britain's greatest threat, and in the age of air power
threatened the security of the home front. The Royal Navy's command
of the English Channel could no longer ensure British security, which de-

pended on denying the Germans access to the airfields in northern France—*and British civilians knew this*. In other words, British civilians recognized Germany as the primary threat, yet they repeatedly refused to adopt a continental commitment. It was not until the eve of the war that the British Cabinet discarded the policy of limited liability.

For the preceding two decades British civilians had given a continental commitment the lowest priority. The Ten-Year Rule, initiated in 1919 and extended until 1933, specifically forbade the preparation of a force for intervention in Europe, and the Geddes Report in 1921 reinforced this directive.[14] The principal discussions on British rearmament and strategic policy in the mid-1930s again limited preparations for a European campaign.[15] The White Paper issued in March 1936 gave a continental commitment the lowest priority (after defense of the British Isles and maintaining garrisons in the Empire). In his diary in 1936 Chamberlain explained the reasoning behind his position: "I cannot believe that the next war, if it ever comes, will be like the last one, and I believe our resources will be more profitably employed in the air, and on the sea, than in building up great armies."[16] The implication was that Britain would limit its participation in a European conflict to air and naval support.

The British Cabinet's adoption of Sir Thomas Inskip's proposals in 1938 again reflected the British civilians' reluctance to prepare for a European land war.[17] Inskip, the minister for the coordination of defense, stated that "the defense of Imperial commitments, including defense at home," was the army's primary role. Only as a last objective, "which can only be provided after the other objectives have been met," did Inskip list cooperation in "defense of the territories of any allies we may have in war."[18] Even following the Anschluss in March 1938 the policy of limited liability remained. It was only in March 1939—six months after Munich—that Chamberlain half-heartedly approved the preparation of a small field force for Europe.[19]

It was not ignorance of Britain's strategic position that prevented London from adopting a continental commitment. British civilians knew they had to keep German forces out of the Low Countries. Even before World War I, many civilian elites believed that, irrespective of Belgian and French security, British security and especially the maintenance of British naval superiority required keeping German troops away from the channel ports.[20] With the rise of air power this preference became a necessity. If Britain could contain Germany within its northern borders, English air space would remain relatively free of German bombers, and the industrial areas in the Midlands and northern England would be beyond their range. Failing to contain Germany would dramatically increase the frequency and intensity of German air attacks. If Germany occupied the Low Countries, the Luftwaffe would have to fly only 40 miles through hostile airspace in its 120-mile journey to London, while the RAF would have to fly 120 miles through hostile territory in a 240-mile trek to vital German targets. If British forces occupied the Low Countries, Germany would be placed at a similar strategic disadvantage.[21] In 1923, Prime Minister Baldwin explained that Britain could not "cut herself adrift from Europe," for "we must remember that our island story is old . . . and that with the advent of the aeroplane we ceased to be an island. Whether we like it or not, we are indissolubly bound to Europe."[22]

Baldwin was not alone in recognizing that British frontiers had been moved to the Rhine. Before the House of Commons in 1925, the foreign secretary, Austen Chamberlain, declared, "All our greatest wars have been fought to prevent one great military Power dominating Europe, and at the same time dominating the coasts of the Channel and the ports of the Low Countries." During the initial rearmament discussions in 1934, the secretary of the Cabinet, Sir Maurice Hankey, said, "The Low Countries are vital to our security from the point of view of both naval and air defense." The Cabinet agreed that British security required the defense of Belgium. Civilians believed that the most threatening German attack would be an advance into the Low Countries and the use of this area as a launching pad for air strikes against England.[23]

Leading members of the British armed services understood the implications of the rise of air power and repeatedly warned civilians of the dangers of staying aloof from the continent. As early as 1925, the General Staff called for engagement in Europe: "[This] is only incidentally a question of French security; essentially it is a matter of British security. . . . The true strategic frontier of Britain is the Rhine; her security depends entirely on the present frontiers of France, Belgium and Holland being maintained and remaining in friendly hands." The chiefs of staff also reminded the Cabinet that the army had not been given the directives that would allow it to honor British commitments in the Locarno Treaty.[24]

The services' support for a continental commitment continued in the 1930s. In 1935 the General Staff argued that the military exercises should be based on European—as opposed to colonial—warfare, and numerous editorials in the *Army Quarterly* in the mid- to late 1930s decried the policy of limited liability.[25] As Major General Henry Pownall explained, "If we got embroiled in a major European war sooner or later, and I believe *sooner*, British troops would go to France." In the 1935 Annual Review, the chiefs of staff officially stated their support for a continental commitment: "The integrity of the Low Countries is, with the advent of air power, of greater importance than ever in our history, and the Army must be prepared in conjunction with the French to attempt to deny those countries to German invasion." In January 1937 the chiefs of staff again informed the Cabinet that the defense of Belgium could not be left to France alone, and after the Anschluss, the General Staff called for the preparation of an expeditionary force. After Munich the army proposed a modest reorganization in order to better prepare it for continental warfare and conducted an active campaign for the adoption of a continental commitment—even asking the British military attaché in Paris to urge the French government to put pressure on London.[26]

The military's support for a continental commitment does not mean it viewed this contingency with enthusiasm. Few officers wanted to return to the trenches in northern Europe, and many privately expressed apprehension about repeating the "horrors of Passchendaele."[27] Several senior serving officers even pushed for the adoption of a maritime strategy that would rely primarily on a naval blockade and limit the British army's role to small, diversionary land operations. Nevertheless, as military advisers to the government, the chiefs of staff attempted to overrule the Cabinet's stubborn adherence to the policy of limited liability.

The assessment of British defense "deficiencies" and the planning for rearmament that began in 1933 best illustrates the tension between the strategic rationale for a continental commitment and the government's reluctance to adopt this policy. The first report (1934) of the Defence Requirements Committee—a body composed of Hankey, Robert Vansittart of the Foreign Office, Warren Fisher from the Treasury, and the three chiefs of staff—proposed a drastic revision of the services' priorities that included the preparation of an expeditionary force capable of intervening promptly in a continental war.[28] From the start of the discussions of this proposal, Chamberlain objected to a continental commitment. The chiefs of staff responded that a German air offensive would be 80 percent stronger if launched from bases in the Low Countries and that the Belgian frontier was of only secondary concern to the French. However, marshalling financial considerations in his defense, Chamberlain successfully defeated the proposal for an expeditionary force, and instead concentrated resources on building up the RAF to provide a deterrent force.[29]

As the German threat increased, British civilians did not intervene in doctrinal developments to turn the army away from pursuing its parochial interests. To the contrary, by adhering to a policy of limited liability, civilians *frustrated* the British army's efforts to prepare to defeat its continental adversary—despite the army's repeated and early support for such a policy. This was no trifling matter. Without a continental commitment, the centerpiece of British strategy could collapse: British civilians chose to entrust British security to strategic bombing while simultaneously discarding the very element that might keep the German air force at bay.

COMPARING 1914 WITH 1939

The British Cabinet's refusal to endorse a continental commitment before 1939 is all the more puzzling for balance-of-power theory when
compared with British policy in 1914. Whereas the British Cabinet
waited until the last possible moment to rescind the policy of limited liability before World War II, by 1909, British policy focused discreetly on
meeting the German threat.[30] Negotiations with France on an expeditionary force began in 1905, and the need to prepare for continental
warfare was one of the reasons for the creation of the reserve military
force, the Territorials, in 1909. These years of preparation paid off—
while in 1914 the British could send five well-equipped and organized divisions within two weeks of mobilization, in 1939 France could expect
only three divisions after thirty days.[31]

This comparison illustrates the weakness of a systemic explanation: if
balance-of-power imperatives were compelling, the opposite should have
occurred: British civilians should have been more willing to make a continental commitment before World War II than before World War I.
Denying the Germans access to channel ports was important to British
security in 1914, but the importance of controlling the Low Countries
rose exponentially with the rise of air power. But British civilians—who
were able to make a continental commitment in 1909—proved unwilling
to respond in the 1920s and 1930s. When a continental commitment
was finally made in February 1939, there was hardly time to do more
than cobble together several poorly trained and ill-equipped divisions.

Although some aspects of Britain's strategic environment changed between 1914 and 1939, many of the differences between these two periods are precisely those that made the need for a continental commitment
even more compelling in 1939. As already mentioned, the rise of air
power increased the importance of keeping the Germans (and German
air bases) out of the Low Countries. France's loss of its pre–World War
I ally, Russia, also meant that France would be less able to confront a
German adversary without British assistance. Finally, differential
birthrates in France and Germany had further shifted the distribution of
power against France—again increasing the importance of British assistance. In short, the most important changes from 1914 to 1939 created
even greater strategic incentives for a robust continental commitment,
yet British civilians went in the opposite direction. As the historian Correlli Barnett commented, "It is not easy to see why it followed that, because the British had to place a large army in France by 1916–17 in order
to save the French from collapse, we should not need to do so again."[32]

This comparison points to a larger, more general problem with using
balance-of-power theory to explain British doctrine. From 1914 to 1939,

Britain's position in the international system changed little, yet British army doctrine changed dramatically. During both periods, the system was multipolar, and Britain was relatively weak and faced similar alliance patterns: Germany as probable adversary and France as probable ally.[33] This similarity in the structure of the international system is not reflected in British army doctrine. While the British army charged forward in 1914 with an offensive doctrine, two decades later, and facing similar international constraints, the British army adopted a defensive doctrine. Balance of power does not explain this radical doctrinal change in a relatively static international system.

AIR FORCE PRIORITIES

Balance-of-power theory also expects civilian intervention in air force developments. Barry Posen argues, for example, that when the British air staff was left to its own devices during the 1920s and early 1930s, it adopted an offensive doctrine (strategic bombing) that served its organizational interests. However, with the resurgence of the German threat, civilians intervened in 1937 and overruled the RAF's long-standing support for strategic bombing, forcing the RAF to concentrate on fighters—that is, on a defensive doctrine. "Prompted by systemic pressures, constraints, and incentives," Posen explains, "civilians refashioned the doctrine of the Royal Air Force."[34] In other words, while the RAF is blamed for myopically pursuing its organizational interests by clinging to strategic bombing, British civilians get credit for developing the defensive potential that defeated the German air assault.

This argument neglects three important factors: the tremendous support *civilians* gave to strategic bombing, civilians' lackluster support for many aspects of the air defense programs, and the *air force's* role in the development of the air defense system.[35] The argument that British civilians redirected the RAF away from its self-serving (and offensive) doctrine neglects the determined civilian support for that very same doctrine. Unlike many air forces, the RAF did not have to struggle very hard for recognition. Its future was in question immediately after World War I, but in 1922 the Cabinet announced the permanent establishment of a separate Air Ministry and its formal responsibility for the defense of the United Kingdom. In fact, as early as 1921 the British Cabinet endorsed deterrence through strategic bombing, and in 1923 the Cabinet adopted the principle of parity in air striking forces.[36]

Tight budgets prevented the air force from achieving parity, but when rearmament began in the early 1930s civilians gave the air force, and in particular strategic bombing, pride of place. The Cabinet radically revised the rearmament program drafted by the Defence Requirements

Committee in 1934 and gave the priority to offensive bombing. Sir Robert Vansittart and the Foreign Office also pushed for a more rapid expansion of the bomber force.[37] Civilians, and particularly the chancellor of the exchequer, Neville Chamberlain, led the successful campaign to designate strategic bombing as the linchpin of British strategy.[38] Baldwin, Alfred James Balfour, Anthony Eden, Fisher, David Lloyd George, Viscount Edward Halifax, Hankey, Sir Samuel Hoare, Sir John Simon, Inskip, Vansittart, and Lord Weir all championed strategic bombing. Baldwin's comments to the House of Commons in 1932 captured their sentiments: "There is no power on earth that can protect him [the man on the street] from being bombed. Whatever people may tell him, *the bomber will always get through*. The only defence is in offence, which means that you have to kill more women and children than the enemy if you want to save yourselves."[39] British civilians did not stand passively by as the air force developed strategic bombing. The Cabinet eagerly accepted and promoted Trenchard's vision of offensive air power.

In contrast, British civilians showed little enthusiasm for air defense. A.J.P. Taylor states that although Secretary for Air Lord Swinton supported Henry Tizard's plan for the development of radar, "most ministers did not, even if they troubled to listen. They went on believing that the bomber would always get through." As Tizard himself explained, "[Swinton] was the only Air Minister that I have had to deal with who could understand the recommendations and take action on them. I have had no help from the others; indeed, obstruction rather than help."[40]

The Air Parity Sub-Committee formed by the Cabinet in April 1935 recommended increasing the procurement of medium and heavy bombers and advised *against* the mass procurement of fighter aircraft (Spitfire and Hurricane).[41] Even the Biggin Hill Experiment, the experiment led by Tizard and his associates that put in place the basic system of air defense in the summer of 1936 and 1937, received tepid official (civilian) support.[42] Furthermore, Swinton—the civilian who received the most praise for supporting the development of radar—opposed Inskip's proposal to increase fighter procurement, explaining, "There is no question of altering the ratio of fighter and bomber squadrons in the sense of reducing bomber squadrons to make fighter squadrons."[43] In short, British civilians heralded strategic bombing and paid little attention to air defense.

Posen's argument also shortchanges the extent to which the air force itself supported the development of defensive capabilities. The air staff supported strategic bombing, but it did not ignore the needs of air defense until civilians forced the issue. Stephen Rosen has shown that British air force officers were instrumental in the development of the two major components of air defense: radar and fighter planes.[44] Even before the creation of a separate Fighter Command, many air force officers and in particular Sir Hugh Dowding, actively supported the development of air defense.[45] In 1931, for example, Dowding objected to the international competition in seaplanes because the contests would, in his view, contribute little to the combat value of aircraft. Dowding explained, "I wanted to invite private tenders from two firms to cash in on the experience that had been gained in aircraft construction and engine progress so that we could order two of the fastest machines which it was possible to build with no restriction except landing speed and that had to be on grass airfields." The Air Ministry accepted his proposal and the Hurricane and Spitfire were the eventual consequence.[46] In addition, as Rosen argues, after Trenchard's retirement the new heads of the air staff supported many aspects of defensive air power, including the creation of "shadow" aircraft factories and the training of additional fighter pilots.[47]

Dowding and others in the air force also promoted the development of radar; again, civilians did not force the technology on the RAF.[48] When the scientific adviser at the Air Ministry reported the preliminary results of the radar test in February 1935 to Dowding (who was then air member for supply and research), Dowding guaranteed him adequate budgetary support. The chief of the air staff, Sir Cyril Newall, also supported Tizard's efforts, and while Fighter Command led the development of radar, all of the commands were interested in its development.[49] In fact, Rosen argues that the RAF's long-standing interest in command, control, and communications paved the way for the effective integration of radar. The technological discovery of radar was instrumental, but it was not enough. As Rosen explained, "It was a round technological peg going into a round doctrinal hole."[50] Without years of preparation, the technological discovery might have had little strategic payoff.

Dowding and Fighter Command's pivotal role in the development of air defense should not obscure the fact that the air force, as a whole, always placed the highest priority on strategic bombing. For example, despite some support for fighters within the RAF, Trenchard emphasized bombers as early as 1923. The air staff was not pleased with the shift in priorities in 1937 to fighters. In their view, this change was tantamount to surrendering before the war began. In a speech to the House of Lords in 1939, Trenchard proclaimed that the development of offensive air power should not be limited by "devoting too large a proportion of the country's resources to defence work, like air raid shelters and fighter aircraft."[51] Nevertheless, many air force officers were instrumental in developing the essential components of the British air defense system. Most important, British civilians were not the wise directors of British defense priorities depicted by balance-of-power theory: civilians actively supported strategic bombing yet resisted the very policy that would have prepared the British army to defeat German assaults on the Low Countries.

The Military's Parochial Interests

Much of the British armed services' behavior during the interwar period does not fit the expectations of a functional analysis of military organizations. The British army had the need and the opportunity to use the adoption of an offensive doctrine to get additional resources, but it adopted a defensive doctrine and marginalized the officers calling for an offensive orientation. The other British services also displayed a budgetary modesty that baffles a conventional explanation of organizational interests. However, the RAF's support for strategic bombing illustrates that military organizations can manipulate the adoption of an offensive doctrine to augment or ensure their autonomy.

Throughout the 1920s and early 1930s all three British services were on a strict budgetary diet. The Ten-Year Rule, adopted in 1919 and reaffirmed every year until 1932, worked on the assumption that there would be no war for the next ten years. This policy, combined with the budget-cutting "Geddes Axe" in 1921, so restrained military expenditures that total defense spending during the interwar period did not equal that of the prewar period.[52] British military expenditures as a whole remained relatively modest even after rearmament began. For example, from 1935 to 1938, the British military budget (as a percentage of national income) never reached one-third of the percentage rate of its continental adversary.[53] This financial stringency hit the army the hardest. When rearmament began in 1935, the army continued to suffer from a chronic lack of funding.[54] The Cabinet slashed the budget originally proposed for the army by one-third and placed the army as the lowest priority. As Hankey explained six weeks after Munich: "Chamberlain will give freely to the Navy and Air Force, but he is very niggardly, I think, to the Army."[55]

THE ARMY'S DEFENSIVE DOCTRINE

The logic of a functional analysis would lead us to expect each British service to have advocated the adoption of the military doctrine that would enhance its autonomy, resources, certainty, and prestige. We would expect, for example, the British army to have endorsed an offensive doctrine and in particular, to have embraced the armored warfare concepts of Liddell Hart, Fuller, and the other champions of the offensive use of massed armor. This new doctrine could have been a potent justification for increasing expenditures: going on the offensive requires materiel superiority, and mechanized warfare depended on the procurement of new and expensive technology—tracked vehicles. However, the British army rejected the possibilities of armored warfare and instead adopted a more traditional and defensive doctrine.

The British army adopted a defensive doctrine not because it had little knowledge of offensive possibilities; the ideas were there for the taking. The British army had been first to create tank units during World War I, and two British officers, Giffard Martel and John Fuller, wrote prophetic accounts of armored warfare.[56] Influenced by Fuller, yet rejecting an all-tank approach, Liddell Hart also outlined his ideas for mechanized warfare.[57] The British army officers Charles Broad, Frederick Pile, and Percy Hobart also strongly supported mechanized warfare.[58]

Nor was the British army a passive recipient of civilian directives. British civilians did not force the army to adopt a defensive doctrine despite its apparent preference for an offensive doctrine. To the contrary, British army officers from the traditional regiments actively discouraged the development of (offensive) mechanized warfare and only reluctantly financed armored activities. In 1937, for example, the army budgeted 20,000 pounds to train 38 students at the equitation school, while 550 students at the tank corps school had to make do with 46,000 pounds.[59] Similarly, the British army consistently refused to place officers with an understanding of tank warfare in command of armored units.[60] With the formation of the Experimental Mechanized Force in 1927, for example, the army gave the command to Colonel Collins, an infantry man.[61] Again, when the army created the Mobile Division in 1937, its command did not go to Hobart, Broad, Pile, or one of the other officers with armored experience.[62] Indeed, many of the most articulate advocates of offensive armored warfare either left the army altogether or took their case to the public. If they remained officers, the army ensured that they stayed at the margins. Fuller retired in 1930, George Lindsay served in administrative posts until the army posted him and Broad to India, and Pile commanded an antiaircraft command. The army sent Hobart to Egypt in 1938, placed him on the retirement list after the German invasion of Poland, and brought him back to active duty only on Churchill's insistence.[63]

When the British army made progress in mechanization, it was often due to outside pressure, not army policy.[64] For example, the army established the Mechanized Force in 1927 only after Liddell Hart publicly questioned in print why it had not been formed.[65] Even then, the army planned the armored experiments in such a way that the offensive use of massed tanks was doomed to fail. For example, unimaginative direction and the heterogeneous collection of vehicles hindered the experimental trials of mechanized forces in 1927 and 1928.[66] In fact, in 1934, Hobart refused to participate in the exercises of an experimental armored division because of all the barriers placed in the way of its possible success.[67] In 1935 the army once again frustrated the armored exercises.[68]

The British army's reaction to French pressure for the creation of a small, hard-hitting mobile force provides further evidence that the British army itself checked the development of an offensive doctrine. In the 1930s, General Gamelin pressured British civilian and military leaders to design a small but highly mobile expeditionary force to fill the gap in the French order of battle. If military organizations prefer offensive doctrines and use their adoption to gain more resources, we would have expected the British army to take advantage of the opportunity provided by the French request to push its government to create this offensive force. But what happened? The British army leadership ignored French demands and persisted in its preference for a defensive doctrine.[69]

THE MILITARY'S BUDGETARY RESTRAINT

Still more puzzling for a functional analysis of military organizations is the British army's general reluctance to request more resources. Not only did the army staff forfeit an ideal justification for more resources by scorning the offensive potential of mechanization, but it also exhibited a reluctance to demand greater resources that belies the standard view of organizational interests. Surprising as it may seem, the Cabinet did not reaffirm the Ten-Year Rule over the shrill objections of British military leaders. The chiefs of staff quietly accepted the limitations imposed on them in the 1928 budget and commented that otherwise the burden of national defense "would be well-nigh insupportable." Commenting on the reticence of the military services, a historian noted: "One is left with the impression that, even had the money been saved on social services in the 1920s, there would not have been adequate pressure from any quarter to divert the savings so achieved to national defense."[70]

The services' budget requests were also modest in the 1930s. The programs adopted after the Defence Requirements Committee debate in the Cabinet were less than thought necessary by the Foreign Office, but they *exceeded* what the services considered sufficient.[71] Throughout the process, Sir Robert Vansittart, the representative of the Foreign Office, chided the service's budgetary passivity, but the service chiefs disregarded Vansittart's pressure and continued to request modest resources.[72] For example, the chief of the Imperial General Staff, General Sir Archibald Montgomery-Massingberd, resisted Fisher and Vansittart's pressure. Requesting additional funding, the head of the army explained, "would unbalance the Report as between various items and as between three services."[73] The former chief of naval staff, Admiral Sir Ernle Chatfield, acknowledged the services' passivity: "So brow-beaten had been the then Staff for the last decade, so little sympathy had they received, so hopeless did the struggle appear that there was a feeling, even in my committee, that it was almost improper to be too insistent, to make more than the most moderate demands."[74]

The British military's intelligence reports on German military power again show the chiefs of staff's reluctance to lobby for greater resources. Whereas we might expect the military to exaggerate its adversary's strength in order to justify increased expenditures, both the army and the air force *under*estimated German military power.[75] In fact, both Fisher and Vansittart disparaged the chief of staff's apparent complacency about German power. The War Office questioned the Foreign Office's menacing portrait of Germany's future strength, and the RAF was reluctant to exaggerate the Luftwaffe's power.[76] In defending the air staff's intelligence reports, Sir Maurice Hankey explained to the Foreign Office in March 1934, "I am as much concerned as you are at the German air menace. It is only one of degree or rather of imminence. The Germans are efficient people but they are not supermen. They have also to build up a navy and that is not going to be done very quickly."[77] Later, in his diary, Hankey wrote, "The Chancellor of the Exchequer and most of the cabinet have become rather over-obsessed with the danger from Germany, though warned by the CAS [chief of the air staff] that it would take Germany a long time to become a menace."[78] Air Marshal Ellington also attempted to calm what he saw as excessive anxiety about German air strength by assuring the Cabinet that the German air force would not reach parity until 1945. In fact, the historian Donald Watt referred to "the slowness with which the Air Staff adjusted to reality."[79]

Instead of conducting worst-case analyses to satisfy its organizational interest in greater resources, the British military attempted to temper what it saw as exaggerated civilian concerns. These actions are especially striking during a period of financial stringency. We would expect a functional logic to hold when there is a pressing need for greater resources and an easy way to attain it, but the British services did not behave as anticipated. The British army ignored the organizational advantages that adopting an offensive doctrine could have brought, and all three services chose not to capitalize on or stoke civilian fear of German power.

THE RAF'S INDEPENDENCE

The establishment of the air force as an independent service was not a foregone conclusion. Many within the military assumed that the introduction of the airplane meant little more than a new means to accomplish traditional missions. To the army, the airplane could enhance the cavalry's reconnaissance capabilities and augment the firepower of long-range artillery. Assigned these missions, there would be little need to create an independent service. However, strategic bombing was an entirely new mission and was, as Posen argued, an ideal vehicle to justify a new and autonomous service.[80]

The RAF gained some independence during World War I, but upon demobilization, budget cuts and attacks from other services threatened its survival. Lloyd George told Winston Churchill to "make up your mind whether you would like to go to the War Office or the Admiralty, and let me know by tomorrow. You can take the Air with you in either case; I am not going to keep it as a separate department." However, by stressing air power's unique and new roles air advocates were able to ensure the maintenance of an autonomous air service.[81]

From the start of his appointment as chief of the air staff in 1919, Trenchard argued that the RAF's primary role should be the defense of Great Britain through the threat of a counteroffensive from the air. The air force was, the air advocates argued, a substitute for and not an auxiliary to the other services. Strategic bombing was a new and autonomous mission that the navy and army could not accomplish. The RAF could also undertake missions already assigned to the other services—such as coastal defense and imperial air policing—but more cheaply.[82]

Despite its claim that it could counter a German attack, the RAF had little evidence that the German air force intended to launch a strategic bombing campaign against the British Isles. The first study of the probable German air strategy was not completed until 1936, and the air staff could do little but assume that the Luftwaffe would conduct an air offensive against Britain. Throughout the 1930s, the air staff produced only one paper that specifically discussed evidence that supported their contentions about German air doctrine. This lack of evidence is not surprising: the Luftwaffe did not examine the operational implications of an air offensive against Britain until mid-1936, concluding then that such an attack would have little if any effect on the war.[83] In short, the RAF created the enemy it needed to justify an offensive doctrine that it wanted for organizational reasons.

The RAF's failure to develop the capability to implement strategic bombing is further evidence that the air force adopted the offensive doctrine to contend with attacks on its autonomy at home, not its adversaries abroad. The RAF's targeting policy emphasized striking oil plants and railroad yards, but it had not studied whether doing so would be feasible;[84] it had not begun to address problems of navigation, night bombing accuracy, and marking techniques.[85] In fact, it was not until 1937 that the RAF began to assess the damage that it could inflict on Germany.[86] "It remains one of the most remarkable facts in the whole history of British defense policy," Michael Howard explains, "that the RAF, which since 1918 based its entire strategic doctrine and raison d'être on the vital part which strategic bombing would play in future wars, had before 1937 carried out no studies as to how this was actually to be done." Britain entered the war, according to Tizard, "with the most inadequate bombs, with rudimentary ideas of accurate bombing under the conditions of war, and with little, if any experience of the problems of flying in a 'black-out.'"[87]

The transformation of Trenchard's views after he became the chief of the air staff is some of the most compelling evidence that the adoption of strategic bombing was a function of organizational opportunism. As the head of the Royal Flying Corps in France during World War I, Trenchard resisted calls for offensive strikes against Germany; he demanded that the air wing directly support the army. However, once head of the air force and driven by the desire to retain the force's independence, Trenchard converted to the doctrine that he had so strenuously opposed during World War I.[88]

THE FRENCH AIR FORCE'S AUTONOMY

The RAF was not alone in using strategic bombing to justify institutional autonomy. The United States Air Force also took advantage of this new offensive doctrine to gain and maintain its status as a separate service.[89] Similarly, during the interwar period the French air force used strategic bombing to fight off the army and navy's opposition to the creation of a separate air ministry. In the army's view, aviation should be used to support ground operations, not to run independent missions deep in enemy territory. The army repeatedly stressed that the air force's primary role should be to provide intelligence and ground support. For example, in 1933 the minister of the army labeled the air force's proposal to reduce the number of reconnaissance planes as "inadmissible." The air force proposals, he argued, were based on an erroneous hypothesis: that the air war would take place several days before the land attack.[90] The French army resisted the aviators' attempts to gain independence from army missions.[91]

Some French aviators realized that their hopes for real institutional autonomy might be realized only through the development of independent missions, and, like many of their counterparts abroad, they used strategic bombing to justify their autonomy. They stressed the service the air force could provide in missions that were independent of the ground war.[92] But this functional argument cannot explain several other important aspects of doctrinal developments in the French and British air forces. For example, if the desire for independence drove the RAF's doctrine, why did the British airmen also adopt a defensive doctrine? Similarly, if the quest for autonomy is the impetus behind the adoption of strategic bombing, why were the British airmen much more ardent advocates of strategic bombing than their French counterparts when it was the French air force's autonomy that was the more precarious?

Whereas the French air force struggled for more than two decades to gain and maintain its status as an independent service, administrative recognition of a separate air force occurred in Britain as early as 1918. The Cabinet reaffirmed the RAF's independent status in 1922; thereafter its autonomy was never seriously questioned.[93] The contrast with France is striking. The French government did not create the separate Air Ministry until 1928, and even then the air force acquired little real autonomy. The decree establishing the ministry specified that the units for "tactical use in cooperation with the Army" be placed at the permanent disposition of the Ministry of War. The air force could use the general reserve only with the prior approval of the War Ministry. Only the principle of independence had been recognized, and the first battle engaged. The services continued to fight over the independent status of the air force before and after the creation of the air force in 1934. Even after liberation in 1944, the controversy recurred.[94]

One of the more poignant examples of this incessant turf battle is the procurement of what was called the BCR (bombardment, combat, reconnaissance) airplane. It met the air force's desire for a plane capable of strategic bombing and also satisfied the army's operational requirements. Designed to do everything, however, the BCR was really good for nothing; it was outclassed by the planes built specifically for each service.[95]

Given the constraints on the French air force's autonomy, one would have expected it to embrace an offensive doctrine to justify its fledgling independence. Yet it was the British air force—the institution that had gained its autonomy relatively easily—that was the strongest advocate of offensive air power. There was some support within the French air force for targeting industrial centers, population centers, and the adversary's morale, but French aviators' enthusiasm for strategic bombing paled next to that of the Bomber Command. Indeed, not until the late 1920s and especially the early 1930s did the debate about the value of strategic bombing develop within the French air force. Previously, the air force had accepted its role as an auxiliary to the other services and ignored the possibility of an offensive and independent role for air power.[96] In other words, during some of the most bitter debates between the French services about the future status of this new service, the air force did not attempt to use strategic bombing to justify its autonomy. In fact, there was never a consensus about the value of strategic bombing.[97] As Pascal Vennesson has documented, only brief passages in Giulio Douhet's influential book *The Command of the Air* were translated into French, and the French air force never produced a powerful advocate of strategic bombing like Douhet in Italy, Billy Mitchell in the United States, or Hugh Trenchard in Britain.[98] In fact, French air force officers often critiqued this new offensive mission. During the Spanish Civil War a report by the chief of the air staff downplayed the importance of strategic bombing: "Contrary to Douhet's theories, during the war in Spain the air force did not relentlessly attack vital targets in the rear."[99]

When the strategic bombing mission dominated the French air force, it was not due to the airmen's efforts or to any consensus that had emerged about its benefits. As minister of the air in the fall of 1936, Pierre Cot, a civilian, shifted the emphasis of the French air force from ground support to strategic bombing; he reorganized the air force and doubled the number of bombers assigned an offensive role.[100] Later, in 1937, Cot refocused on ground support, but it is important to emphasize that the offensive air doctrine was promoted by civilians, not by the military.[101] In short, there was little relationship between the degree of organizational support for strategic bombing and the desire or need for institutional autonomy. The French air force, desperately fighting for autonomy, displayed only lukewarm support for strategic bombing, while the British air force, confident in its autonomy, championed offensive air power.

Unlike in France, in Britain the external environment helped guide civilian intervention in doctrinal developments. As discussed in Chapter 6, London's desire to keep defense expenditures to a minimum, and so to ensure Britain's peacetime deterrent and wartime strength, influenced strategic priorities. Financial considerations drove early civilian support for strategic bombing and the later switch to fighters. However, many of the British civilians' choices seemed immune to international events. Although aware of the German threat and worried about strategic bombing, civilians refused to make a continental commitment or to take rudimentary steps that would have placed the army in a much better position to deny the Germans access to the airfields in northern Europe. Rarely in international politics has the external environment been as compelling, yet British civilians responded inadequately.

Nor did the British military pursue their parochial interests, as a functional analysis of military organizations would have predicted. The air staff used strategic bombing to ensure its institutional autonomy, but the contrasting decisions of the British and French air forces and the RAF's additional adoption of a defensive doctrine raise questions about the usefulness of this argument. The British army's behavior is even more surprising from a functional perspective. On its own initiative the army adopted a defensive doctrine, and all three services showed a budgetary modesty that confounds a conventional evaluation of organizational interests. As I argue in Chapter 6, understanding this puzzling behavior, as well as making sense of civilian choices, requires understanding both the political culture and the military's organizational culture.

6

Culture and British Doctrine

> Unhappy Nations have lost that precious Jewel
> *Liberty* . . . [when] their Necessities or Indiscretion
> have permitted a Standing Army to be kept
> amongst them.
> *(John Trenchard)*

BRITISH CIVILIANS agreed on the parameters of British defense policy. Unlike France, which was still battling over the position of the military in society, Britain had long resolved the fundamental question about the role of the armed forces in the domestic arena. Whatever their political persuasion, British civilians did not want an army with a strong military caste independent of legislative control. This consensus also meant that British civilians were more likely than their French counterparts to respond to systemic imperatives. In London's eyes, British security depended on the strength of its economy; a healthy economy would deter adversaries in peacetime and defeat them in war.

The importance accorded to the economy as the "fourth arm of defense" and the fear of the despotic power of a professional army set important constraints on doctrinal developments in the British army. First, civilian refusal to make a continental commitment because of its potential cost robbed the army of the one area in which offensive mechanized warfare made any sense. The concern about costs also shaped doctrinal developments in the Royal Air Force. Second, civilian fear of a professional army meant that civilians never forced the British army's officer corps to modernize or professionalize. As a result, the British army's organizational culture continued to prize the gentleman-officer over the professional soldier. This anachronistic culture prevented the army from grasping the potential of massed armor. Although war was no longer the business of amateurs, the dominant branches of the British army continued to view professionalization as something unbefitting gentlemen. Nearly every aspect of the army's culture reflected another age of warfare. Whether it was their view of the nature of war or the preferred command structure, British officers were ill prepared for the demands of offensive operations dominated by mechanized vehicles and massed firepower. As a result, these gentleman-officers could only imagine using these new technologies to fight in a traditional, and defensive, manner. Adopting an offensive doctrine on the modern battlefield required an organizational culture that they did not have.

Although civilian choices constrained subsequent doctrinal developments, they did not determine the defensive orientation of British army doctrine; another army could have responded differently to constraints set in the domestic political arena. However, the British army's culture could not recognize the potential for the offensive use of massed tanks. The British army's organizational culture intervenes between civilian decisions and army doctrine.

Consensual Political Culture

No Standing Army!

Since Cromwell and his "ironsides," the British upper class were suspicious of any military force that could threaten the state.[1] Whereas the French Left feared the professional army that the French Right preferred, the British Left, Right, Labor, Liberal, and Conservatives agreed that a strong and efficient standing army *might not* serve British interests. As the historian Correlli Barnett observed, "the history of the British army, then, is the history of the institution that the British have always been reluctant to accept that they needed."[2] Although resigned to its maintenance in peacetime, British elites ensured that the British army remained a domestically weak actor.

As early as 1628 the English gentry drafted the Petition of Right to protest the Crown's maintenance of a peacetime standing army. The suspension of liberties under Cromwell's New Model Army and the excesses of the throne cemented their aversion to strong peacetime armies. The settlement of 1688 determined the basic distribution of power in the British state and society: the existence of the army depended on the annual approval of the Parliament. Only the militia, viewed as unlikely to endanger English liberties, received statutory status. The House of Commons gained sovereignty and henceforth controlled the ultimate source of domestic power. The British had settled one of the fundamental themes of their political culture: parliamentary control of a relatively weak army.[3]

For the next three centuries the British Parliament secured its victory. The parliamentarians kept the army small, ensured an apolitical officer corps, and guaranteed that it would not become a strong centralized institution with corporate interests at odds with the state. Although Britain was at war for most of the eighteenth century, the Parliament permitted neither a permanent commander-in-chief nor a separate secretaryship for war.[4] It was not until 1755 that the parliamentarians would refer to the "army" as such. Before that time, only the "guards and garrisons" could be spoken of in the House of Commons.[5] Throughout the nineteenth century, British civilians continued to limit the army's potential power. Queen Victoria and most politicians, particularly the Liberals and Radicals, opposed the creation of a modern General Staff. "For over two generations," an analyst commented, "Whig politicians had done all in their power, by institutionalizing the anarchy of military administration and command, to prevent it from coalescing into a neo-Cromwellian threat to the State."[6] Twenty years after most European states had copied the Prussian army model, the British secretary of state Henry Campbell-Bannerman commented that there was "no room for 'general military policy' in this larger and more ambitious sense of the phrase" where a body devoted entirely to planning for war might accordingly prove "some danger to our best interests."[7]

The fragmentation of army command and organization might have weakened the army's strength beyond English frontiers, but it bolstered parliamentary supremacy within England. Even during the French Revolutionary Wars, both Whigs and Radicals had rebuffed the Duke of York's calls for the creation of a more efficient army.[8] After 1870, the government conducted numerous official inquires into military affairs, but little was done.[9] It was not until after the army's disastrous performance in the Boer War that British civilians approved the creation of a General Staff.[10] In fact, a report commissioned after the Boer War reached the same conclusion as a report completed fifty years earlier: Britain lacked a professional army.

British civilians wanted to keep the army from becoming an insular group, separate from the general society, and with its own corporate interests. While the Prussian army adopted promotion by merit and seniority in the mid-eighteenth century, the British retained the purchase of commissions until 1871. In an inquiry into this system, Earl Henry George Grey, a Whig politician and former secretary-at-war, explained that, "officers in the army do not look to it entirely as their means of existence. They trust to private fortune . . . and the existence of a large number of persons of that kind in the army . . . seems to me to be a very great political advantage, and to render the maintenance of a considerable standing army much more safe than it would otherwise be."[11] With promotion and recruitment divorced from merit, only elites could aspire to the higher offices in the army. This system encouraged the officer corps to identify with what were seen as national interests, not the military's corporate interests. The Parliament also rejected proposals for the creation of a separate Army Club out of fear that it would encourage the development of a military caste.[12]

Little changed in the British army after World War I. Historically, most military organizations did not take the initiative to professionalize, and many even opposed professionalization.[13] The British army was no different; it did not call for the type of internal reform necessary to become a professional body, and civilians—who viewed professional military officers as a manifestation of militarism and a danger to civilian control—saw little reason to push for reform. British civilians also resisted proposals aimed at creating a more centralized military structure. Despite military calls for the creation of a formal organization to better coordinate strategic policy, the creation of a single defense ministry was not politically feasible.[14] Proposals to centralize military authority clashed with British notions of civilian supremacy.[15] In short, despite revolutionary changes in warfare introduced during World War I, British civilians did little as the army returned to regimental soldiering.

Whereas British civilians prevented the officer corps from becoming a separate military caste, they encouraged the development of a large gulf between the common soldiers and British society. Only in dire circumstances would British liberalism accept military conscription. In contrast to the French, who stressed the ideals of honor and duty to the state and saw the citizen army as an essential source of the republic, British civilians felt that universal military service was an affront to English liberties. England filled its forces with volunteers trying to escape starvation and unemployment. The Duke of Wellington described the British army as "the national and filthy receptacle . . . for the misfits of society who could only be held in check by punishment and repression." According to the *Westminster Review*, by accepting the bounty for enlisting, the soldier lost his right of citizenship and his claim to individualism.[16] During the nineteenth century, for example, public parks, gardens, and music halls were off limits to the rank and file.[17]

For much of its history, Britain's position as an island nation meant that it could afford the civilians' aversion to a strong standing army and peacetime conscription. The English Channel sheltered Britain from the prospect of invasion. British geography made those civilian preferences possible; but it did not require them. Cuba and Japan in the nineteenth and early twentieth century are two examples of island nations that relied on military conscription and a professional officer corps.[18] More important, the rise of air power threatened British security. Strategic bombing directly and immediately exposed Britain to continental warfare. Still, British civilians' beliefs about military policy persisted.

Many European states had reformed their armies to correspond with the Prussian model of universal conscription and a professional officer corps, but British civilians were content with a small amateur army. No major political group wanted either a professional military caste or citizen soldiers. The army remained a weak political actor led by amateur officers who identified with the national interest. The British army might never have been the most efficient fighting force, but it also had neither the power nor the inclination to threaten the balance of power within the state. Although perhaps beneficial for domestic stability, the absence of army reform meant that during the 1920s and 1930s the British army had an organizational culture that predated the modern era. This gentleman-officer culture prevented the army from recognizing the potential of armored warfare.

The Fourth Arm of Defense

The reluctance of the British to create a professional army should not be mistaken for a lack of interest in their national security. To the contrary, the civilian consensus about the role of the military in the domestic arena leads one to expect that civilians would have been attuned to international considerations when making decisions about military policy. This appears to be the case. British civilians worried about their relative power, and in particular were careful not to undermine the strength of the economy. Whereas the French emphasized amassing military materiel and continued to finance large defense budgets even during periods of economic crisis, the British refused to rearm if doing so would interfere with the normal course of British business. In London's view the maintenance of an army, air force, and navy would not guarantee British security; a healthy and growing economy was the "fourth arm of defense."

Rearmament had to strike a delicate balance between meeting an emergent threat and avoiding undue strain on the peacetime economy. If trade-offs were necessary, maintaining economic stability took priority over balancing an adversary's military power. The minister for the coordination of defense, Sir Thomas Inskip, explained, "Nothing operates more strongly to deter a potential aggressor from attacking this country than our stability." Successful deterrence required social and economic stability. "This reputation stands us in good stead," Inskip stressed, "and causes other countries to rate our powers of resistance at something far more formidable than is implied merely by the number of men of war, aeroplanes and battalions which we should have at our disposal immediately on the outbreak of war."[19]

Even if deterrence failed, the strength of the British economy was as important as the outcome of military engagements. In the House of Commons in November 1936, Inskip reminded his colleagues, "We depend upon the resources of finance for the successful fighting of a war as much as upon the production of munitions."[20] In peacetime, as in war, the strength of the City of London was as important as the production rate of the armament factories. Clinging to the precepts of orthodox finance, successive British Cabinets believed that ensuring the fourth arm of defense required avoiding deficit spending and the ensuing inflation. Before the House of Commons, the chancellor of the exchequer explained, "It is not part of my job . . . to put before the House of Commons proposals for the expenditure of public money. The function of the Chancellor of the Exchequer . . . is to resist all demands for expenditure . . . and, when he can no longer resist, to limit the concession to the barest point of acceptance." The British Treasury and the Cabinet as a whole resolved to stay within the "limits of decent finance" and avoid American or French budgetary methods.[21]

London's determination to avoid a peacetime military buildup also had domestic roots. The Conservative government worried about the domestic dislocation that an economic crisis might bring. In the government's eyes, especially after the disastrous experience of Weimar Germany, it was better to underarm than to risk hyperinflation and its attendant social and economic costs, especially if the latter could result in the fall of the government and the reorganization of the British economic and social structure. As Robert Shay, a historian of British rearmament noted, "Inflation was not only a threat to national security, but to the whole social order." The historian Gustav Schmidt argues that domestic considerations were the primary determinant of British policy. Even in the late 1930s, "security policy was still subject to the directive that Britain could rather afford to take risks over the defense issue than run the risk of dividing the country along class lines."[22] Zara Steiner critiques Schmidt for slighting the importance of international factors, but she also stresses that "recent work on Treasury policy and on industrial and labor attitudes gives added weight to Schmidt's contention that policy-makers were more willing to take risks abroad than at home."[23] The "Watch on the Tyne" (symbolizing unemployment and economic crisis) was as important as the "Watch on the Rhine."[24]

This concern about domestic unrest meant that the balance of peacetime expenditures favored social programs; the only way to avoid deficit spending while also satisfying some of the demands of the disadvantaged sectors in English society was to sacrifice the defense budget. The percentage of the public expenditure devoted to defense and social services in 1913 and 1933 captures the dilemma facing British governments. In 1913, 30 percent of the public expenditure went to defense and 33 percent to social services. By 1933, the percentage devoted to social services had jumped to 46.6 percent and defense spending had decreased to 10.5 percent. In 1936, Baldwin explained before the House of Commons, "In the postwar years we had to choose between . . . a policy of disarmament, social reform and latterly financial rehabilitation and . . . a heavy expenditure on armaments."[25] In the 1930s Alfred Duff-Cooper, secretary of state for war, commented that the British Cabinet had the choice between altering the "whole of our social system or the whole of our foreign and imperial policy."[26] Faced with this choice, the British government chose to preserve the domestic status quo.

For both domestic and international reasons, British civilians wanted to keep defense expenditures to a minimum and gave at least rhetorical support to collective security and disarmament negotiations.[27] In the first decade following World War I, defense expenditures fell dramatically, from 766 million pounds in 1919–20 to 189 million in 1921, and to 102 million in 1932.[28] British defense spending remained small until 1938 and never approached one-third of the percentage rate of national income spent by the Germans.[29]

After the Japanese invasion of Shanghai, the Treasury explained its resistance to increased defense expenditures: "Today financial and economic risks are by far the most serious and urgent the country has to face and . . . . other risks must be run until the country has had time and opportunity to recuperate and our financial situation to improve." The Cabinet concurred: although it canceled the Ten-Year Rule, the government made no commitment to increase defense expenditures.[30] Throughout the rearmament process, the Cabinet would fund the military only up to the point where its expenses would not interfere with the normal course of trade and business. Going beyond that would have, in their view, jeopardized Britain's long-term security.[31]

Civilian reluctance to create a ministry of supply was symptomatic of the British government's unwillingness to interfere with the normal course of business. The government did not think that it should impose controls on labor or the level of profit. Indeed, Swinton and Inskip's stubborn demand for the new ministry cost them their jobs in January 1939. Even when the government finally created the Ministry of Supply in May 1939, it had only limited powers.[32]

The demands of the fourth arm of defense meant that the cheaper option invariably won out. Concern about the size of the defense budget prompted early civilian support for strategic bombing. Wanting to keep costs down but guarantee British security, civilians advocated the one option that appeared to allow them a way out: strategic bombing. Following Chamberlain's advice that rearmament should not disrupt the peacetime economy, the Cabinet amended the proposals drafted by the Defence Requirements Committee in 1934 and shifted the priority toward an expansion of the RAF. Chamberlain argued that Britain could get "more bang for its buck" by expanding the strategic air force.[33] Strategic bombing would buy deterrence on the cheap.

As bombers became more expensive, civilian enthusiasm waned, and in 1937 the civilians chose the cheaper alternative to bombers: fighters.[34] At the time, Inskip explained to the Cabinet that they must not allow rearmament to interfere with the British economy.[35] Britain should not overly tax its economy for the sake of military hardware, and in particular, Inskip wished to reduce the proposed defense programs by 1.5 million pounds. For him, the choice was simple: bombers cost four times more than fighters and the production of fighters was less disruptive of Britain's industrial base.[36] Both Chamberlain and Simon agreed that focusing on bombers would tax the economy excessively.[37] The desire to avoid large defense expenditures also determined the army's role. Worried about the cost of an expeditionary army, British civilians refused to make a continental commitment until the last possible moment. And without this responsibility for the European theater, the British army did not have the one role that would have been a powerful incentive for the adoption of an offensive doctrine based on massed armor.

The British Way in Warfare?

The reluctance to make a military commitment on the continent may seem to have been a fundamental tenet of British strategic culture. The "British way in warfare" referred to a peripheral or maritime strategy premised on Britain's geographic position as an island nation. The Royal Navy would protect the British Isles, the colonies, and British commerce. Preparing large land forces for continental warfare was, according to this position, unnecessary and potentially disastrous; Britain preferred to limit its participation in a European conflict to imposing economic pressure through a naval blockade or diverting an adversary's land forces through a small land operation. Britain's allies and Britain itself would be best served if London kept to its "traditional" strategy and strengthened the Royal Navy.

The notion that there was a British way in warfare was particularly potent during the interwar period. The well-known military correspondent Basil Liddell Hart publicly introduced this theme at a lecture at the Royal United Services Institution in 1931 and led an active campaign on its behalf in the (London) *Times* and his own publications. As the unofficial adviser to War Minister Leslie Hore-Belisha in 1937–38, Liddell Hart argued for Britain's traditional maritime strategy and against a continental commitment. According to Liddell Hart, 1914 was an aberration; before World War I, Britain's land commitment to the continent was limited.[38] British strategic policy during the 1920s and 1930s seemed to reflect this essential tenet; for most of this period, the British Cabinet gave a continental commitment the lowest priority. The policy of limited liability began as early as 1919 and continued until the eve of the war despite continuous calls by the chiefs of staff for an expeditionary force and civilian awareness of the importance of keeping the Germans out of northern Europe. This dogged persistence in the face of important and persuasive counterarguments would seem to indicate that a policy of limited liability was an essential ingredient in Britain's strategic culture.

However, British civilians manipulated the notion of a British way in warfare to justify a policy that they desired for other reasons. Proponents of the British way in warfare heralded this policy as part of British tradition, but financial reasons, not a cultural legacy, drove the choice. London did not want to spend the resources required to prepare an expeditionary force tailored for continental warfare, and invoking the legacy and wisdom of history was a convenient way of justifying their position. There was a strong policy preference for remaining aloof from the continent, but this is different than arguing that the British way in warfare was part of the strategic culture. There were too many violations of the "cultural precept" and too much controversy to claim that this principle was taken for granted.

Both British strategic theory and practice challenge a British way in warfare. Since Elizabeth I's reign, English policymakers had debated the merits of the maritime and continental school.[39] While many argued that Britain could limit its military involvement on the continent, others maintained that a navy alone would not secure the British Isles. In their eyes, Britain would need an army capable of defeating a European land power; imposing a naval blockade could not win the war. Nor has Britain consistently adhered to the British way in warfare. Many potentially hegemonic continental powers could not be brought to their knees with an economic blockade or diversionary land tactics. Britain sent large expeditionary forces to the continent during the revolt in the Netherlands, the War of Spanish Succession, the Seven Years' War, and the Napoleonic Wars.[40] Liddell Hart may have argued that it was "not until the first major war of the twentieth century that Britain departed from her historic strategy," but Britain had long sent large forces during great continental wars of vital importance to British security.[41] As Michael Howard explained, a continental commitment "on the largest scale that contemporary resources could afford, so far from being alien to traditional British strategy was absolutely central to it."[42] In fact, a recent article on this strategic concept began with the simple sentence: "There has never been a British way in warfare."[43]

Although this policy was not a fundamental tenet of British strategic culture, the British way in warfare was politically effective. Few in the British electorate desired a repetition of World War I, and leading members of the Cabinet, including the foreign secretary, assumed that the preparation of an expeditionary force would be politically unpopular.[44]

The government avoided using labels like "expeditionary force" in official publications out of fear that it would arouse public opposition.[45] The final Cabinet report of the Defence Requirements Committee explained its reasoning: "In the present case it happened that the general trend of public opinion appeared to coincide with our own views as to the desirability of considerable expansion of the RAF for home defense" [and the corresponding low priority given to an expeditionary force].[46] The Cabinet knew that a continental commitment was politically unpopular and used this knowledge to its advantage.

British civilians packaged their policy in the strategic rhetoric of a "British way in warfare," but concerns about the budget led to the policy of limited liability.[47] Restricting the army's missions to antiaircraft defense at home and imperial defense saved substantial expenditures on the equipment that would be necessary to conduct a European campaign. Elimination of the expeditionary force, for example, allowed Chamberlain to shave 21 million pounds from the army estimates proposed by the Defence Requirements Committee.[48] Three years later, the Cabinet's support for a limited liability forced the army to cut its expenditures significantly over the next two years; much of this saving came from cuts in the army's "Field Force."[49] General Pownall's indignant reaction to this outcome captures the Cabinet's rationale: "Therein lies the fallacy of his [Inskip's] argument. And see how the role is altered to fit the purse. The tail wagging the dog."[50]

Without a continental commitment there was little reason to adopt the organization, training, equipment, or doctrine necessary for meeting a threat in Europe.[51] In the nineteenth century, the Cardwell reforms linked every battalion at home to one serving overseas.[52] As the chiefs of staff explained, this system subordinated the needs of Europe and home defense to those of overseas garrisons: "Neither the size of the Regular Army nor that of the Expeditionary Force has any relation to the size of foreign armies. The size of the Regular Army is therefore conditioned by the number and strength of the garrisons maintained overseas." The training and equipment of the British army responded to the needs of policing the empire, not to European warfare. Interchangeable before the advent of the increased mobility and enhanced firepower of the modern age, units organized for the defense of the empire were no longer adequate for the demands of continental warfare. As one commentator explained at the time, "Everything in the Army is dependent upon the Cardwell system. . . . We thus have a situation in which the greater portion of the British Army is regulated by the conditions prevailing on a portion of one of the frontiers of one of the Empire's constituent parts."[53] Armored units capable of thwarting a German assault made little sense in this context.

For the British civilians, the army was the least cost-effective way to deter Britain's "ultimate enemy." The desire to limit defense spending led to the initial preference for the air force over the army in 1934 and the growing support for the policy of limited liability in the British Cabinet after May 1937. Even when the Cabinet made a continental commitment in February 1939, it did not allocate money for the preparation of an expeditionary force. The army went to France equipped for imperial duties.[54]

The determination to prevent the development of a professional army and the principle of a buoyant economy as the fourth arm of defense set limits on doctrinal developments in the British armed services during the 1920s and 1930s. The government's decision to avoid a continental commitment because of its high cost encouraged the army to focus on colonial warfare and not the role best suited to offensive mechanized warfare. More important, bereft of the reforming arm of the state, the British army continued to have an organizational culture reminiscent of nineteenth-century warfare. Although these beliefs did not threaten the state, they were ill suited to the revolutionary changes taking place on the battlefield. As an amateur army with an imperial role, the British army had little proclivity for or need to adopt mechanized, offensive warfare.

The British Army Adopts a Defensive Doctrine

The British army could have adopted an offensive doctrine in the years preceding World War II. British civilians did not intervene and force the high command to accept a defensive doctrine; the army had the freedom, knowledge, and funding to do as it wanted. Other military organizations facing the same domestic constraints could have acted differently; an offensive doctrine similar to the German army's blitzkrieg doctrine was "objectively" possible. However, the British army's culture could not assimilate this new type of offensive warfare; the army adopted a defensive doctrine consistent with its organizational culture.

British civilians were not involved in decisions about doctrine. Unlike during the post–World War II period, public interest and participation in military affairs was minimal, and at no time during the interwar period did the Parliament discuss mechanization.[55] Neither the Cabinet nor the Parliament concerned itself with army doctrine.[56] As Campbell-Bannerman put it: "Leave the old Army alone and don't make war."[57]

The successive extension of the Ten-Year Rule handicapped all three services, and especially the army, but the army had sufficient funds for mechanized warfare. It was, after all, almost completely converted to motor transport by 1939 and had the resources to organize two to three armored divisions. In May 1937, for example, Liddell Hart outlined how the army could be reorganized (not expanded) to accommodate four armored mobile divisions.[58] In addition, army leaders could have enhanced the armored units in Egypt or used tanks to defend India.[59] The British army's decision about what kind of tanks to procure and how to deploy them, not a deficit in tanks themselves, prevented offensive attacks spearheaded by armored formations. As Michael Howard noted, the German army had fewer resources than the British army until 1934, but when money began to pour in, the German army knew how to use it.[60]

The British army also had immediate access to the ideas themselves: the concepts of armored warfare were there for the taking. As discussed in Chapter 5, Britain had led developments of mechanized warfare in the 1920s and early 1930s, and some of the most persuasive advocates of an offensive doctrine were British. Liddell Hart may have exaggerated his influence on the German army, but it was not the lack of knowledge about offensive possibilities that forced the British army to adopt a defensive doctrine.[61] Instead, the British army itself marginalized the officers who advocated a more offensive orientation.

Although financial stringency and the lack of a continental commitment limited doctrinal developments in the British army, the military organization itself played a role. As Brian Bond pointed out, it was "precisely when financial stringency was at its tightest in the early 1930s that Britain carried out her most progressive experiments with the world's first tank brigade."[62] While it is too much to expect the British army to have undertaken fundamental reform given its meager resources and the chronic uncertainty over its role, it could have developed a more progressive doctrine for the use of tanks. In other words, it mattered which military organization operated under those constraints; all armies would not have reacted the same way to the same civilian choices.

The Army's Dominant Culture: An Officer and a Gentleman

> They taught us to mount our bicycles in a
> soldierly manner—that is, by pretending
> the bicycles were horses and we a troop
> of cavalry.
>   (John Masters)

The British army's organizational culture valued the gentleman-officer over the professional soldier; it could not capitalize on the revolutionary implications of massed armor. Whereas the German army's organizational culture paved the way for the adoption of a blitzkrieg doctrine, the British army could not imagine how the technology introduced in the trenches of northern Europe could open the battlefield to mobile and offensive warfare.[63] On numerous different issues—skills, technology, command structure, and relationship between the officers and the rank—the British army preferred the orientation that it thought would maintain the army's morale. Although appropriate to nineteenth-century wars or imperial policing, those aspects of its culture no longer corresponded to the modern battlefield, and as a consequence the army was blind to the offensive potential of new technology.

THE AMATEUR OFFICER

British army officers traditionally came from the landed gentry, and the army's culture reflected and reinforced this history. Hunting, horses, silver, and fine crystal filled regimental life. "Attracted more to their class than to their profession," an observer remarked, British gentlemen were drawn to this part-time occupation that mirrored life on country estates.[64] Even after the right to purchase commissions was abolished in 1871, regimental life remained the preserve of the privileged.[65] Military service offered a pleasant and collegial home away from home. In 1901 an army officer wrote that he did "not like soldiering, though I very much like the life—the fun of always being with a lot of nice people of one's own age. . . . I feel I never want to leave this jolly battalion."[66] Military life allowed the gentleman-officer the leisure to manage his estates, participate in local government, and delight in the sporting pleasures of country life.

The British army had changed very little by the 1920s and 1930s.[67] Whereas most European states had a professional officer corps, the British officer clung to his amateur status.[68] Even after World War I and the deadly effects of enhanced firepower, the British army returned to regimental soldiering. As one officer remarked, "There was something agreeably amateur about the Services, perhaps particularly about the Army, in those days [1930s] . . . it was certainly different from the attitude of mind in most foreign armies."[69] The battlefield had undergone remarkable changes, but life at the center of the army remained the same: "In many respects, life in an officers' mess has changed little in the past 150 years or so. New members now [1977], as in 1811 and certainly in 1931, are expected to behave as though they are guests in a country house."[70]

During the interwar period, a member of the French high command visited the British army and was surprised by what he observed. A British officer explained:

> The Directing Staff returned from a reconnaissance for an outdoor exercise, attired in the usual neglige of the British officer at his ease in the country—corduroys or grey bags, ancient tweed coats and rather villainous felt hats or

cloth caps—to find in the hall no less a person then General Weygand, being shown around the Staff College by the Commandant. The dapper little General did not conceal his surprise at the arrival of this gang of *sans-culottes*, whom he might have been excused for taking as poachers or dog-robbers.[71]

British officers displayed a cultivated amateurishness unfamiliar to their foreign counterparts.

An officer's pay was no longer an honorarium, but it did not cover the costs of regimental life.[72] Men of modest means could not make a career in the most prestigious regiments.[73] Instead, they attracted men seeking a part-time and agreeable occupation. General Wavell explained in 1933 that "in the profession of an officer there is, still, more leisure granted than in any other."[74] In his memoirs, an army officer describes his fellow cadets at Sandhurst, the military academy: "Their only common denominator was that few had any intention of permanently pursuing a military career. They were on their way to spend a few years in the Guards or the cavalry, because it was traditional, or because it passed the time while they were waiting to inherit estates."[75] During the interwar period, the British army was, once again, a pleasant home for a gentleman, a world of sporting and social events in the country and minor military duties in the barracks.[76]

Most British officers thought of soldiering as a way of life or an agreeable job, not a serious profession or a salaried career.[77] Their attention to military matters, and especially any traces of professionalism, were kept to a minimum. "The British army has to a certain extent still kept its amateur status," said General Wavell in 1936.[78] A government report twenty years later repeated this conclusion: "The pattern of an officer's career is anachronistic. It presupposes that the typical officer will be a public school man who after twenty years of service life can retire to manage his estates and interest himself in the public affairs of his neighborhood."[79] Whereas in the air force "the ground crews had received the finest training obtainable and were deeply imbued with professional pride and love of their work for its own sake," in the army, the breeding of a gentleman was the essential qualification for service.[80] Writing disparagingly about officers in the air force, an army officer commented, "In any event it was unseemly to go barnstorming in flying machines, in the company of cranks and exhibitionists. If a man must break his neck, let him break it on a horse, like a gentleman."[81]

THE IMPORTANCE OF MORALE

For British officers, morale was the fundamental aspect of war. Victory favored not materiel, mass, or tactical skill, but personal courage and the qualities of a gentlemen. Just a year after the end of World War I, the first chapter in the *Field Service Regulations*, entitled "The Principles of War," explained that "success in war depends more on moral than on physical qualities. Neither numbers, armament, resources, nor skill can compensate for the lack of courage, energy, and determination."[82] The introduction to the 1926 manual *Infantry Training* declared that "battle is, above everything else, a struggle of morale."[83] Whether discussing training or military hardware, army officers thought first about the development and maintenance of morale. After reviewing the introduction of tanks, a British officer concluded, "New weapons are useful in that they add to the repertoire of killing, but be they tanks or tomahawks, weapons are only weapons after all. . . . It is the spirit of the men who follow and of the man who leads that gains the victory."[84] The infantry training manual also downplayed the importance of skill and materiel: "It must . . . be remembered that the development of morale, which includes fighting spirit and discipline, is the first object to be attained in the training of an Army."[85] In the army's view, the nature of war remained as it had always been.

This vision of war was not well adapted to the possibilities of massed armor. The British officer could generate little enthusiasm for new technologies that promised to enhance mobility, mass, or firepower. Whereas some officers saw these new capabilities as a way to break out of the trenches, the gentleman-officer continued to allow the premium on morale to shape his training and preparation for war. These officers could not understand that the newly found mobility could dramatically alter the conduct of operations.

CHARACTER, NOT INTELLECT

The British army valued the abilities and skills that it believed contributed to and enhanced morale. As gentlemen, army officers valued good manners, bravery, courage, honor, and above all, character. In contrast, these amateur officers thought little of ability, merit, push, cleverness, and ambition. An army officer described the attitude at Sandhurst: "We were expected to be efficient and win competitions, especially at riding, but we were on no account to be seen as *trying*."[86] As gentleman-officers, British officers had little time for the "vulgar careerism" of the professional armies on the continent. Horsemanship, and sporting in general, were the only highly regarded skills. For the British army, the human side of war—stamina, courage, gallantry, character, and above all morale—rated above the acquisition of professional skills. The following comment in an article in the *Cavalry Journal* in the 1920s reflects this attitude: "It has always appeared to me that Englishmen seem to naturally dislike the revolver as much as the knife, considering both the weapons of the assassin." The author explained that it was "very often difficult to make officers carry revolvers and ammunition and they generally carry them so uncomfortably that they may be excused for refusing to do so, except under pressure."[87] An army is in the business of killing, yet British officers could be excused and even praised for being "uncomfortable" carrying weapons and ammunition.

The British army cultivated character in its officers, not expertise or intelligence. The social mores of regimental life discouraged the development of a professional ethos. "Shop talk" was strictly forbidden at meals; officers occupied themselves with discussions about racing, horses, and other gentlemanly pursuits. It was while dining that an individual's abilities as an officer could be appraised.[88] "For the newly joined," the officers' mess allowed the others "to take their measure of him; to note his table manners and his ability to hold his liquor; to discover his interest and conversational fluency; to see how he reacted to a bit of friendly ragging; in fact to assess his rating as an 'officer and gentleman' and his suitability to join the family."[89] What mattered was the officer's breeding and demeanor, not his skill or professionalism.

Officer training also did not encourage a professional aptitude. The British army had established military schools, and by the interwar years examinations in the military academies had advanced beyond the questions typical of the nineteenth century (e.g., "Describe the general character of the flora of the Carboniferous period").[90] However, in contrast to other European academies, which stressed professionalism and a purposive school curriculum, British institutions continued to emphasize character training as the educational aim. A British officer writing in 1932 explained, "There is no place for the mere bookworm. Let us keep in mind, therefore, throughout this talk on personal study that the goal at which we aim is men of character and sound judgement with the capacity for leadership, and not mere pundits."[91] Devoted study and practice of the military profession were not "good form" and would only interfere with polo matches and hunting expeditions. "If there is any specially sterling characteristic of life at the Staff College," an officer observed in 1927, "one would say it is the peculiarly British spirit of humor bubbling through it. Everyone is expected to do a job of work without making heavy weather, or taking it, or himself, too seriously."[92] The social round and the preservation of customs, status, and prestige dominated army life. One officer remarked, "There can have been few forms of existence more pleasant than life at the Staff College in the early thirties."[93]

The British army did not study the philosophy of war or its theoretical foundations; it instead looked to practical experience as a guide. While recuperating in the hospital, a British officer was visited by his colonel who, upon seeing two military books by his bedside, exclaimed "What the devil are you reading those for? You are a horse artilleryman; what more do you want?"[94] In 1936 General Wavell also downplayed the relevance of military science: "All military learning must be based on a solid foundation of common sense. . . . It is the lack of this knowledge [of logistics] that puts what we call "amateur strategists" wrong, not the principles of strategy themselves, which can be apprehended in a very short time by any reasonable intelligence."[95] In the early 1920s, the chief of the Imperial General Staff disapproved of active officers' writing books on military subjects.[96] What mattered were questions of breeding—or at least the appearance of breeding—not acquired skills or theorizing about the conduct of war.

THE PARADE GROUND

When the British army focused on military questions, drill and ceremonial duties dominated the agenda.[97] The 1926 infantry training manual covers two topics: the first 153 pages review the various aspects of drill (squad drill, saluting, platoon drill, company drill, etc.), and the last 64 pages address the "ceremonial."[98] Ten years later, the infantry manual again focused on the spit and polish of military life: in a section entitled "things that should be covered in training," "Be able to turn out correctly in every 'order of dress,' have a thorough knowledge of barrack room duties, be capable of carrying out the duties of a sentry on guard, and be able to carry out a short route march in marching order," were all listed before "Have fired prescribed weapons training course."[99] Coming out of one of the most devastating wars, a conflict dominated by firepower and new technology, the British officer persisted in believing that the best preparation for warfare was additional hours on the parade ground.

As one officer explained in 1921: "The tactical value of steady ranks, orderly movement, and uniformity of method has always played in the past, and must continue in the future to play a profound part in the conduct of war."[100] Commenting on his experience after arriving in India, a British officer reveals how little drill had to do with the actual conduct of war: "I found to my surprise that the Duke of Cornwall's Light Infantry thought rifles were for firing, not just for drill. . . . I unlearned my Sandhurst drill and learned a new type, light-infantry drill, where all movements were executed with extreme speed and a minimum of orders."[101] The British army devoted endless hours to drill and ceremonial duties because those exercises would develop discipline—the foundation of morale.[102] For example, in an evaluation of the lessons of World War I, a British infantry officer returns to the importance of ceremonial duties:

> The vital importance not only of steady close-order drill but of a due proportion of ceremonial, should receive full recognition in the future. . . . Drill should be regarded . . . as the handmaid of discipline; and ceremonial should

be given its rightful place as the manifestation of something higher still, and as the outward and visible sign of the spiritual life of the Army. . . . There are probably many who will freely acknowledge now that, had the scarlet thread of ceremonial been entwined a little more generously in the drab texture of war-time training, it would have more than made up in morale, mental and physical value for an hour or two subtracted from the normal weekly programmes.[103]

For the army to fight effectively, they believed, its members must, above all else, have a firm spiritual foundation.

In contrast, tactical training received little attention.[104] In 1936 a British soldier described tactical training as consisting of "a few lectures annually interspersed with some elementary sand table exercises; a modicum of military history, probably with a regimental bias; and finally, of perhaps four weeks of practical work in the handling of a platoon on training, of possible strength of eighteen men. . . . for a considerable, but indefinite period of years, unrelieved by any further excursions into the ramifications of military art."[105] The table of contents of both the cavalry and infantry training manuals hardly mention the tactical employment of modern weapons. For example, the 377 pages of the 1924 cavalry training manual devoted 212 pages to equitation, 96 to drill and ceremonial, 8 to machine and hotchkiss guns, and 28 to training in field operations.[106] In the army's view, because morale dominated the battlefield, character building and discipline, not tactical training or military science, should govern peacetime activity.

The British army's apparent disregard for the development of professional skills does not mean that the British officer corps was cavalier about its responsibilities. The officers did care about winning wars but viewed war as fundamentally a question of morale; as a result, the officers' and soldiers' training focused on what they thought would develop character and discipline.

The contrast with the air force is striking. The RAF's training manuals focused almost exclusively on technical issues and rarely discussed the drill that so dominated infantry manuals.[107] In the RAF, "airmen were inclined to resent the time spent on drills as it took them away from their normal work." More precisely, "the airman at the cadet college who dared try for excellence at drill was a bullshitter, a bobber, a creeping c—." Yet this was "nothing to the scowls dispensed by his fellows to the squadron pilot who was not up to standard, whose air shooting let the squadron's average down, or whose unprofessional standards reduced its readiness for action." Fascinated with flying and technical issues, the airman had little patience for the stuff of army life.[108]

The RAF valued discipline, but in the airman's view, endless repetition of close formation drills would not produce the desired type. An air force officer explained, "By discipline I do not mean what one sees on the parade ground. In the air force we need discipline from within one's self, ingrained deep in the mind." Indeed, the air force's culture highlighted a concept that would seem outlandish to the army: individuality. Having left the army and joined the air force, T. E. Lawrence explained, "We identify the army with its manner of life and already sincerely despise and detest it. . . . Soldiers are parts of a machine and their virtue is in subordinating themselves within their great company. Airmen are lords and masters, when not slaves, of their machines, which the officers indeed own in the air but which belong to us individually for the longer hours they are on earth."[109] In contrast, in the army's mind, war was a team sport.

THE PLAYING FIELD

Despite the advent of the industrial age, the British army continued to view war as a test of wills; the battlefield was like the playing field. In the words of a British officer, "War was like any other outdoor sport, only rougher and more dangerous."[110] Another commented that "the life of a soldier in those days was a very happy one, for war really was more sport than business."[111] In 1936, Wavell drew a parallel between the soldier and the sportsman when he explained that the British army "still has to be prepared for the 'village cricket' type of campaign as well as for the 'timeless test' type of the Great War. The timeless test," Wavell explained, "suits the safe and cautious batsman who can keep an end up and take no risks; village cricket requires the light-hearted type, who will take chances and hard knocks on a rough wicket."[112] Wavell knew that European war was different from imperial duties, but both missions could be understood through sporting analogies.

For the British army, engaging in sports was excellent preparation for the battlefield, and sports became an integral part of army life. Writing in 1931, an army officer commented on the changes in the late nineteenth century, and in particular, on the increase in cricket and football in the daily lives of the soldiers. He concluded that "the advent of these recreations was in due course to bring about a new standard of military efficiency."[113] The 1924 *Cavalry Training* manual explicitly instructed the commander to organize sporting competitions and concluded that "a troop which plays games will not be found wanting in the fight."[114] Even an officer who advocated more tactical training argued that "the games playing officer is the man who can best stand the strain of active service."[115] To the British army, a good sportsman was a good soldier.

For the officer, there was polo in the summer and hunting and racing in the winter, and for the soldier, cricket in summer and football in the winter. As Percy Hobart discovered, sporting events consumed army life. He explained, "Unless one upsets all their polo . . . it's so hard to get anything more into them or any more work out of them. 3 days a week they come in six miles to Gezirah Club for polo. . . . Non-polo days it's tennis or something."[116] Discussing life at the Staff College in the 1920s, an army officer remarked that "sport remains as marked a characteristic of life there as ever. . . . The Drag remains the mainstay of the life of the Staff College."[117]

This fascination with sports was lost on the air force officer, for whom most of the competitions that took place related directly to competence in military tasks (navigation, aerobatics, and air gunnery.)[118] The number of pages devoted to sports in the *Royal Air Force Journal* pales next to that in the infantry and cavalry publications. Indeed, an army officer's memoirs disparaged the RAF's neglect of sports. After noting that in the army "any officer not taking part in games was to be found shouting for his team . . . [while] the station commander and his dutiful wife nobly shivered it through," he complained that when he was commanding RAF ground defense officers he "once tried to ensure that an officer was always there to watch and encourage when his team was playing . . . and when I suggested that he [the senior officer] should 'detail' one for the job each week, he was aghast."[119]

TECHNOLOGY AND THE BATTLEFIELD

The British army officer also had little time for the technology of the modern battlefield. The public schools and universities, the breeding ground of the army officer, accorded minimal attention to science and technology. Indeed, the members of the prestigious infantry and cavalry regiments did not regard the officers in the technical branches as proper soldiers.[120] When questions about technology arose, they were put in terms that corresponded to the British officer's view of war. An author in the *Cavalry Journal* explained that "it is not intended in this article to make incursions into matters of technical detail, but to attempt to reduce them into terms of the human element and to endow them, as far as possible, with flesh and blood." Similarly, a somewhat positive discussion of tanks concluded that "machines neither make nor win wars, it is the man who uses the machine who is the dominant factor."[121]

A comment in 1927 by the chief of the Imperial General Staff reflects the army's discomfort with this new product of the industrial age. "I have been much struck by the fact that an officer who can successfully command his mechanical units is exactly the same class of officer, the same type and the same character as one who can successfully command a cavalry unit; he has exactly the same characteristics and above all he has quick decision. Certain people seem to imagine, because you have a mechanical vehicle you have got to let your hair grow long and go dirty."[122] When Duff-Cooper submitted a project for the mechanization of the cavalry he observed that "it is like asking a great musical performer to throw away his violin and to devote himself in future to the gramophone."[123]

Tanks, or "those petrol things," had little place in the British army officer's vision of war. In his eyes, winning and fighting wars was a question of morale, not materiel, mass, or mobility. If this new technology could foster morale or in other ways be incorporated into the "human side" of war, then it could be accepted with enthusiasm. Otherwise it could only be incorporated into the existing doctrinal approach, and even then, it was done reluctantly. The cavalry came to accept the replacement of horses with tanks, but slowly. Until 1969 the most senior regiment in the British army, the Household Cavalry, benefited from the "privilege" of serving in armored reconnaissance units and not having to work with tanks. However, in the words of an observer, "The Household Cavalry themselves began to feel that however noisy, dirty and smelly an animal that tank might seem, they were missing out by never serving a fully armoured role."[124] This comment was made in the 1960s; in the interwar period, it was even more difficult for army officers to imagine how one could be an officer, a gentleman, *and* a tankman.

This unfamiliarity with modern tactics and technology would have bewildered an air force officer. The RAF prized technological expertise. In 1935 an airman explained that "the secret of good work in the air is well founded confidence of the individual in his own personal skill and superiority of his equipment. . . . The first requirement, and the foundation of all our work, is flying skill."[125] Whereas army officers often created a hierarchy between men and machines, the air force officer envisioned a majestic melding of the two: "It was a little golden age when the practice of war seemed to have lost its real meaning, and to have found another and a better in the poetry of the control of machines by men."[126] References to the beauty of technology and the glories of the new mechanical age fill the RAF journal.[127]

LEADERSHIP AND COMMAND

Army officers were not encouraged to think for themselves. The British army's command structure was authoritarian and highly centralized, and subordinates were not expected to show initiative.[128] In discussing his two years at the Staff College, Hugh Dowding said that he was "irked by the contrast between the respect paid in theory to freedom of thought and the tendency, in practice, to repress all but conventional ideas. Nonconformists who challenged the accepted notions were labelled 'bad boys' by a staff aghast at their temerity." Another officer spoke similarly of his experience in the army during the interwar period: "As for expressing an opinion which differed from the general point of view, that was almost unheard of. . . . It would have been considered very bad manners not to agree with the senior officer."[129]

According to the British army, the ability to lead men derived from being a gentleman, not from acquired competence. Honor, courage, and character, not sophisticated knowledge of tactics or new technology would inspire confidence. "Leadership," the 1924 cavalry training manual explained, "depends on simple and straight-forward human qualities." In the army's view, skilled horsemanship produced good leaders. A 1934 article in the *Army Quarterly* argued that infantry officers should know how to ride and that the "mechanization mania" was "adverse to efficiency and to the creation of leaders." The author continued, drawing a direct relationship between expertise in equitation and military aptitude: "Looking through the list of those who were in my batch at the Staff College. . . . I note the names of several officers who were perniciously bad riders: not one of these 'made good' on active service, whereas nearly all those who rode well became leaders and several of them now hold high rank in the Army." Knowledge of horses was not necessary to fight well (the cavalry was in the process of being mechanized), but expertise in equitation enhanced the qualities of a gentleman, and it was the latter that counted when commanding troops.[130]

In contrast, the air force encouraged individuality, freedom of thought, and a close working relationship between the officers and the rank and file. In the early years of the RAF, for example, the chief of the air staff, Hugh Trenchard, ordered that each squadron receive an experimental machine without standardized mountings so pilots could experiment with their own ideas.[131] Coming from the army, Lawrence was surprised to find that an air force corporal "had spoken decently [to us]. . . . The army has a rule that NCOs may not consort with privates—or rather, there was such a rule before the war. In the R.A.F. all men are equal."[132] Responding to a question about the foundation of the "morale of leadership," an air force officer explained that "first and foremost is the pioneer spirit, the quest after achievement in the uncharted spheres of air activity. Secondly, there is the love and enthusiasm for the work itself, keenness to succeed, to excel, to create; the ideals of efficiency and perfection."[133] To be an effective leader in the air force, an officer had to win the respect of his soldiers by demonstrating professional excellence.

The tidiness of person and surroundings and the apparent respect for authority symbolize the contrast between the army's authoritarian and collective spirit and the more democratic and individualistic culture in the air force. After arriving at the air force college in 1925, a new recruit made his bed and went outside. He said that on returning to his room "my neighbor was regarding the bed with disfavour. 'You bobbing, mate? . . . Where do you come from, anyhow?' 'Depot, Corporal' I rejoined, bringing my heels together as I'd been taught. 'Well, just you forget it, see? And put your bed like this [messed up]. . . . And you don't stand to attention in the Air Force when you talk to an N.C.O.' 'Right O Corporal,' I laughed, daring to pounce at this new easy manner."[134]

The air force's "easy manner" provoked dismay on the part of army officers. As the product of a culture that put a premium on regimentation and a collective spirit, this army officer disparaged the airmen's way of dress:

> One could perhaps forgive the undone top jacket button of the "fighter Boy," but not the slovenliness so widespread on some RAF stations. . . . Where the Army officer would usually do all he could to smarten his up by the lining of lapels, creasing of trousers and sleeves, and so on, many RAF officers (and, of course, the habit quickly spread to the men) seemed deliberately to set out to be as untidy as possible. I remember talking to a fairly senior RAF officer whom I knew well and he told me that many young fighter pilots were deliberately negligent in their turn out, considering, for some reason, that this showed their individuality![135]

The army officer was also disturbed by the lack of authority that he found in the air force. "At one [air force] station," an army officer recounted, "the discipline generally had become very slack. Officers were not doing their jobs, NCOs were weak and station orders were not being carried out. At long last the station commander was constrained to move and told his adjutant to call a meeting of all officers. It was termed a 'conference,' and when the notice came round it 'requested' officers to 'make it convenient to attend personally.' The Army equivalent would have been 'all officers will meet the Commanding Officer.'"[136]

The advertisements in the army and air force publications typify the different worlds in which these two services lived. Whereas the infantry and cavalry journals appealed to the tastes of nineteenth-century gentlemen, the ads in the air force journal appealed to the airmen's professional ethos. Although the cavalry was being mechanized, the *Cavalry Journal* included advertisements for Salter Polo Stick, Lloyd's Bank, Charles Heidsieck Champagne, and an investment company. The infantry journal's advertisements reflected similar sensibilities: tickets for the theater and sports meetings, announcements of international horse shows, hunting and riding kits, and a tailor on Savile Row. In contrast, the advertisements in the RAF's journal spoke to the modern age and professional officers. They included a publisher "of works of the most important German institution of research in the field of flying techniques," the Armstrong Siddeley Tiger IX engine, and the British Burnelli medium bomber. The marketing appeal was to the airman's sense of professionalism, not to his leisure hours.[137]

Secluded within the familiar bounds of the regimental system, the British army had preserved its pre-1914 mentality.[138] War between great industrial powers was different from sporting matches or skirmishes in the empire, yet the army's culture did not value the skills that could have equipped the army for this new age. As Barnett explained, the values and attitudes of British army officers were "very different from those of managers, scientists and technicians of industry. Cleverness, push, ruthlessness, self-interest, and ambition were considerably less prized than modesty, good manners, courage, a sense of duty, chivalry and a certain affectation of easy-going non-professionalism."[139] Understanding the implications of the revolutionary changes in warfare required more than common sense and pragmatic solutions. Given the practice of avoiding "shop talk" in the mess, the premium placed on character rather than expertise, and the disdain for theorizing or the study of war, the British army had little appreciation of the potential for armored warfare. Whereas the German army immediately began to study the lessons of World War I, it was not until 1932 that the British army even formed a committee to consider the question.[140] The gentleman-officer could not make sense of a doctrine that required a type of preparation that was virtually unknown in the British army. Believing that drill and ceremonial duties instilled important values in the soldier, the British officer did not appreciate the value of tactical training.

The increased firepower, mobility, and mass of modern warfare had exploded the traditional dimensions of the battlefield. To respond with fast-moving and decentralized operations required a conception of command that the gentleman-officer did not have; subordinates with little or no initiative could not easily implement a blitzkrieg doctrine. Such an offensive doctrine demanded unprecedented freedom of action in order to capitalize on surprise, search out weak points, and exploit tactical advantages. Operational opportunism clashed with the British army's rigid and centralized command structure. Instead of seeking to capitalize on the potential fluidity of modern conflict, the British army reinforced the "human factor" in warfare; it demanded more discipline and more order. It subordinated the mobility of tanks to the pace of the infantry and stressed painstaking preparation and tight control over the battlefield.

The regimental system in the British army was a powerful means of assimilating the young officer, whatever his social background. Once within its grasp, the officer learned its ways. Although it promoted high morale, this approach to war blinded its officers to the potential of the mechanized battlefield. To an army officer who regarded amateurism as gentlemanly and desirable, and professionalism and technical and tactical skill as either degrading or unnecessary, the mechanization of war was inconceivable and incomprehensible. Senior officers wanted to fight as effectively as possible and procure the best equipment, but they simply could not see the relevance of the industrial revolution. The British officer did not have the skills, understanding of technology, or command structure necessary to understand or implement the tactical sophistication of a decentralized mobile battlefield. As Michael Howard put it, adopting armored warfare "meant the destruction of an entire way of life."[141] The regimental officer, with his rural and gentlemanly culture, could not adjust easily to a "garage mechanics" war. Another organizational culture would have allowed a more generous response to the introduction of tracked vehicles.

The Gentleman-Officer and the Garage Mechanic's War

"The Tank Driver"
In his overalls so oily
He is not a pretty sight,
And a Guardsman in disgust
would turn away

But when ordered to "get Cracking"
For a march by day or night,
He will be there with his tank
without delay.
 (A. W. Davis)

The British army was not so much an army as a collection of regiments.[142] An officer or soldier joined a regiment, learned its history, customs, and traditions, and stayed there throughout his career. "The word 'army' in our language," a historian of the British army explained, "means nothing more than a loose federation of small elite warrior groups, often extremely jealous of each other, together with some larger groups of lower caste auxiliaries who unite only for war. . . . The structure is tribal; each tribe with its own unique mores, totem and rituals and of course eligibility for membership. Its officers are the heads of families, sects and tribes. The group exists for itself. Loyalty to it is total and religious in its intensity."[143]

Because of the regimental system, the British army did not develop a corporate spirit, and an officer's allegiance was to his regiment, not the army or a particular branch: "There is no existing *esprit de corps* of 'infantry' as such—at any rate not in our Army. Can any Line officer honestly say that he is proud of being an 'infantry' man? He is proud of being a Buff, a Fusilier, a Green Howard, but not of being 'infantry.' "[144] In other words, although the the gentleman-officer culture was the dominant culture in the British army, it was not the only one.[145] The less traditional branches of the British army *had a different culture and a different reaction to mechanized warfare.* Unlike the infantry and cavalry regiments, the technical branches welcomed the offensive use of massed tanks. However, they had little power, and as a result, the gentleman-officer culture shaped doctrinal decisions.

Remember that the absence of a corporate spirit is what civilians wanted. Fragmentation ensured that the army would not coalesce as a powerful whole.[146] As Michael Howard explained, "The regimental system may isolate the military but it also tames them, fixing their eyes on minutiae, limiting their ambitions, teaching them a gentle, parochial loyalty difficult to pervert to more dangerous ends."[147] Divided into separate regiments and lacking a corporate spirit, the army was unlikely to aggregate its interests and become a powerful political actor.

The Technical Branches and Mechanization

The British army's technical branches and the infantry and cavalry regiments recruited from different parts of British society, and they sought to imbue a different culture into their units. While "social suitability" was an important criterion for the prestigious infantry and cavalry regiments, the technical branches ranked candidates according to professional standards, such as math scores. The infantry and cavalry officers received their training at Sandhurst; the technical branches were taught in a technical and professional program at Woolwich and in general had more of a careerist orientation.[148]

A comparison of the professional journals of the traditional regiments with those of the technical branches illustrates the gulf between their cultures. Even at first glance, there is a marked difference between the *Royal Engineers Journal* and the *Cavalry Journal.* The engineers' journal is immediately recognizable as a professional journal, with sophisticated analytical articles, surveys of other books and journals, and in general an up-to-date and professional appearance. In contrast, the simplicity of the writing and the portraits of famous horses and cavalry charges make the *Cavalry Journal* seem antiquated.

The differences between the two publications also run deeper. The *Cavalry Journal* rarely discussed any of the professional aspects of army life. For example, the April 1922 edition contains six articles under the subheading "training and instruction"; one is on lion hunting, another on jumping, and another on the height of polo ponies.[149] There are numerous articles on World War I, but they are descriptions of battles, not analytical discussions intended to draw lessons from an earlier conflict. Articles on mechanization occasionally appear, but they are sandwiched between a plethora of articles on the care of horses, descriptions of hunting expeditions, and endless pages devoted to "sporting news." Even after the motorization of the cavalry in the mid 1930s, the *Cavalry Journal* did not become a modern professional journal; it was still filled with sentimental short stories about riding, hunting, panther shoots, and tiger hunts. There was little discussion of modern warfare and the mechanization of the battlefield, and even less of tactical or other professional training. The sporting news continued to receive enormous attention, and reviews of books on horses, the hunt, and polo filled the section on recent publications.

The editorial in the January 1939 edition of the *Cavalry Journal* began remarkably with these words: "It is rather difficult to find very much to write about in this editorial." There is no mention of the crisis in Europe, German capabilities or doctrine, the politics of defense expenditures, mobilization potential, tanks or tactical training, systems of fire control, or the use of wireless. There are instead the typical drawings of cavalry charges and chatty discussions about horses.

In the *Royal Engineers Journal* there was no sporting news, and there were few of the historical narratives that dominated the cavalry's publication. The historical articles rarely discussed events before World War I, and the accompanying drawings and diagrams clarified the topics rather than recording a gallant pose. The engineers' publication tracked developments in other countries, translated foreign publications, and focused on issues of professional interest. It included articles such as "Graphical Method of Mapping from Lateral Oblique Air Photographs" and "Road Surfacing by the Mix-in-place Method in India."

Reading the *Cavalry Journal*, one might never know that World War I happened. The Great War saw the introduction of many new technologies, the transformation of the battlefield, and the mobilization of the entire society, yet the cavalry officer remained fixed on individual heroism and the gentlemanly pursuits of a country squire. Europe had entered the age of total warfare, yet the only article that even hinted at the economic aspects of war is entitled "The Horse as a National Economic Factor."[150] The same year, the *Royal Engineers Journal* featured an article called "Economic Readiness for War."[151] For the officers from the technical branches, warfare had entered a new age. As the poem at the beginning of this section illustrates, the "tank man" did not take pride in affecting the stance of a relaxed amateur or view a professional spirit as vulgar careerism. He belonged to a culture that took pride in hard work, readiness to act, and technical aptitude.

In short, not all branches of the British army displayed the cultivated amateurishness prevalent in the infantry and cavalry regiments. More important, not all branches of the British army had the same response to the mechanization of the battlefield; only the traditional regiments remained resolutely opposed. In an extensive survey of more than two hundred articles in a variety of professional army journals during the interwar period, Brian Hacker found a systematic bias in support or opposition to armored warfare according to the branch affiliation of the author. As one would expect, authors from the traditional branches overwhelmingly opposed mechanization, whereas relatively few authors from the technical branches were against armored warfare.[152] There is a strong correlation between the contrasting organizational cultures discussed above and each branch's evaluation of mechanization. This variation in organizational responses provides additional evidence of the power of the army's organizational culture. It also helps eliminate several alternative explanations for the British army's adoption of a defensive doctrine. Both the technical branches and the traditional regiments fought in World War I and faced the same domestic political and international constraints. In other words, British army officers who were not members of the traditional regiments—but who had fought in World War I, worked within the British political system, and faced the German threat—recognized the potential of massed armor.

Despite the diversity in opinion about mechanization, the offensive potential of massed armor never moved beyond the conceptual phase; the infantry and cavalry regiments determined the pace and direction of mechanization.[153] Instead of viewing this newfound mobility as an advantage or a challenge, officers from the traditional regiments ensured that the introduction of armored vehicles would cause the least possible disruption of traditional methods. They worried that proceeding too quickly with mechanization would disturb the morale of the traditional regiments and so cause irrevocable damage to their fighting effectiveness.[154]

The British army, led by infantry and cavalry officers, would not risk taking steps that might jeopardize morale. While watching the 1928 exercises of mobile forces, Montgomery-Massingberd concluded that, "although invaluable for experimental purposes, it [mechanization] was definitely affecting adversely the morale and training of the Cavalry and Infantry." He decided that it would be better to gradually mechanize the traditional arms than to create new units. During the 1934 training exercises, Burnett Stuart's sense "that the traditional arms needed to have their morale restored" led to the apparent defeat of the independent armored force. Many army officers worried that too rapid an acceptance of tanks would "overwhelm the mystique of confidence based on traditional discipline and morale." As the chief of the Imperial General Staff, Lord Gort, observed, "We mustn't upset the people in the clubs by moving too fast." Whatever armor's value for firepower and maneuverability had to take a back seat to securing the essence of the army's strength—its morale and traditions.[155]

The less traditional branches of the British army could make sense of the modern battlefield, but the dominant regiments (with the gentleman-officer culture) could not understand the potential value of the offensive use of massed tanks. In their view, it was better to integrate the new machines into traditional ways of fighting than risk undermining the traditional regiments' morale by giving undue independence or resources to "those petrol things." One of the leading advocates of tanks, Hobart, pointed to the need for a conceptual change: "It is not, I think, at all fully realized yet that the mechanization of the Army is not only a matter of supply of vehicles, and training in their use, but demands a fundamental *mental* change as great as the change in the navy from wooden sailing ships to steamer ironclads."[156] A memorandum on army training in 1927 seconded this sentiment: "We must not allow the threat of action by a mechanized enemy to upset all our preconceived notions of war."[157] They did not, and as a result, an offensive battlefield was unimaginable.

Doctrinal Dogmatism?

The British case does not provide a good test of the proposition that hostility in an organization's external environment increases the strength of the organizational culture and so encourages doctrinal dogmatism. At no period during the 1920s and 1930s did the British army or air force experience a high degree of threat or doctrinal dogmatism. Without variation, I cannot make strong claims about a relationship between the presence or absence of hostility in the external environment and the presence or absence of doctrinal dogmatism. Nevertheless, the British case provides limited support for the hypothesis about the relationship between threat perception and doctrinal dogmatism.

The British army and air force's perception of threat remained constant in the interwar period; both retained easy relations with the external (domestic) environment. For example, despite the flood of antiwar literature in Britain after World War I, the army did not experience recruitment problems. In the seven years after the armistice, enlistment remained above pre–World War I levels.[158] The army may have resented its meager budget allocations, but it did not feel under siege or question the state's abilities. The external (domestic) environment posed even less threat to the RAF. It was not implicated in the horrors of World War I, and on the whole received the support and enthusiasm of the government and the public alike. The Cabinet repeatedly assigned it the highest priority, and the general public was fascinated with barnstorming and aerial antics.

Throughout the interwar period, both British services remained relatively free of doctrinal dogmatism. In the air force there was conceptual room for both an offensive and a defensive doctrine, and although the army rejected the proposals of the armored advocates, it allowed the publication of their views. The French army had reacted the same way in the 1920s when it also perceived little threat in its external environment. However, unlike the French army, the British services' perception of threat in their external (domestic) environment never changed, and thus they never became dogmatically attached to their doctrinal orientations.

Explaining doctrinal developments in the British army requires an understanding of cultural factors. The varied reactions within the British army to the potential for massed armor shows how different cultures affect choices. Frozen within the world of regimental soldiering, the offensive use of tanks fell on deaf ears in the gentleman-officer culture. In contrast, officers within branches of the British army with a different organizational culture responded enthusiastically to these new ideas. The British case also sheds light on the role of cultural factors when there is a consensus among civilians about the use of force in the domestic arena. British civilians tacitly agreed that a strong military caste might threaten English liberties. In this sense, the British case resembles France in that domestic, not international, factors determine the basic organizational form of the army. However, because of the consensual nature of the culture, British civilians' role differed from the French in two important ways.

First, the consensus about the domestic ramifications of military policy made it more likely that British civilians would respond to international imperatives. Unlike their French counterparts who were preoccupied with domestic battles over military policy, British civilians did not have to worry about defending their domestic flanks. As we saw, London's desire to keep defense expenditures to a minimum reflected strategic calculations about how to best enhance Britain's deterrent strength. Second, a consensual culture sets less explicit constraints on policy. In the French case, the two competing cultures contained explicit policy prescriptions; they were more like ideologies than common sense. The British situation was different; British civilians agreed that a professional military caste was not in Britain's best interests. Rarely challenged, this tenet was taken for granted; it shaped civilian decisions, but it more closely resembled common sense, not a policy option. British civilians did not actively decide not to create a professional army; it seemed natural to them to continue doing what they had always done. The British army's gentleman-officer culture may seem extraordinary, but British civilians rarely thought that reform might be necessary.

A consensual culture not only allows civilians to be more attentive to international conditions; it may also provide greater flexibility. Whereas the competing cultures in France prescribed precise policy choices, British civilians shared certain assumptions about the role of the military in the domestic arena, but their beliefs, rarely explicitly expressed or defended, were a looser set of ideas. This vagueness could leave policymakers with greater room for maneuver. Proposals for reforming the army would have to be carefully packaged to avoid arousing suspicions about the power of a strong standing army, but there would be some flexibility.

This flexibility in reforming the military may not, however, lead to actual reform. Because a consensual culture is more like common sense than an ideology, policymakers are not likely to actively consider alternatives. It might seem ill advised for an advanced industrial society to fight a continental adversary with an army whose organization and ethos date from the nineteenth century, but British civilians saw nothing unusual in their army. There was an unconscious, natural acceptance that the gentleman-officer best met British needs. With little debate or controversy, no alternatives were considered, and so no change occurred.

As a declining power with overextended commitments, Britain was in a strategic bind. But it had options. Civilians in other states might have reacted differently. London could have created a conscript army to respond to European conflicts and retained the long-serving army for imperial duties. Indeed, every major continental state (and many minor ones) had adopted a system of national military service by the early twentieth century. But this was not possible for British civilians; compulsory military service was unacceptable to British liberalism. Enacting universal military service might not have solved the dilemmas facing British strategic policymakers during the 1920s and 1930s, but it could have eased the problems that arose from the competing demands of Europe and the empire. Yet British reluctance to consider conscription or to reform the army shows the power of cultural understandings about the use of military force. Those beliefs were influential precisely because they were taken for granted. The British may have been less visibly and explicitly constrained by their cultural understanding than were the French, but they nevertheless had little room to maneuver.

7

Conclusion

THIS BOOK challenges the conventional wisdom about the origins of offensive and defensive military doctrine by arguing that military doctrine is best understood from a cultural perspective. As the empirical chapters on Britain and France during the 1920s and 1930s explained, conventional explanations are indeterminate of a country's choice of military doctrine, and civilians and the military do not behave as hypothesized by realist and functional analyses. Instead, it is the distribution of power at the *domestic* level and a military's organizational culture that are the key determinants of civilian and military preferences. In other words, civilian and military choices are not just a reflection of structural conditions or functional needs; culture has causal autonomy.

The Role of Civilians: Domestic, Not International Power

In downplaying the role of the international system in the development of military doctrine, I do not ignore power or argue that realists are misguided in their focus on power. But by concentrating on the distribution of power in the international system we often miss an equally important aspect of military policy: its domestic political implications. This is the first principal theme in this book. Civilian policymakers endorse certain military policies that they believe will ensure the maintenance of the preferred *domestic* distribution of power. These civilian choices then constrain a military organization's perception of what is possible. For example, because British civilians feared a professional army, any potential increase in military efficiency would have to yield to civilian insistence on stifling the growth of a strong military caste whose interests might be at odds with the state. Civilians did not push for reforms to create a more modern army and, as a result, the gentleman-officer culture was allowed to flourish within the elite branches of the British army.

In the French case, concerns about the domestic repercussions of military power were acute. Although France feared German power, perceptions of domestic threats, not international ones, shaped many civilian decisions about the French army. The Left feared that a professional army would do the bidding of the antirepublican forces in society, and the Right worried that a conscript army would be unwilling to enforce internal stability. French civilians' version of peace at home took precedence over sources of instability abroad. As the Germans were approaching Paris in 1940, General Weygand revealingly declared: "Ah! If only I could be sure the Germans would leave me the necessary forces to maintain order!"[1]

Although the international system is indeterminate of choices between offensive and defensive doctrines, civilian decisions are more likely to correspond with realist expectations if civilians agree about the role of the armed forces in the domestic arena. In other words, although the structure of the international system does not determine doctrine, civilians are attuned to systemic constraints. For example, while French civilians fought for military options that they believed best protected their domestic interests, British civilians agreed about the basic form of the military. Freed from domestic battles, British decisions responded to systemic constraints. Although the desire to keep defense expenditures to a minimum partially reflected the Conservatives' desire to guarantee the domestic social and economic status quo, financial constraints also reflected international factors: a buoyant economy would buttress Britain's peacetime deterrent and wartime mobilization. In short, the greater the civilian consensus about the position of the military in the state, the more likely it is that international threats and opportunities will shape their decisions.

Cultures versus Ideologies

The contrast between competing and consensual cultures illustrates the different ways culture affects outcomes. In Britain, the consensus about the military's role in society resembled common sense: it was so taken for granted that actors had difficulty imagining that things could be different. Consensual cultures do not need to justify or defend their beliefs against a set of competing beliefs. They also express less explicit policy objectives than do competing ideologies. The British did not actively debate whether to reform the officer corps; they took it for granted that they did not want a strong military caste. In contrast, the competing French cultures were more like ideologies. Constantly in conflict with each other, the cultures of the Left and Right contained explicit policy prescriptions: the Left wanted short-term conscription, the Right a professional army. Unlike Britain, where reform of the army was not considered, French policymakers actively rejected alternative policies.

Competing political cultures may be more detrimental to policy formation than consensual political cultures. The domestic conflict distracts attention from the conditions in the international system, and explicit policy preferences leave little room for compromise or bargaining. In contrast, the implicit nature of consensual cultures provides greater flexibility. As Peter Hall argued in his study of the influence of Keynesian ideas, ambiguity "[became] a cloak with which to cover or dress up a wide variety of economic practices."[2] Because a consensual culture does not explicitly prescribe or proscribe specific policies, policymakers have room to maneuver in designing military policy. However, this picture may be too rosy. British policymakers hardly excelled during the 1920s and 1930s. Despite the apparent flexibility, British civilians considered few alternatives precisely because of the nature of a consensual culture—it is hard to question common sense. British civilians had experienced modern warfare, but during the 1920s and 1930s they gave little thought to reforming their army. French civilians may have wasted energy on the domestic conflict, but they considered alternatives. Constrained by what seemed "natural," British civilians had few options.

Consensual and competing cultures constrain policymaking in different ways. Competing cultures (ideologies) constrict choices to the prescriptions contained within the culture, while a consensual culture (common sense) often ignores alternatives. Each process limits civilians' ability to formulate flexible policies attuned to changing international conditions.

Preferences Are Not Given

This book's other important theme is that there are not definitive meanings attached to an objective empirical reality. We should not assume that similarly situated groups in different national settings have similar preferences. Culture helps explain why parallel interest groups in different countries believe different policies to be in their interest. For example, similar actors in different countries evaluate conscription differently. While the British Labour Party opposed conscription for fear that it would militarize society, restrict individual freedom, and encourage expansionist policies, the French Left supported conscription, viewing it as an expression of community spirit, equality, and insurance against the growth of a praetorian guard. These contrasting beliefs, despite similar socioeconomic positions, belie a structural determination of preferences.

The contrasting positions of the French and British delegations at the Versailles negotiations are another example of actors' having different beliefs despite similar objective conditions. France and Britain had the same goal in the same context: they were in accord on the need to reduce Germany's military potential, yet they proposed opposite prescriptions. The French prime minister, Georges Clemenceau, proposed that Germany rely solely on a conscript army. A French officer wrote, "[It] would be better to let Germany have a relatively numerous army, without seriously trained officers, than a smaller army of well-tried, proven officers that Germany will have and which I fear she will know how to make use of."[3] France feared that a small professional force would threaten the European balance of power.

Britain reached the opposite conclusion. The British prime minister, Lloyd George, worried that, with a conscript army, "Germany will train 200,000 men each year, or 2 million in ten years. Why make a gift to them of a system that in fifteen to twenty years will give Germany millions of trained soldiers?"[4] Lloyd George insisted that only the imposition of a professional army would harness German military power.[5] Both civilians and the military in Britain feared that universal military service would militarize Germany, prepare its young men for war, and place a dangerous weapon in the hands of future German leaders. In fact, an eminent British historian dismissed the French objections to a professional force: "It is more difficult to accept the French contention that a voluntary long-service army will, if maintained in accordance with the terms of the Treaty, prove a greater menace to the peace of Europe than a compulsory short-service army, in which, sooner or later, the entire manhood of Germany would be trained for war."[6]

The assumption that similarly placed actors have the same interests ignores the different meanings that actors can give to similar military policies. In addition, though realists rightly stress that concerns about power drive civilian intervention in doctrinal developments, often it is power politics at the domestic level, not at the level of the international system, that shapes civilian decisions. In designing military policy, civilians address their concerns about *domestic* threats and stability.

The Role of the Military: Cultural, not Functional Preferences

Just as civilian preferences cannot be deduced from the structure of the international system, military preferences cannot be deduced from the functional needs of military organizations. The military is not as consciously shortsighted or self-serving as commonly portrayed. This does not mean that militaries are "objective" rational actors; the organization's culture constrains the formation of military policy. All militaries do not share the same collection of ideas about armed force, and their beliefs shape how the organization integrates changes in its external environment with its doctrinal orientation. In the French case, the civilian decision to reduce the length of conscription limited what the French army thought was possible. The French officer corps could only imagine short-term conscripts executing a defensive doctrine.

The British army's officer culture also constrained doctrinal developments. The gentleman-officer could not recognize the revolutionary potential of the modern battlefield and integrate the new means of warfare into an offensive doctrine. Convinced that war was, above all else, a battle of wills, the British army officer did not have the necessary skills, command structure, view of technology, or relationship between officer and rank that would have allowed him to imagine a mechanized and offensive battlefield. The gentleman-officer in the prestigious and influential infantry and cavalry regiments could only integrate the new technology within a defensive doctrine. While the regiments in the British army with the gentleman-officer culture developed a defensive conception of a mechanized battlefield, officers within the culture of the technical corps were more receptive to the offensive possibilities of massed tanks. Both groups operated with the same international and domestic political constraints, and both had fought the deadly defensive warfare of World War I. Yet they had different organizational cultures, and those differences account for their different reactions to the modern battlefield.

Static Cultures and Change

To understand how culture affects doctrinal developments I adopted Swidler's view—that culture provides means, not ends; culture provides a particular (and limited) "way of organizing action." For example, the French army did not adopt a defensive doctrine because its culture put great value on defensive doctrines; that would have been end-driven behavior. Instead, the French army's culture contained a finite set of elements (or means) that limited the types of possible action. Given the constraint of short-term conscripts, the French officer corps could only imagine a defensive doctrine; the army chose the doctrine that corresponded with the (perceived) means at its disposal. In Swidler's words, "Action and values are organized to take advantage of cultural competences. . . . What endures is *the way action is organized*, not its ends."[7]

Swidler's view of culture permits change in the dependent variable (doctrine) despite continuity in the intervening variable (culture). In France and Britain, the armies' cultures remained relatively static from the late nineteenth century until the outbreak of World War II. During this period, both armies' doctrines shifted radically from offensive in World War I to defensive in World War II. Explaining this change requires looking at how the (static) organizational culture incorporates changing variables in its external environment. The way of organizing their behavior (the means contained in their organizational cultures) stayed the same, while the outcome (the doctrines) changed.

With this view of culture, the change in French doctrine is straightforward. In 1913 the Parliament increased the length of conscription to three years; in 1928 it reduced it to one year. After 1913 the French army had the type of conscript that its culture thought capable of conducting offensive operations. After 1928 and the reduction in the term of conscription, the French officer corps could only imagine defensive actions. Throughout both periods, the army's culture contained, in Swidler's words, the same "strategies for action." Outside constraints, however, determined which strategies would be activated.

We see a similar pattern in the British army, except this time the exogenous change comes from the introduction of new technology. When going on the offensive was a matter of bravery and morale, the British army could conceive of charging forward and overcoming opposing forces by drawing on the courage and morale of the units. The British army entered World War I confident its morale would overcome the enhanced firepower of modern warfare.[8] But the defensive stalemate in the trenches of World War I showed that the old types of offensive operations were no longer feasible. The British army could have responded by incorporating radical technological or tactical changes into an offensive doctrine. Such doctrinal innovation would have been a case of value- or end-directed behavior—the army would have changed its means in order to continue achieving the same valued end (an offensive doctrine). But this is not what the British army did. Making the technological or tactical changes necessary to maintain an offensive doctrine would have required strategies of action that were not part of its organizational culture. The British officers incorporated the enhanced speed and firepower into their existing ways of organizing action, and in their view, this modernization could only result in a defensive doctrine. As in the French case, the means (or culture) stayed constant; the end (or doctrine) changed as the culture responded to exogenous factors.

The role that culture plays in civilian and military choices between offensive and defensive military doctrines demonstrates the danger of creating a distinction between interests and culture. The British and French armies did not cling to precious cultural precepts while ignoring their organizational interests. Nor did their civilian counterparts place ideological goals above the defense of the British and French empires. Their cultures shaped what they imagined to be in their interest.

Doctrinal Dogmatism

A military's culture also helps explain why some military organizations become dogmatically committed to their doctrinal orientation. Borrowing from organizational theory, I hypothesized that the more the military perceives a threat in its external domestic environment, the stronger its organizational culture becomes, and as a result, the more likely it will become dogmatic. Both the French and British cases support this argument. In France, doctrinal dogmatism coincided with the army's enhanced threat perception, while in Britain the armed services were not dogmatic about doctrine and did not perceive an escalating threat. While these correlations between doctrinal dogmatism and threat perception seem to confirm my hypothesis, without tracing the causal relationship or testing it in a statistically significant number of cases, these findings remain only suggestive. Does this dynamic occur in other militaries? For example, in the 1930s Stalin subjected the Soviet army to vicious purges. If my argument is correct, we should find a corresponding increase in the rigidity of the Soviet army's culture and as a result, doctrinal dogmatism. Similarly, these same outcomes should occur whatever the source of the hostility. This study tested whether the state of civil-military relations affected doctrinal dogmatism, but we should also expect that the greater the hostility in the international environment, the greater the potential for military dogmatism.

Testing Culture's Causal Autonomy

Culture can have explanatory power, but political entrepreneurs often use culture instrumentally. Although the extent of conscious political manipulation differs, both the British and French cases provide illustrations of "manipulated myths." For example, many analysts believe that, unnerved by the memory of the bloody trenches of World War I, the French army could not and would not consider anything but a defensive doctrine: the "lessons of World War I" determined doctrinal developments. However, for ten years after the armistice the French army maintained offensive war plans, and many officers advocated the offensive use of fortifications and massed tanks. These are not the actions of an army so devastated by the trench warfare of World War I that it shunned all offensive possibilities.

Contemporary beliefs may not mirror past attitudes. Myths may appear causal only in hindsight. The legacy of Verdun took on legendary proportions in France, but only *after* it is said to have influenced doctrinal developments. One could also mistakenly assume that the unwillingness to adopt a continental commitment was part of the British strategic culture. The "British way in warfare" called for a maritime strategy and gained considerable currency during the interwar period. But this "tradition" was not a genuine belief about British national interests but a myth manipulated by British civilians to push for the adoption of a policy that they desired for other reasons.

Political entrepreneurs use culture as much as they are unknowingly constrained by it. The myth of the "British way in warfare" was politically inspired, not culturally determined. Similarly, the French may have created and fanned the myth of Verdun to serve certain political purposes; encouraging the idea that the army really had no choice but to adopt a defensive doctrine may have helped exonerate both the regime and the army for the humiliating defeat in 1940. The myth-making may also have had less purposive origins; the legacy of Verdun may have slowly and unconsciously developed in the collective memory of France. Either way, these examples serve as warnings about the potential difficulty in separating embedded myths with causal autonomy from apparent myths without explanatory value.

Because of this possibility, Chapter 2 outlined three issues that should be addressed before making claims about culture's causal autonomy. This section reviews these issues to see how well my cultural explanation fares in the British and French cases. First, it is important to show that factors other than culture do not explain the outcome; I had to provide evidence that an alternative, or offensive, doctrine was "objectively" possible before I could claim that a military's culture shaped the adoption of a defensive doctrine. In both the French and British cases, alternative doctrinal orientations were possible: civilians did not demand the adoption of an defensive doctrine, the military had experimented with or been exposed to offensive alternatives, and adequate resources were available (although the latter is less true in the British case).

Second, culture must do more than reflect structural conditions or other "objective" criteria; there must be actors in similar positions who hold different beliefs. In these cases, the Left in Britain and France viewed conscription differently. It was also important to show that the French army's opinion of short-term conscripts was not universal. For example, the German officer corps did not share the French army's evaluation of conscript or reserve forces and used nonprofessional soldiers in offensive operations. As Michael Vlahos explained, the French army's belief about conscripts was a "prejudice" that stemmed from "the corporate ethos of the officer corps, still simmeringly royalist, that denied the combat equality of nonprofessionals."[9] It was not an objective evaluation common to all military organizations. The case studies also showed that even though the French and British armies served similar types of states and had fought in both World War I and the colonies, they had a different set of basic assumptions, values, norms, beliefs, and formal knowledge.

Third, culturally derived beliefs must not be used instrumentally to achieve other goals. We must have confidence that the culture was not invoked as a justification or rationale for the preferred policy. For example, how can we know that the French army really believed that short-term conscripts and a defensive doctrine were inseparable—could this belief have been instrumental? Some of the best evidence comes from the French army's estimate of the German army before World War I. The French army's belief that conscript forces could not undertake offensive actions prevented it from seriously considering the possibility that the Germans would attack with the forces that they did. Because they could not imagine short-term conscripts or reserves leading offensive operations, the French army dismissed intelligence reports showing that the Germans would use "young troops" in the front lines. Whatever the outcome of the future battle, the French army's belief in the relative incompetence of short-term conscripts was not in its interest; it is not in the military's interest to underestimate the strength of opposing forces by, in this case, more than 680,000 soldiers.

One can make a similar argument about de Gaulle. De Gaulle was convinced that the defense and ultimate *grandeur* of France depended on the adoption of an offensive doctrine. De Gaulle also knew that the creation of a professional force was politically impossible. Yet he continued to advocate the coupling of an offensive doctrine with a professional army. If de Gaulle's estimation of the value of short-term conscripts had not been genuine, he would have dropped it in order to pursue what he believed was in France's national interest—an offensive doctrine.

The British army during the interwar period is another example of a military organization making decisions that were not in its interest as commonly understood. Although it had the lowest financial priority among the three services, the British army rejected the ideas of the advocates of armored warfare even though adopting them would have given the army a stronger rationale to increase its expenditures. In other words, where its bureaucratic interest in greater resources diverged from its cultural beliefs, culture won. If the British army's culture had led it to adopt a doctrine that required greater resources (that is, if cultural and bureaucratic interests had converged), we would be less confident that the culture led to its doctrinal choice.

The Sources of Military Culture

This book examines organizational culture as an intervening, not a dependent, variable. Once one is confident that the culture is not epiphenomenal or a reflection of situational factors, it is possible to trace its causal role without knowing the origins of the culture itself. However, understanding the sources of a military's culture is important, especially for those interested in changing an organization's culture. The following discussion addresses some of the possible sources of an organization's culture and suggests that the characteristics of military organizations limit the extent to which we can make assumptions about the military on the basis of research on organizational cultures in private companies.

The Total (Institution) Is Different from the Sum of Its Parts

Many organizational theorists argue that the values and attitudes of the larger society are an important source of an organization's culture. A study of absenteeism, for example, concluded that societal beliefs about the legitimacy of not going to work partially explained cross-national absence rates within organizations.[10] Similarly, Michel Crozier demonstrated that authority patterns in French society infuse French organizational life, and Arthur Stinchcombe argued that the social structure or ideology that existed in the wider society when an organization was created often continued to shape its behavior.[11]

Although aspects of an organization's culture may reflect the values and attitudes of the wider culture, there is reason to believe that this is less likely to be true in the armed services. The military's powerful assimilation processes can displace the influence of the wider society. For example, landed gentry and aristocrats constituted the majority of the officer corps in the British and German armies during the 1800s, but only in the former did the officers' social origins manifest themselves in the organization's command structure and the relationship between the officers and the rank. While the British army encouraged aristocratic values and beliefs, the German army fostered different values and attitudes.

The British army's command structure resembled the hierarchical arrangement of the English gentry; the idea of a subordinate exercising initiative was practically unthinkable. Centralized authority ensured that subordinates received little power, respect, or trust. Wellington, for example, did not allow his generals to design their own operations.[12] Relations between the officers and the rank were also feudalistic. In 1887, General Wolsely described the typical British officer: "The relations between the officer and the private, with us, have always partaken very much of the patriarchal and feudal character. Looked at in this light, our regimental officer was, and still is, all that he should be amongst his men, namely a kind, indulgent, outspoken, liberal, and generous master."[13] British officers had at best a paternalistic relationship with their men. As one analyst put it, the "inbred distrust of labouring masses by the gentry was inevitably duplicated in the relationship between the officers and the men."[14]

In discussing life in the army after World War II, a British officer observed, "The farther away we were from England, the more we resembled the traditional prewar concept of an English regiment. . . . In a word, officers were once again thought of as 'gentlemen,' and once again began to conduct themselves as such. They expected to be deferred to and obeyed, and for the time being they were."[15] A British officer described one of his fellow officers, a product of Sandhurst, as rejecting "the democratic view that soldiers, being individual human beings, must be treated with a certain reverence for their dignity as such. . . . He liked his men, he studied their individual peculiarities, he was sometimes even indulgent to them; but he could not take them seriously as adults and autonomous persons."[16] British army officers viewed the rank as the gentry might regard commoners: with the proper degree of discipline, they would behave as expected.[17]

In contrast, the German army encouraged contact between the officer and enlistee and endorsed a degree of decentralization, initiative, trust, and mutual respect unheard of in the British army.[18] Helmuth von Moltke explained why individual initiative was so important: "A favorable situation will never be exploited if commanders wait for orders. The highest commander and the youngest soldier must always be conscious of the fact that omission and inactivity are worse than resorting to the wrong expedient."[19] The German army encouraged its officers to think independently and offer suggestions to their superiors. Moltke stressed that "adherence to a battle plan must not be allowed to crush the initiative of individual commanders and that the *Feldherr* must have the courage and the wit to change his dispositions as the situation required."[20] Although German officers were products of a hierarchical and authoritarian background similar to that of their British counterparts, they adopted beliefs and attitudes inimical to their social milieu; the German army's culture displaced the Junkers' social background.

While the German army replaced some of the values and attitudes that would have been part of the childhood socialization of its officers with aristocratic lineage, the opposite process occurred in the German navy. By the early twentieth century, only 10 to 15 percent of the officer cadets in the German navy came from noble backgrounds, but the resulting influx of cadets from professional families did not lead to the adoption of more liberal or middle-class attitudes. Instead, the navy officers became "feudalized" by adopting the manners and outlook of the Prussian nobility.[21]

Some analysts argue that the British army's social conservatism and aristocratic values cannot be responsible for its failure to mechanize because the officers with aristocratic backgrounds no longer dominated the officer corps by the 1920s and 1930s.[22] But the percentage of aristocratic officers is irrelevant; the British army's culture is different from the sum of the childhood socialization of its members. The British military historian Correlli Barnett explains that socialization in the British army erases differences of birth: "Among modern armies the British officer corps remains the last donjon keep of neofeudalism because the manners, values and attitudes of the aristocratic past have become institutionalized. After ten years in the British army, the grammar school [middle-class] boy is to be distinguished only by the expert, if then, from the son of a country gentleman educated at a famous public school."[23] A contemporary account of life at Sandhurst also illustrates that the army's culture was not simply the product of the social background or childhood socialization of its members: "The hooting and tooting of the traffic in Camberly, and along the A30 [a highway], merely buttresses the sense of unreality, but the surrealism is an essential part of the British army itself, which no longer insists in the least that you are a gentleman by birth, but rigidly insists that you are a gentleman by behavior."[24] The British officer corps was no longer the preserve of the privileged classes, but the culture institutionalized within the army assumed these values.

Military sociologists also argue that the values and attitudes within a military organization are independent from those of the wider society. In examining the U.S. officer corps, Morris Janowitz stressed the dominance of organizational experience over social background:

> Differences in political behavior between services or within services cannot be accounted for by social background. In the past, the military profession has recruited those whose social backgrounds have inclined them toward conservative commitments. Yet, analysis of social origins of the military elite demonstrates that there has been a progressive decline in the importance of social heritage and a rise in the importance of organizational experiences.[25]

Other studies found that the Norwegian military overcame differences in social background and imposed "common attitudes and standards of behavior," and that a medieval feudal tradition, not the modern democratic tradition, was influential in the U.S. army in the early post–World War II period.[26] In short, just as "all cops are blue," the culture of a total institution like the military can override wider societal influences or early socialization patterns.

Founders and Individual Entrepreneurs

Many organizational theorists argue that key founders and entrepreneurs shape an organization's culture by creating the initial culture and choosing members and ceremonies that reinforce it.[27] The dark suits,

crisp white shirts, and narrow black ties of IBM employees were em-
blematic, for example, of the IBM founder's attempt to inculcate a distinctive culture.[28] Similarly, Burton Clark argues that charismatic leaders
of Antioch, Reed, and Swarthmore Colleges played a key role in creating
those schools' distinctive cultures.[29] This process may also occur in the
military. For example, some analysts argue that Admiral Hyman Rick-
over successfully imposed his vision on the U.S. Navy's Reactors Branch
through his strong leadership and personal selection of officers who
shared his focus on engineering excellence.[30] Hugh Trenchard, the head
of the Royal Air Force during its initial years, may have also had a strong
impact on the RAF's culture.

Although founding leaders may play an important role in creating a
military's culture, individuals may be a less important source of culture
in the military than in the private sector. If creating an organizational
culture from scratch is easier than changing an existing one, there are
few opportunities for individuals (other than founding members) to play
a pivotal role in shaping a military's culture. While roughly three hundred new firms are created every year in Silicon Valley alone, there are
only three services in most countries' armed services, and once established they endure for generations.[31] New subdivisions, like the U.S.
Navy's Reactor Branch, provide opportunities for key individuals to play
a consequential role in shaping values and attitudes within that subdivi-
sion, but even in those cases, the individual's efforts are unlikely to affect
the culture of the service as a whole.

Similarly, the organizational culture is not the sum of the values and
beliefs of a few individual members. Replacing a few leading officers is
unlikely to give rise to a new organizational culture. In 1937 the British
secretary of war, Leslie Hore-Belisha, decided that the only way to advance the mechanization of the British army was to undertake a large-
scale replacement of the senior generals in the Army Council. In justifying his intentions to the prime minister, Hore-Belisha argued that he
needed to eliminate, as he put it, "the 1914–18 mentality." Hore-Belisha
proceeded with his "purge" only to find that within a few weeks, his
hand-picked successors were displaying similar behavior.[32] In other
words, although individuals have beliefs, values, and attitudes, and are
the carriers of a culture, organizational cultures are features of organizations, not of individuals. A culture is the property of a collectivity.

Structure and Function are Indeterminate of Culture

Some of the variation in organizational culture may stem from the specific needs of a certain type of industry, the degree of technological
complexity, or the nature of the competitive environment. For example,

Salomon Brothers' compensation structure probably best explains what has been called its "fractious culture of greed." By instituting limitless bonuses, Salomon encouraged its traders to develop an attitude of everyone (or at least each department) for himself.[33]

However, cultures may vary across organizations that face similar functional or structural imperatives: often industries in the same sector do not share the same characteristics. For example, a study of industries using different production technologies (mass production, small batch, and process) in three different countries (Britain, France, and Germany) found greater similarities within each country than among the firms with similar production processes.[34] Similarly, after US Air and British Airways formed an alliance in January 1993, executives instituted programs to "help key employees deal with cultural shock."[35] Japanese and American car firms show similar cultural differences. Whereas junior executives in American companies are expected to show decisiveness and self-assurance, an executive search firm explained that "in recruiting for Japanese automakers, you have to listen hard during the interview to avoid a person who is arrogant or whose style is 'do it my way.' "[36] Structural, functional, or technological requirements within an industrial sector are unlikely to explain the sources of an organization's culture; I would expect this to also be true of military organizations.

Military cultures are not a codification of the values and attitudes necessary for the way a particular service fights. The individual and collective ethos of the British air force and army respectively may appear to echo the nature of their mission: the army fights in mass, while air force officers fly as individuals. As T. E. Lawrence said, "Soldiers [in the army] are parts of a machine and their virtue is in subordinating themselves within their great company."[37] In contrast, the air force "ace" battles one-on-one in the vast skies. It is tempting to claim that these values and attitudes are functional and so generalizable: all air forces would have a more democratic, individualistic ethos; all armies a more authoritarian, collective spirit.

However, as discussed above, individual initiative was an important value in the German *army's* culture. German army officers—like officers in the RAF—were encouraged to criticize the actions of their equals and superiors. The 1887 German field regulations stressed the importance of individual initiative: "This regulation intentionally leaves freedom of action in the field, which will develop initiative in officers at all ranks. This initiative is absolutely necessary, and must not, under any circumstances, be limited by more precise orders."[38] The official army manual in 1936 again endorsed this democratic command structure: "Thus decisive action remains the first prerequisite for success in war. Everybody, from the highest commander to the youngest soldiers must be conscious of the fact that inactivity and lost opportunities weigh heavier than do errors in the choice of means."[39] The German word *auftragstaktik* refers to this concept, and not surprisingly, has no counterpart in English army lexicon.

In short, a military's culture does not simply mirror functional or structural requirements. Different services may share similar approaches, and similar services can endorse different values and attitudes. Armies and air forces fight differently but may share the same values and beliefs, and armies with the same responsibilities may have different cultures. As in the case of France and Britain, armies with similar responsibilities and access to the same technological base had different organizational cultures; the German and the French armies' cultures were also distinctive.[40]

The Military Is a Natural Monopoly

Selection processes are another possible source of an organization's culture; environmental constraints may select for those cultures best adapted to current competitive pressures. There are, however, at least three reasons to question whether the source of militaries' cultures is to be found in their efficient adaptation to selection processes. First, just as most houses on fire offer several escape routes, most environmental constraints allow for numerous adaptive responses. In other words, environmental constraints may matter, but there may be more than one way to be functional in the face of competitive pressure. More than one type of culture is possible given any one set of environmental constraints.

Second, the adaptation expected from an evolutionary model often does not occur. Organizational theorists repeatedly find firms whose cultures are ill suited to the current business environment.[41] For example, a team of researchers found several large American companies with organizational cultures that had developed during the days of scientific management, even though many of the values and beliefs of that management style are poorly adapted to the demands of today's world economy.[42] AT&T's organizational culture also resisted adaptation despite dramatic changes in its competitive environment after the breakup of the Bell system.[43] Antiquated beliefs can persist even when an organization recognizes that it should change. Maryann Keller's study of General Motors, for example, concluded that GM "recognized it needed to change, but found itself hopelessly tangled in a complex corporate culture that resisted change."[44]

Finally, a selection process is especially unlikely to explain the origins of a military's culture because the military occupies a monopoly position within the state. Simply put, the military's existence does not depend on its outperforming its competitors. Military organizations have no competitors.

The environment cannot select for the most appropriate organizations if there are no competitors.[45] If an army fails to adequately adapt to a new form of warfare, there is not an auxiliary army ready to assume its place when the unprepared army is defeated. The U.S. Army's inability to adapt to counterinsurgency warfare during the Vietnam War did not lead to its replacement by another army better suited to this new challenge on the battlefield. The military organization may suffer a decline in its prestige, and it may lose resources, but it will not disappear and be replaced by another organization that fulfills the same function. Armies may lose wars, but unlike firms, they do not go bankrupt; they are not dismantled and their facilities sold to the highest bidder.

Only if defeat in war leads to the elimination of the state does the military organization disappear. Thus, if efficient adaptation is to occur it must be within the military organization itself and not because a more successful organization replaces it. This requirement for organizational learning (rather than replacement) makes efficient cultural adaptation unlikely. When a successful firm replaces a bankrupt one the selection process takes places automatically; no one has to identify the reasons one firm is more successful than another or try to change the organization in line with environmental constraints. Not so with the military. Military organizations must both determine the reasons for defeat and engineer the necessary changes within the organization. Because armies are natural monopolies there are even fewer reasons to expect their cultures to adapt efficiently to environmental constraints.

This conclusion may underestimate the selective incentives that military organizations face. Military organizations may not go through the same birth-to-death cycle of firms in a competitive market structure, but they are not immune to competitive pressures. As anyone familiar with the bureaucratic maneuvering of the American armed services will testify, military services often compete with each other for certain roles and missions. More important, it is hard to imagine a more competitive environment than the battlefield itself. In other words, the military's monopolistic position may ensure that it is not eliminated, but competitive pressures from other services and on the battlefield may force organizational learning and a concomitant change in culture. Although examples of military organizations' inability to adapt to battlefield conditions cast doubt on this argument, the contrast between the military's monopolistic position within the state and the Darwinian pressures of the battlefield suggests some possible directions for further research. For example, if the battlefield does force cultural adaptation, we should find much greater cultural change in military organizations that are often engaged in warfare, and conversely, cultural continuity in services with little battlefield experience.

The Political Origins of Military Cultures

Perhaps because organizational theorists focus on organizations in the private sector, they do not examine the political origins of organizational cultures. But this may be an important source of a military's culture. Government policies affect private firms, but military organizations depend on the government in a way that is unparalleled in most parts of the private sector. Most private companies do not depend on Congress for their labor force, budget, and goals. This intense interaction and bureaucratic maneuvering with the government and the other services may shape the content of the military's culture. Deborah Avant argues, for example, that state structure and civilian incentives shape the military's "institutional bias."[46]

Similarly, aspects of the military's culture may have started as politically expedient arguments that came to be taken for granted through the continual process of political bargaining. Social psychologists have shown that stating an idea often leads to changes in personal convictions. During World War I, for example, a group of soldiers who had caused problems at an army camp showed a marked improvement in morale after participating in a public speaking contest in which they were asked to invent speeches that championed army life. In other words, getting people to commit themselves publicly to a particular belief can lead them to internalize that belief.[47] A similar process may explain the French army's low estimation of short-term conscripts. Arguing that short-term conscripts were poor soldiers was politically more palatable than arguing against a conscript army because it might strengthen the Left and the Socialists' power. But having repeatedly made this argument in political battles to increase the length of conscription, the French army may have come to believe what it said. Since the military bargains continually with the government, and if "saying is believing," many aspects of the military's culture may have originated as politically expedient strategies.

Policy Implications and Areas for Further Research

The importance of culture is an empirical question. My argument that culture is well suited for studying the military is based on a limited test of doctrinal developments in Britain and France during the 1920s and 1930s. Increasing the number of cases studied would provide additional tests of my argument and help evaluate the potential impact of nuclear weapons, war, and the "civilianization" of the officer corps. Additional cases could also better test the relative impact of international and domestic issues on civilian decisions, as well as the generalizability of my argument. In addition, with confidence that military culture has explanatory power, we should begin to investigate the origins of military cultures and how they change.

Contemporary Military Organizations in Wartime

The nuclear revolution might weaken my argument that culture strongly affects the choice between an offensive and a defensive military doctrine. The unspeakable consequences of a nuclear war may so focus the mind that military officers in different branches and different countries may hold the same beliefs about nuclear weapons and the conduct of war. This finding would challenge my proposition that the type of technology used is unlikely to explain the origins of a military's culture; because nuclear weapons are singular in their effects, only one cultural response may be possible. More important, if the presence of nuclear weapons leads to similar military cultures, then military cultures are epiphenomenal; cultural explanations are unnecessary if actors facing the same conditions reach the same conclusions.

Examining doctrinal developments during wartime could also shed light on the importance of military culture. I needed access to an extensive written record in order to check and double-check the embeddedness of certain basic assumptions, values, norms, beliefs, and formal knowledge. For this reason, I looked at the development of doctrine during the time when the military generates the largest written record: in peacetime. Looking at cases of doctrinal change during wartime could be, however, an important test of my argument.[48] Contrary to the prevailing view, this book argues that the international system has a limited effect on the choice between an offensive and a defensive doctrine. Yet, if there is any time when the adversary (or external environment) should matter, it is during war. Examining wartime doctrinal change would either show the limits of this study's argument or make an even stronger case for the explanatory power of military culture.

It would also be valuable to examine the extent to which "civilianization" of the officer corps has occurred and, to the extent it has occurred, whether it has reduced the importance of a military's culture. The military sociologist Morris Janowitz argued that changes in the military after World War II, such as the influx of technology and shifts in officer recruitment, dissolved many of the differences between military and civilian life.[49] Janowitz also argued that there are limits to how far this process can go, but if civilianization has advanced in most military organizations, my claims about the limited effect of the wider culture on the military's culture may need revision, or at least be limited to states that have retained an insulated military caste. More important, if the civilian and military worlds have merged, the organizational culture itself may be less important.

The civilianization of the armed services may not, however, be widespread. A recent account of the British regimental system, for example, shows that the army continues to be insulated from the wider society. Members of a regiment have few if any friends outside the regiment, and their children marry into other families belonging to the same regiment. In the words of a recent analyst, "This completeness of association forms a psychology of the regiment such that it is a complete social system, much the same way a religious sect or culture controls every minute detail of its members' lives."[50] Many Latin American militaries remain an elite society isolated from the larger society.[51] The exposure of sexual harassment at the U.S. Navy aviators' Tailhook convention in 1991 also attests to the degree to which a military organization's values and attitudes can be out of sync with wider society. Further research on the military's culture could systematically address the civilianization of the officer corps and its impact on the points made in this book.

Domestic versus International Factors in Doctrinal Development

Further research could also contribute to our understanding of the relative importance of domestic and international factors. My argument about the role of civilians in the development of doctrine supports Jack Snyder's claim that "it is by no means obvious that vulnerability to international pressure is more worrisome than vulnerability to domestic pressure."[52] However, we disagree about when domestic or international forces predominate. Whereas Snyder suggests that smaller and more vulnerable states are more responsive to international conditions, I argue that civilian responsiveness to international conditions is a function of whether there is a civilian consensus on the role of the armed forces in the domestic arena.[53]

There are several ways to address this disagreement. First, additional research could examine whether there is a relationship between international vulnerability and domestic consensus. Perhaps only countries that are relatively invulnerable can allow themselves the luxury of domestic controversy over the armed services, and conversely, states in high threat environments quickly resolve domestic debates that could hinder state survival. Although this argument is plausible, the French and British cases suggest otherwise. As an island nation, Britain was historically relatively invulnerable yet also enjoyed domestic consensus about the military, while in France, despite the proximity of the German threat, domestic controversy over the armed services persisted. Furthermore, as the perception of a German threat receded during the cold war, so did French domestic debate over the armed services. In short, international vulnerability correlated with domestic debate, not with internal cohesion. Nevertheless, if there is a systematic relationship between the degree of domestic debate and a state's relative vulnerability to international pressures, Snyder's argument would trump mine.

Second, confirmation of my proposition about the relative importance of international and domestic factors may be an artifact of my case selection. Since I looked exclusively at great powers—France and Great Britain in the interwar period—I could not see whether international factors overrode domestic considerations in relatively weak or exposed states. Although France was hardly invulnerable during the 1930s, research on the relative importance of international and domestic factors in small and vulnerable states would help address this unresolved question. If Snyder's proposition is correct—that small powers adapt their domestic circumstances to international conditions—this finding would not show that my argument was wrong. However, it would limit its generalizability to civilians in invulnerable states or great powers.

Typologies of Military Cultures

The inclusion of more cases might also lead to the ability to identify different typologies of organizational culture in the military. With only the British and French cases, it is difficult to sort out the general from the unique. For example, the French army's emphasis on the length of conscription has no meaning in the British context: the categories that make sense to the British officer would not make sense to the French officer. But this contrast does not mean that the French culture is unique. Looking at other countries, especially those where conscription is a much more integral part of the military system, might lead to the identification of different typologies of military culture for volunteer and conscript armies. In addition, because many of the militaries in the developing world were either initially European and then passed on to the state at independence (such as India), or strongly influenced by military advisers from a regional power or former metropole (such as France in Africa and

South America, and the United States in Central and South America), it might also be useful to think in terms of a typical American, French, or British military culture.

In addition, can military cultures help us explain other military actions besides the choice between offensive and defensive doctrines? For example, Jeffrey Legro argued that military culture explains why some restraints on the conduct of war were respected during World War II.[54] Can military culture also explain the adoption of counterinsurgency doctrines? During the post–World War II period, the French and American armies had very different doctrinal reactions to their defeat in Indochina. While the French army adopted a counterinsurgency doctrine, the American army resisted civilian attempts to reorient its doctrine away from conventional mechanized warfare.[55] Indeed, the American army's recovery from the Vietnam War led to a doctrine even more highly attuned to combat on the inter-German border. France and the United States faced similar strategic requirements—both had entered the age of limited warfare with far-flung commitments, and both remained committed to the defense of Western Europe. Yet their armies appear—if one examines their doctrine—to be facing different adversaries. Could organizational culture help us understand why such apparently similar armies react so differently to the same battlefield threat? Military culture may also provide an important key to explaining why some military organizations are more reluctant than others to intervene in politics.

Changing Military Cultures

Further research could develop and test some of the propositions made in the previous section about the origins of military cultures, as well as shed light on how to change a military's culture. These issues are important to policymakers interested in intervening in the development of doctrine, and they are particularly important in democratic states in which military values and attitudes should echo, not challenge, the principles on which the country is based. For example, does the American armed services' relative success in dealing with racism provide valuable lessons for those interested in changing aspects of a military's culture?[56] Why have some branches of the U.S. armed services been more successful than others, and what do these successes or failures say about the services' ability to address the aspects of its culture that foster sexual harassment or hinder the open integration of homosexuals? In short, what does it take to change a military's culture?

There is considerable disagreement among analysts about the difficulty of changing an organization's culture.[57] While some management consultants line their pockets by claiming to change corporate cultures and so enhance organizational effectiveness, others present a less optimistic scenario. A partner in the consulting firm McKinsey and Company noted that changing an organization's culture could take five to ten years and observed in 1992 that no one had yet done it successfully.[58] Most organizational theorists agree that it is difficult to change an organization's culture. A 1985 review of research on cultural change, for example, argued that companies should not attempt to change their corporate culture unless they had lots of time and resources and little choice.[59]

It may be equally difficult to change a military's culture. Although the American military has made great strides in changing racist attitudes and behavior, examples of military resistance to change abound. For example, at the turn of the century, the French minister of war, General André, attempted to "republicanize" the French officer corps. André abolished the dowry required of officers' brides in the hopes of attracting different types of men, and brought new instructors to the military academies to alter the socialization of new members. André also encouraged contact with civilians by abolishing the obligatory mess for unmarried officers and did away with many of the symbols of the officers' more privileged life, such as tennis courts and skating rinks. But despite these and many other efforts, André's reforms ultimately failed to induce the desired change.[60]

The difficulty of changing a military's culture may indicate that its strength is a double-edged sword. On the one hand, the consistency of beliefs in total institutions like the military means that most of its members have difficulty imagining that things could or should be done differently. On the other hand, the military's powerful assimilating mechanisms mean that once an organization gets behind an initiative to change aspects of its culture, change may be more feasible than in a private company, which has more limited ways to control and shape its members' beliefs. After all, the military can go beyond pronouncing new goals or strategies and redesigning the internal layout of their buildings; militaries have the power to intervene at the lowest level to get members to challenge cultural beliefs that have become objective truths. Although it may be more difficult for leading officers to overcome the initial hurdle of recognizing that a change in the organization's culture is necessary, once this barrier has been crossed it should be easier to impose a change in the military's culture.

Focusing on the cultural aspects of organizations may also help us better understand how to eliminate sexual harassment in the armed services. Ironically, on the same page as a 1995 *New York Times* article acclaiming the U.S. military's success in racial integration was an article entitled, "Study Says Sexual Harassment Persists at Military Academies."[61] This contrast may be because integration of the U.S. armed services has been an important objective since the late 1940s whereas combating sexual harassment did not receive much attention until the 1980s; it might also say something about sexism in the military. Assimilating a culture is not only about what is written and taught. It is also about what one lives and what one hears and sees in myths and visual images. As long as women are excluded from the military's raison d'etre (combat) and so excluded from its rostrum of heroes, stories, and myths, they may continue to face discrimination. If the larger, though implicit, message in an organization is that some of its members are not fully qualified to fulfill its primary mission, it may be very difficult for sensitivity training to teach otherwise.

This discussion raises the larger issue of the extent to which civilians can force the military to change its culture. The contrast between the French minister of war's failure to change the army's culture and the U.S. Army's success in overcoming racism might provide testable propositions about the necessary conditions for changing a culture. Although most of the French officer corps resisted André's reforms, it would be interesting to know whether most officers in the U.S. Army supported efforts to integrate African-Americans into the armed services. Similarly, although the French army did not believe that changing the political orientation of its members would increase its battlefield effectiveness, did American military officers feel that successful integration of minorities was a military necessity? In other words, is cultural change more likely if the military believes that the new value or attitude will strengthen its ability to fight wars?

Much of the earlier work on the origins of military doctrine contained one overriding message for policymakers: "Watch your generals!" Scholars worried that, left on their own, military organizations would adopt offensive military doctrines that served organizational goals rather than the national interest. Civilian intervention was seen as the most likely avenue to well-formulated doctrine tailored to strategic incentives. However, expecting civilians to respond to conditions in the international system is unrealistic and as potentially risky as leaving the conduct of foreign policy to a few chosen elites in Washington, London, and Paris.

Much of the recent work on military innovation paints a generally positive portrait of military organizations. For example, Stephen Rosen argues that militaries innovate without civilian intervention, and Kimberly Zisk shows that the Soviet military, although bureaucratic, was responsive to international threats and opportunities throughout the cold war. Other work has cast doubt on civilians' strategic wisdom. In her study of political military integration, for example, Deborah Avant argues that short-term political interests also affect civilian decisions.[62] I also endorse a more balanced view of the role of civilians and the military. After all, it was the British military, not civilians, who showed greater strategic vision on the question of a continental commitment. Policymakers must recognize their own political agenda and the highly political nature of any enterprise to restructure the armed services. Certain organizational forms of the military appeal to certain sectors of society for reasons of power. These preferences may reflect contemporary stakes or they may be outdated. In either case, they constrain policy options and must be taken into consideration.

These conclusions do not lead to the advice that we should watch our civilians (and ignore our generals). Policymakers should resist blaming the military for adopting offensive doctrines and recognize that military resistance to defensive doctrines may not stem from the officer corps' attempt to protect the offensive doctrine itself. It may not be the offensive aspect of the doctrine that the military seeks to safeguard, but instead components within its organizational culture that they believe are integral to the successful implementation of their mission. If defensive doctrines could be designed to incorporate those components of the military's culture, then military resistance to the change would decrease.

In addition, the barriers to changing a military's culture suggest that we should be careful not to allow the officer corps to become a separate caste, isolated from society, and permeated with its own values and attitudes. The more we encourage interaction between the military and civilians, as well as militaries in other countries, the more likely that the basic assumptions, values, norms, beliefs, and formal knowledge that shape collective understandings within a particular military organization will have to face competing and contrasting cultural beliefs. One of the best strategies to encourage actors to recognize that their objective truths may be cultural beliefs is to put them face to face with contrasting truths.

However, there are drawbacks to attempting to weaken a military's culture. If military organizations are more likely to be able to change their culture because of their powerful control over the socialization process, encouraging contact with outsiders may weaken the institutions' control and so their ability to change when they think change is necessary. In addition, organizational cultures are valuable; organizations need predictability. This is especially true for the military. Fighting is a group task; the military must ensure coordinated action even while it is asking its members to put their lives in jeopardy. Collective understandings, or a culture, make this possible. This point serves as an important reminder that, to some degree, a military's culture is functional.

Nevertheless, some of the policies that could be expanded in order to expose the military to alternative visions include continuing officer education within the universities and extending military exchanges with other countries. For example, many universities routinely host foreign and American military officers. Exposure to the theories and methods popular in civilian universities makes it more likely that the military could imagine doing things differently, and so be both more apt to consider alternatives and more receptive to civilian-directed change.

This book argues that a military's culture shapes its choice between an offensive and a defensive military doctrine but does not provide a recipe for changing a military's culture. We must first be certain that military cultures have explanatory power before it makes sense to try to understand the sources of a military's culture or how to change it: demonstrating that military culture matters is a prerequisite to providing policymakers with advice on how to change a military's doctrine. I presented some of the possible sources of a military's culture and suggested some implications of changing a military's culture, but this discussion is just a beginning. Developing methods for successful intervention in military cultures will require research focused on the determinants of cultural change.

I do not advocate the wholesale adoption of cultural analyses. In the case of the development of military doctrine, making sense of military and civilian choices requires understanding the cultural context, but this does not mean that cultural analyses are always necessary or that more traditional approaches are unimportant. Structural and functional analyses are valuable tools in understanding international politics.[63] Indeed, the normative and political rationale for pursuing the question of the origins of military doctrine stems from a structural constraint. It is because offensive military postures are structural impediments to cooperative relations among states that the determinants of the choice between an offensive and a defensive doctrine are important. Defensive doctrines may also be preferable because they often consume fewer resources, but fears about the extent to which offensive military doctrines exaggerate the dangerous dynamics in the security dilemma motivate much of the research on the origins of military doctrine.

I believe that international relations scholars should take a closer look at the ideational side of international politics. This book joins a growing body of literature in international relations that uses a sociological or constructivist approach to explain questions in international security.[64] Material structures are important, but their meanings often vary. Sometimes it is appropriate to take preferences as given and interests as self-evident. But often we cannot understand how structure matters or what incentives it provides without understanding the meanings that actors attach to their world. And we can further our understanding of these meanings by appreciating the central role that culture plays in our lives. A culture makes some things possible, some things desirable, and some things unimaginable. Recognizing this simple truth is the first step toward a better understanding of the origins of military doctrine.

Notes

Introduction

1. On the destabilizing consequences of offensive doctrines see Jervis, "Cooperation under the Security Dilemma," 167–214; Levy, "The Offensive/Defensive Balance," 220–22; Posen, "Inadvertent Nuclear War?" 28–54; Quester, *Offense and Defense*, 7; Van Evera, "The Cult of the Offensive," 58–107. For critiques, see Sagan, "1914 Revisited," 151–77; Tractenberg, "The Meaning of Mobilization," 120–50.

2. For the classic discussion of social construction, see Berger and Luckmann, *The Social Construction of Reality*.

3. van Creveld, *Fighting Power*, 32–33, 39–40; Vial, "Les doctrines militaires," 121; Travers, "The Offensive and the Problem of Innovation," 536.

4. Cotton, "Institutional and Occupational Values in Canada's Army," 99–110; Henderson, *Cohesion*; Janowitz, *The Professional Soldier*, 8–15; Janowitz, *Sociology and the Military Establishment*, 36, 39–40.

5. Luttwak and Horowitz, *The Israeli Army*, 117.

6. Posen, *The Sources of Military Doctrine*; Snyder, *The Ideology of the Offensive*; Van Evera, "Causes of War."

Chapter 1

1. Many analysts argue that military organizations are inherently difficult to change. For example, see Howard, "Military Science in an Age of Peace," 4–5; McNeill, *The Pursuit of Power*, 262–306; Morison, *Men, Machines, and Modern Times*, 17–44; and Simpkin, *Race to the Swift*, 5. Deborah Avant argues that a military's ability to change is not an inherent property but a function of the degree and type of civilian control. See Avant, *Political Institutions and Military Change*, 15.

2. Many analysts argue that technology drives military strategy. For example, see Evans, "The Impact of Technology," 40–47; and Macmillan, "Technology," 16–22. However, Posen concludes that technology and geography are weak explanations. See Posen, *The Sources of Military Doctrine*, 50–51, 65–67, 236–39. For additional discussions of the relationship between technology, doctrine, and strategy, see Brown, *Flying Blind*; and Holloway, "Doctrine and Technology in Soviet Armaments Policy." Some argue that defeat in war stimulates innovation. See Mandelbaum, *The Fate of Nations*, 126–27; and Paret, *Innovation and Reform in Warfare*, 8. In contrast, Stephen Rosen argues that defeat in war is neither necessary nor sufficient for innovation. See Rosen, *Winning the Next War*, 8–9.

3. Posen explains two additional aspects of military doctrine: the extent of

political-military integration and the degree of innovation. See Posen, *The Sources of Military Doctrine*; and Snyder, *The Ideology of the Offensive*. The quantity and quality of work that Snyder and Posen's work has generated testifies to the power of their ideas. See especially Avant, *Political Institutions and Military Change*; and Zisk, *Engaging the Enemy*.

4. Unlike Waltz, who refined balance-of-power theory to explain why balances recur, Posen uses balance-of-power theory to explain specific states' military doctrines. I use "realism" and "balance-of-power theory" to refer to the realpolitik theory of military doctrine that Posen developed. See Posen's discussion in *The Sources of Military Doctrine*, 34–35; for the classic statement of contemporary realism, see Waltz, *Theory of International Politics*.

5. Posen, *The Sources of Military Doctrine*, 141–78.

6. Snyder, *The Ideology of the Offensive*, 196.

7. On the importance of civilian intervention, see Alexander, *Decision-Making in Soviet Weapons Procurement*; Betts, *Cruise Missiles*; Katzenbach, "The Horse Cavalry in the Twentieth Century," 360–73; and Kaempffert, "War and Technology," 431–44. Several scholars have challenged the argument that military innovation requires civilian intervention. See especially Rosen, *Winning the Next War*. Avant and Zisk also argue that civilian intervention is often unnecessary: see Avant, *Political Institutions and Military Change*, 5, 13; and Zisk, *Engaging the Enemy*, 28.

8. Snyder, *The Ideology of the Offensive*, 30, 200, 209.

9. Snyder, "The Origins of Offense," 190. The operational war plan that formed the basis for the German attack in 1914, the Schlieffen Plan, called for German forces to knock out France in an offensive while Russia was mobilizing, then turn with all force to the East.

10. Levite, *Offense and Defense in Israeli Military Doctrine*, 78.

11. For a discussion of why the relative power of the German army cannot explain this shift, see Chapter 3.

12. Airland Battle stresses maneuver warfare, attacking enemy reinforcements before they reach the front, and seizing the initiative to create pockets of opportunity for offensive ground operations. Given that the conventional military balance always favored the Soviets (even when the American army had a defensive doctrine), Soviet conventional superiority cannot explain this shift in army doctrine. For a discussion of Airland battle, see Romjue, *From Active Defense to Airland Battle*.

13. Rikhye, *The War That Never Was*, 23; Singh, "Let Us Reorganize our Logistical Services," 64.

14. Snyder, *The Ideology of the Offensive*, 39.

15. Zisk argues that successful civilian intervention depends on the broadening of the defense policy community. Zisk, *Engaging the Enemy*, 5.

16. Pognon, *De Gaulle et l'armée*, 95. Unless otherwise noted, the translations throughout the text are mine.

17. B. Crozier, *De Gaulle*, 74.

18. On Cot's policies, see Service historique de l'armée de l'air (SHAA), 2 B 1, "Cot à Daladier," August 3, 1936; Teyssier, "L'appui aux forces de surface," 257–62; and Christienne, "L'armée de l'air française, 187–88. On Guy La

Chambre's policy, see Krauskopf, "French Air Power Policy, 1919–1939." 246–68.

19. Doise and Vaisse, *Diplomatie et outil militaire*, 342; Hébrard, *Vingt-cinq années d'aviation militaire*, 185; Fridenson and Lecuir, *La France et la Grande-Bretagne*, 19; Vennesson, "La Fabrication de l'armée de l'air," 80–83.

20. Posen, *The Sources of Military Doctrine*, 69.

21. For example, see Milward, *The German Economy at War*; and Mason, "The Primacy of Politics," 175–200. For a discussion of "blitzkrieg economics," see Wark, *The Ultimate Enemy*, 156–57.

22. Mearsheimer, *Conventional Deterrence*, 99–133.

23. Murray, "German Army Doctrine," 79, 90–94; O'Neill, "Doctrine and Training in the German Army," 143–95.

24. Geyer, "German Strategy in the Age of Machine Warfare," 559. Murray, "German Army Doctrine," 91, see also 79, 90–94; Murray, "Force Strategy, Blitzkrieg Strategy, and the Economic Difficulties," 39–43; and Overy, "Hitler's War and the German Economy," 272–91.

25. Posen, Snyder, and Van Evera developed this argument. See Posen, *The Sources of Military Doctrine*, esp. 41–59; Snyder, *The Ideology of the Offensive*, esp. 24–30; and Van Evera, "Causes of War," esp. 206–399. Both Avant and Zisk have recently revised this one-sided view of the military. In explaining political military integration, Avant argues that military organizations do not have the same preferences. Avant, *Political Institutions and Military Change*, 12–15. Zisk argues that military organizations are not exclusively interested in their parochial interests. Zisk, *Engaging the Enemy*, 14, 26–27, 180.

26. Van Evera, "Causes of War," 282.

27. Snyder acknowledges that some of these goals might lead to a preference for a defensive doctrine but concludes that the majority of the goals lead to a preference for the offensive. Snyder, *The Ideology of the Offensive*, 24–26.

28. Quoted in Coox, "French Military Doctrine 1919–1939," 108. Indeed, in contrast to his hypothesis that "military organizations will generally prefer offensive doctrines because they reduce uncertainty," Posen argues that the French army accepted a defensive doctrine because it would reduce uncertainty. Posen, *The Sources of Military Doctrine*, 47, 118–20.

29. For discussions of functionalism, see Turner and Maryanski, *Functionalism*; and Stinchcombe, *Constructing Social Theories*, 80–82.

30. Halperin posits that organizations will forgo new roles and missions to preserve the organization's "essence." Halperin, *Bureaucratic Politics and Foreign Policy*, esp. 39–40.

31. Bialer, *The Shadow of the Bomber*, 58–68; Gibbs, *Grand Strategy*, vol. 1, *History of the Second World War*, 108; Howard, *The Continental Commitment*, 106; Slessor, *The Central Blue*, 169–75; M. Smith, *British Air Strategy between the Wars*, 127; Wark, *The Ultimate Enemy*, 34–48, 56.

32. Quoted in Wark, *The Ultimate Enemy*, 29.

33. Quoted in Kennedy, *The Rise and Fall of British Naval Mastery*, 219; also see Semmel, *Liberalism and Naval Strategy*, 138.

34. Frankenstein, "A propos des aspects financiers du réarmement français," 7; LeFranc, *Histoire du front populaire*, 392.

35. Clarke, "Military Technology in Republican France," 178, 192; Doughty, *The Seeds of Disaster*, 164; Hughes, *To the Maginot Line*, 71, 137. Posen states that in 1934 civilians called for greater offensive mobility; see *The Sources of Military Doctrine*, 128.

36. Posen, *The Sources of Military Doctrine*, 144.

37. Quoted in Semmel, *Liberalism and Naval Strategy*, 141–42, also see 139–49; Padfield, *The Great Naval Race*, 144, 150–52.

38. Quoted in Semmel, *Liberalism and Naval Strategy*, 148, also see 144–45; Marder, *From the Dreadnought to Scapa Flow*, vol. 1, 344–57, 373–77; Roskill, *The Strategy of Sea Power*, 101–9.

39. For a discussion of how Durkheim separated the causal from the functional analysis to avoid making a teleological argument, see Turner and Maryanski, *Functionalism*, 96.

Chapter 2

1. See Friedman, "Conscription and the Constitution," 231–96; Whiteclay, *To Raise an Army*, esp. 107.

2. Stockton, "Organizations and Military Doctrine."

3. Bridge, *From Sadowa to Sarajevo*, 255.

4. Beckett, "The Amateur Military Tradition," 410.

5. Kelleher, "Mass Armies in the 1970s," 7–8.

6. Madison quoted in Friedman, "Conscription and the Constitution," 251; also see Hamilton, *Federalist Papers* nos. 8, 24, and 26. Adams quoted in the *Boston Gazette*, December 1798; reprinted in Karsten, ed., *The Military in America*, 18.

7. Dupuy, *A Genius for War*, 311. Similarly, reforms of the French high command in the early twentieth century were designed to prevent a military coup, not to safeguard military efficiency. See Porch, *The March to the Marne*, 170–71.

8. Quoted in B. Hacker, "The United States Army as a National Police Force," 256.

9. A prominent Algerian general declared, "It is within a popular army, and not a professional army, that many freedom fighters in the Third World are trained and hardened." Quoted in Pierre Haski, "L'algérie fête 25 ans d'histoire," *Libération*, June 6, 1987. The official publication of the Algerian army, *El Djeich*, is filled with articles that discuss, praise, and honor guerrilla leaders.

10. René Delisle, "Alger: les milices face à l'armée," *France observateur*, July 16, 1964; Charles Henri Favord, "Le croc en jambe de l'ultime minute," *Gazette de Lausaune*, June 21, 1965; Quandt, *Revolution and Political Leadership*, 220–25; Jean François Kahn, "La lutte contre l'opposition en Algérie," *Le monde*, July 15, 1964.

11. Finer, *The Man on Horseback*, 46; Beckett, "Amateur Military Tradition," 411.

12. Stepan, *The Military in Politics*, 23–27. For a fascinating discussion of how the creation of armed forces during independence struggles helps stave off military coups in Africa, see Frazer, "Sustaining Civilian Control."

13. Quoted in Porch, *The March to the Marne*, 184.

14. Dobbin, *Forging Industrial Policy*, 220.

15. Weir, "Ideas and Politics," 58. Also see Hall, "Conclusion," 383–84.

16. Vlahos, "Military Reform in Historical Perspective," 251.

17. Buffotot, "La politique militaire du Parti socialiste," 88–101. Also see Dournel, "L'armée de l'air en 1946," 266; Kirkland, "Anti-Military Group Fantasies," 31; and Rouquie, "Les processus politiques," 30–31.

18. Quoted in Destremau and Hélie, *Les militaires*, 47, also see 253, 256; and Planchais, "Crise de modernisme dans l'armée," 119.

19. Adams and Poirier, *The Conscription Controversy in Great Britain*, 10–22, 39–42; Chambers, *To Raise an Army*, 80–112; Dabezies, "Milices, conscription," 1083–84; Dennis, *Decision by Default*, 164, 191; Huntington, *The Soldier and the State*, 270.

20. This is especially true in discussions about conscription, but it also influences general discussions about the military and the political role of the officer corps. See Jacques Isnard, "Un sondage CAS Le Monde Fr3 sur les Français et la défense," *Le monde*, May 23, 1989; Dabezies, "Milices, conscription," 1080–84; "Service ou servilité," *Le monde*, May 20, 1988; and Jean Planchais, "Le socialiste et le soldat," *Le monde*, October 4, 1985. Similarly, the fear of the Left continues to haunt the army. See Destremau and Hélie, *Les militaires*, 259; "L'armée s'interroge sur les intentions du nouveau pouvoir," *Le figaro*, May 29, 1981.

21. Swidler, "Culture in Action," 279.

22. Ibid., 279, 284.

23. Deborah Avant makes a similar argument. Avant argues that the degree to which civilians respond to systemic imperatives depends on the electoral pressures they face. Avant, *Political Institutions and Military Change*, 2, 9, 20, 30.

24. For discussions of organizational culture, see Pettigrew, "On Studying Organizational Cultures," 570–82; Schein, "Coming to a New Awareness of Organizational Culture," 3–16; Trice and Beyer, "Studying Organizational Cultures," 653–69; and the following special journal issues: *Administrative Science Quarterly* 28, no. 3 (1983); *Organizational Studies* 7, no. 2 (1986); *International Studies of Management and Organization* 17, no. 3 (1987); and *Journal of Management* 11, no. 2 (1985). Studies of "organizational climate" preceded by twenty years the current work on organizational culture. See Payne and Pugh, "Organizational Structure and Climate"; and Tagiuri and Litwin, *Organizational Climate*.

25. For a list of different definitions, see the appendix to chap. 3 in Ott, *The Organizational Culture Perspective*, 70–73.

26. Discussed in Hedberg, "How Organizations Learn and Unlearn," 3–27.

27. Meyer, "Adapting to Environmental Jolts," 515–37.

28. Halperin, *Bureaucratic Politics and Foreign Policy*, 26–51; Builder, *The Masks of War*, 3; Head, "Doctrinal Innovation and the A-7 Attack Aircraft Decisions"; Snyder, *The Ideology of the Offensive*; Katzenbach, "The Horse Cavalry in the Twentieth Century"; Legro, *Cooperation under Fire*; Avant, *Political Institutions and Military Change*. For a conceptual discussion of military culture, see Applegate and Moore, "The Nature of Military Culture," 302–5.

29. Harrison, "Keeping the Faith," 553.

30. Rochlin, La Porte, and Roberts, "The Self-Designing High-Reliability Organization," 77.

31. Glenn Rifkin, "Andersen Consulting's Culture of 'Clones'," *New York Times*, September 6, 1992, 1F.

32. On "total institutions," see Goffman, *Asylums*. On military organizations as "total institutions," see Chandessais, *La psychologie dans l'armée*, 9–10.

33. Barnett, "The Education of Military Elites," 202–3; Dornbusch, "The Military Academy as an Assimilating Institution," 316–21.

34. Translations: talkative messmate, mental depression, shoddy workmanship. Granville, *A Dictionary of Sailors' Slang*. Also see Brotz and Wilson, "Characteristics of Military Society," 371; and Elkin, "The Soldier's Language," 414–22.

35. van Creveld, *Fighting Power*, 83.

36. Schelling, *The Strategy of Conflict*, 92.

37. For a discussion of the origins of military cultures, see Chapter 7. For a discussion of how social structure affects military power, see Rosen, *Societies and Military Power*. For a review of the literature on strategic culture, see Johnston, "Thinking about Strategic Culture," 32–64; and Johnston, *Cultural Realism*.

38. For example, see Huntington, *The Soldier and the State*, 59–71.

39. van Creveld, *Fighting Power*, 129–32; Moskos, *The American Enlisted Man*, 24. The classic statement on paternalism in the French army is Lyautey, "Le rôle social de l'officier."

40. For a discussion of different methods for determining an organization's culture see Sackmann, "Uncovering Culture in Organizations," 295–317.

41. Mitroff and Kilmann, "Corporate Taboos as the Key to Unlocking Culture," 184–99; Sathe, "How to Decipher and Change Corporate Culture," 237.

42. Swidler, "Culture in Action," 284.

43. Simpkin, *Race to the Swift*, 228–34; Travers, *The Killing Ground*, 258.

44. Swidler, "Culture in Action," 277.

45. Hermann, "Some Consequences of Crises," 61–82; Staw, Sandelands, and Dutton, "Threat-Rigidity Effects in Organizational Behavior," 501–24; Khandwalla, "Environment and Its Impact on the Organization," 297–313.

46. Turner, "The Organizational and Interorganizational Development of Disasters," 378–97.

47. This hypothesis is similar to Snyder's argument that organizational bias is greatest when there is external domestic pressure on the military. Snyder, *The Ideology of the Offensive*, 25.

48. Laitin, *Hegemony and Culture*.

49. Alexander, "Analytic Debates."

50. Kratochwil and Ruggie, "International Organization," 764–66; Neufeld, "Interpretation and the 'Science' of International Relations," 39–62.

51. Almond and Verba, *The Civic Culture*; Pye and Verba, eds., *Political Culture and Political Development*.

52. Hellman, *Journeys among Women*.

53. George, "The Causal Nexus between Cognitive Beliefs and Decision-Making Behavior," 113.

54. Hofstede, *Culture's Consequences*; Laurent, "The Cultural Diversity of Western Conceptions of Management," 75–96.

55. For example, see Adams, "Energy and the Regulation of the Nation-State"; Lodge and Vogel, eds., *Ideology and National Competitiveness*; and Upham, *Law and Social Change in Post-War Japan*.

56. I have used Barry Posen's definitions of offensive and defensive military doctrines. Posen, *The Sources of Military Doctrine*, 13–15.

57. Jepperson and Swidler, "What Properties of Culture Should We Measure?" 368.

58. Corse and Robinson, "Cross-cultural Measurement and New Conceptions of Culture," 313–25.

Chapter 3

1. Fuller was a fascist sympathizer. Fuller, *The Decisive Battles of the Western World*, vol. 3, 386.

2. See Serre, *Les événements survenus en France de 1933 à 1945*.

3. Adamthwaite, *France and the Second World War*; Alerme, *Les causes militaires de notre défaite*, 42; Bloch, *Strange Defeat*; Conquet, *L'énigme des blindés*, 20–23; Duroselle, *La décadence*; Dutourd, *Les taxis de la Marne*; Michel, *Le procès de Riom*, 258; Shirer, *The Collapse of the Third Republic*; Tint, *The Decline of French Patriotism*.

4. See Alexander, "Repercussions of the Breda Variant"; de Bardies, *La campagne*; Cohen and Gooch, *Military Misfortunes*, 201; Ely, *L'armée dans la nation*, 52; Frankenstein, *Le prix du réarmement français*, 9; de la Gorce, *The French Army*; Horne, *To Lose a Battle*; and Possony, "Organized Intelligence," 219–26.

5. For claims of quantitative inferiority, see de Cossé-Brissac, "L'armée allemande dans la campagne de France de 1940," 3–28; Danel, "En mai–juin 1940, ils étaient les plus forts," 68–69; Darcy, *Oraison funèbre pour la vieille armée*; Gamelin, *Servir*, 424–25; and Weygand, *Histoire de l'armée française*.

6. Army training manuals are one of the primary sources on French doctrine. For the most important of the interwar period, see Ministère de la guerre, Etat-Major de l'armée, *L'instruction provisoire sur l'emploi des chars de combat*, 1920; *L'instruction provisoire sur l'emploi tactique des grandes unités*, 1921; *L'instruction sur l'emploi des chars de combat*, 1929; *Règlement des unités de chars légers* 1929–30; and *L'instruction sur l'emploi tactique des grandes unités*, 1936. Five excellent secondary sources on the French army's doctrine are Doughty, *The Seeds of Disaster*; Challener, *The French Theory of the Nation in Arms*; Kiesling, *Arming against Hitler*; Paoli, *L'armée française de 1919 à 1939*, esp. vol. 2; Vial, "Les doctrines militaires françaises et allemandes."

7. Challener, *The French Theory of the Nation in Arms*, 178; Coox, "French Military Doctrine," 17; Doughty, *The Seeds of Disaster*, 21–24; Doise and Vaisse, *Diplomatie et outil militaire*, 284; Service historique de l'armée de terre (SHAT), 1 N 42, File 2, Weygand, "Etat de l'armée" (February 5, 1934).

8. For general discussion of the development of motorization and mechanization in the French army, see Clarke, "Military Technology in Republican

France"; Coox, "French Military Doctrine," 96–185; Delaunay, "Chars de combat et cavalerie"; Doughty, *The Seeds of Disaster*, 136–68; Dutailly, "Motorisation et mécanisation dans l'armée de terre française," 214–27; Ferré, *Le défaut de l'armure*, 29–33, 54–59, 70–79, 140–46, 157; Harvey, "French Concepts of Military Strategy," 142, 157–59; and Perré, "La refonte de la réglementation relative aux chars de combat," 468–84. For Gamelin's position on the use of tanks see his discussion in SHAT, 1 N 22, Conseil supérieur de la guerre (CSG), "Composition à donner à la division cuirassée et création de grandes unités de ce type" (December 2, 1938).

9. On the preponderance of firepower, see Paoli, *Armée française*, vol. 2, 155; and Carrias, *La pensée militaire française*, 318.

10. For discussions of the methodical battle, see Carrias, *La pensée militaire française*, 332–33; and Doughty, *The Seeds of Disaster*, 3.

11. Although most observers at the time perceived that military technology favored the defense, most military historians claim that by 1930 military technology favored the offense. See Levy, "The Offensive/Defensive Balance of Military Technology," 233.

12. For examples of this argument, see Cohen and Gooch, *Military Misfortunes*, 214; Coox, "French Military Doctrine," 12, 130; Delaunay, "Chars de combat"; Horne, *The Price of Glory*, 2, 336; and Young, "French Military Intelligence and Nazi Germany," 300–301. For an interesting critique of this argument, see Kiesling, *Arming against Hitler*, 120–25.

13. The most comprehensive accounts of the development of the Maginot Line remain Tournoux, *Haut commandement*; and Tournoux, "Les origines de la Ligne Maginot."

14. On the two schools of thought, see Doughty, *The Seeds of Disaster*, 47–58; Garret, "La Ligne Maginot et la dissuasion nucléaire," 9, 48–49; and Paoli, *Armée française*, vol. 2, 104–5.

15. For an exposition of Foch's views on the French army, see [Foch], "L'armée qu'il nous faut."

16. Nobecourt, *Une histoire politique de l'armée*, 188.

17. Carrias, *La pensée militaire française*, 330.

18. On the lessons that Pétain derived from World War I, see Harvey, "French Concepts of Military Strategy," 8–16.

19. On the offensive and defensive roles assigned to fortifications immediately after World War I, see the discussion at the Superior Council of War. For example, see SHAT, 1 N 20, "Résumé succinct des séances du CSG" (May 17, 1920); also see Hughes, *To the Maginot Line*, 200–204.

20. SHAT, 1 N 20, "Résumé succinct des séances du CSG" (December 14–15, 1926).

21. Ibid. (July 2, 1927).

22. Quoted in Duroselle, *La décadence*, 244. Also see Mysyrowicz, *Anatomie d'une défaite*, 129.

23. Hughes, *To the Maginot Line*, 200.

24. Tournoux, *Haut commandement*, 36.

25. SHAT, 1 N 20, "Résumé succinct des séances du CSG" (December 15, 1925); Tournoux, *Haut commandement*, 53–54.

26. Doughty, *The Seeds of Disaster*, 27, 52–58; Hogg, *Forteresses*, 144; Tournoux, *Haut commandement*, 36, 182–93.

27. Tournoux, *Haut commandement*, 55.

28. SHAT, 1 N 21, "Procès verbaux de la séance du CSG" (May 28, 1932).

29. Bonnefous, *Histoire politique*, 312; SHAT, 1 N 20, "Procès verbaux du CSG" (March 22, 1922).

30. Delaunay, "Chars de combat," 7.

31. Bond and Alexander, "Liddell Hart and de Gaulle."

32. Quoted in Hoff, *Les programmes d'armement*, 9.

33. Dutailly, "Motorisation et mécanisation," 214–17.

34. Paoli, *Armée française*, vol. 2, 192.

35. For example, see Romain, "La réorganisation de l'armée," 868–71; Langlois, "Cheval et chenille," 27–30, 34; Doumenc, "Puissance et mobilité."

36. Kirkland, "Governmental Policy and Combat Effectiveness," 178. See for example, Grazin, "Essai d'emploi d'autos mitrialleuses"; and Flavigny, "Manoeuvres de la 4e division de cavalerie."

37. Bond and Alexander, "Liddell Hart and de Gaulle," 603.

38. Coox, "French Military Doctrine," 186.

39. Quoted in Doughty, *The Seeds of Disaster*, 137.

40. Adamthwaite, *France and the Second World War*, 24; Doise and Vaisse, *Diplomatie et outil*, 269; Laffargue, *Justice pour ceux de 1940*, 91.

41. For a discussion of the limited offensive capability and intentions of the French army during the late 1930s, and especially in 1939, see Doise and Vaisse, *Diplomatie et outil*, 337–38; Michel, *Le procès de Riom*, 265–66; and Young, "Le haut commandement français au moment de Munich," 193–96. On French war plans during the 1930s, see Doise and Vaisse, *Diplomatie et outil*, 300; Duroselle, *La décadence*, 246; Dutailly, *Les problèmes de l'armée de terre française*, 94–95, 100, 104–5; and Tournoux, *Haut commandement*, 335–39.

42. Doise and Vaisse, *Diplomatie et outil*, 276; Hughes, *To the Maginot Line*, 193; Tournoux, *Haut commandement*, 332–35.

43. SHAT, 1 N 27, file 3, "Rapports de présentation du CSG" (March 9, 1925).

44. Doise and Vaisse, *Diplomatie et outil*, 276; Tournoux, *Haut commandement*, 335.

45. Doughty, *The Seeds of Disaster*, 10, 91; Vial, "Doctrines militaires françaises et allemandes," 120.

46. Further discussion of France's shift from an offensive to a defensive orientation during the interwar period can be found in Doise and Vaisse, *Diplomatie et outil*, 275–79; Doughty, *The Seeds of Disaster*, 67; and Hoff, *Les programmes d'armement*, 153, 268. Hughes also argues that the French army was less defensively minded than is commonly thought. Hughes, *To the Maginot Line*, 198.

47. Kraehe, "The Motives behind the Maginot Line," 110.

48. Horne, *The Price of Glory*, 2, 348.

49. Ibid., 348.

50. Reproduced in *Inroads: Harvard's Socialist Forum* (May 1991): 10.

51. On the availability of other lessons, see Christienne, "Le haut comman-

dement française," 411; Ferré, *Le défaut de l'armure*, 20; Murray, *The Change in the European Balance of Power*, 98.

52. de Gaulle, *Vers l'armée de métier*, 291–92.

53. Horne, *The Price of Glory*, 341.

54. Snyder, *Myths of Empire*, 30.

55. Adamthwaite, *France and the Second World War*, xiii; Carr, *International Relations between the Two World Wars*, 25; Dutailly, "La puissance militaire de la France en 1938," 5; Nobecourt, *Une histoire politique*, 56.

56. Cohen and Gooch, *Military Misfortunes*, 217; Young, "Attaque brusquée," 98.

57. SHAT, 1 N 21, "Procès verbal de la séance du CSG" (December 14, 1932); SHAT, 1 N 35, file 5, CSG, "Note de Gamelin" (March 19, 1935); Goyet, "Evolution de la doctrine d'emploi de l'aviation française," 16; Harvey, "French Concepts of Military Strategy," 66–67.

58. Conquet, *L'énigme des blindés*, 137.

59. Quoted in Alexander, *The Republic in Danger*, 149, also see 46–49.

60. Alexander, *The Republic in Danger*, 255; Buffotot, "La perception du réarmement allemand," 177.

61. Adamthwaite, *France and the Second World War*, 166; Buffotot, "La perception du réarmement," 177; Cohen and Gooch, *Military Misfortunes*, 216–17; Ferré, *Le défaut de l'armure*, 77; Michel, *Le procès de Riom*, 216; Young, "French Military Intelligence and Nazi Germany," 288–89.

62. Cohen and Gooch, *Military Misfortunes*, 210–12; Dutailly, "Faiblesses et potentialités de l'armée de terre," 28; Facon, "Les leçons de la campagne de Pologne," 103–4.

63. Doughty, *The Seeds of Disaster*, 183.

64. Frankenstein, "A propos des aspects financiers," 2–4.

65. Alexander, "The Fall of France," 11.

66. Lee, "Strategy, Arms and the Collapse of France," 65–66.

67. Doughty, *The Seeds of Disaster*, 183.

68. Adamthwaite, *France and the Second World War*, 165.

69. On the nationalization of the aviation industry, see Réquin, *D'une guerre à l'autre*, 248; Armengaud, *Batailles politiques et militaires sur l'Europe*, 24–25; and Langeron, *Misère et grandeur de notre aviation*, 111, 218–20. Others dismiss the importance of the nationalization of the defense industry. See Alexander, *The Republic in Danger*, 113–15; Cot, "The Defeat of the French Air Force," 793; Maroselli, *Le sabotage de notre aviation*, 50, 96, 99–102, 121–22; and Ingraud, *Le chemin de croix de l'aviation française*, 10–11, 25, 130.

70. Hoff, *Les programmes d'armement*, 23. Also see Frankenstein, *Le prix du réarmement français*, 21–23.

71. Frankenstein, "A propos des aspects financiers," 7; LeFranc, *Histoire du front populaire*, 397; Hoff, *Les programmes d'armement*, 154.

72. d'Hoop, "La politique française du réarmement," 4; Gibbs, *Grand Strategy*, vol. 1, *History of the Second World War*, 244; Michel, *Le procès de Riom*, 189, 206.

73. Alexander, "Repercussions of the Breda Variant," 459.

74. Danel, "L'armée de l'air française à l'entrée en guerre"; Stolfi, "Equipment for Victory in France in 1940," 6, 8, 10.

75. Alexander, "Repercussions of the Breda Variant," 461. Also see Doughty, *The Seeds of Disaster*, 183. Cohen and Gooch and Frankenstein argue that Germany had fewer tanks than the French (2,700 vs. 3,500). Cohen and Gooch, *Military Misfortunes*, 201; Frankenstein, *Le prix du réarmement français*, 8. The French emphasized heavy tanks and light reconnaissance vehicles, not the medium-sized tank necessary for offensive armored warfare, but this choice followed their doctrine.

76. Alexander, "Repercussions of the Breda Variant," 461.

77. Cohen and Gooch, *Military Misfortunes*, 201, 206; Michel, *Le procès de Riom*, 264. However, Truelle argues that the French air force was not quantitatively inferior. See Truelle, "La production aéronautique militaire jusqu'en juin 1940."

78. Vaisse, *Sécurité d'abord*, 27–29, 166.

79. Mandelbaum, *The Fate of Nations*, 91.

80. Posen, *The Sources of Military Doctrine*, 105–40. Michael Mandelbaum also argues that France's adoption of a defensive doctrine was due to its relative weakness. Like Posen, Mandelbaum stresses the French desire for British assistance *The Fate of Nations*, 104–5, 121–22.

81. Kirshner, *Currency and Coercion*, chap. 5.

82. Posen, *The Sources of Military Doctrine*, 114.

83. Alexander, *The Republic in Danger*, 236–37; Adamthwaite, "France and the Coming of War," 246–51; Adamthwaite, "Reaction to the Munich Crisis," 172, 191; also see Wolfers, *Britain and France between Two Wars*, 89.

84. Weinberg, *The Foreign Policy of Hitler's Germany*, 57–58, 342–43.

85. Quoted in ibid., 341.

86. Doughty, "The Illusion of Security," 470. Weinberg, *The Foreign Policy of Hitler's Germany*, 85, 315, 341–43.

87. For a detailed account of the French refusal to respond to Soviet requests for a military alliance, see Vaisse, "Les militaires français et l'alliance franco-soviétique"; Doise and Vaisse, *Diplomatie et outil*, 297–98. Also see Buffotot, "The French High Command," 546–56.

88. SHAT, 1 N 20, "Résumé succinct des séances du CSG" (December 14, 1927).

89. Posen, *The Sources of Military Doctrine*, 108. Mandelbaum also stresses the lessons of World War I as a contributory factor. Mandelbaum, *The Fate of Nations*, 63.

90. Mandelbaum, *The Fate of Nations*, 92; Posen, *The Sources of Military Doctrine*, 73–74, 109–10. Adamthwaite also argues that German material superiority determined France's adoption of a defensive doctrine. Adamthwaite, *France and the Second World War*, 8.

91. Martin, "La doctrine française de contre offensive," 340. For an exposition of Pétain's claim that Germany's strength required that France gain time, see Service historique de l'armée de l'air, 1 B 1, "Séance du haut comité militaire" (November 21, 1935).

92. Krauskopf, "French Air Power Policy," 54.

93. Quoted in Tournoux, *Haut commandement*, 334.

94. Mandelbaum, *The Fate of Nations*, 74.

95. Some might argue that France was not a status quo state before World

War I because of the desire to reclaim Alsace-Lorraine. But only after mobilization did the return of this territory become a war aim. Maurice Baumont, *Bulletin de la société d'histoire moderne* (1964): 2, quoted in Mayeur, *La vie politique sous la troisième République*, 234. De Gaulle argues that the revanchist sentiment did not endure after its initial surge immediately following the defeat in 1871. De Gaulle, *La France et son armée*, 203–19.

96. Harvey, "French Concepts of Military Strategy," 119–24; Martin, "La doctrine française"; and Michel, *Le procès de Riom*, 192, 261.

97. Schuker, "France and the Remilitarization of the Rhineland," 299–338; Christienne and Buffotot, "L'armée de l'air française et la crise du 7 mars 1936."

98. Berstein, *La France des années 30*, 164.

99. Coox, "French Military Doctrine," 161; Ferré, *Le défaut de l'armure*, 9, 70. On de Gaulle's memo advocating the creation of a mechanized force, see B. Crozier, *De Gaulle*, 87–90.

100. The French civilians understood that France lacked offensive capabilities. During the remilitarization of the Rhineland in 1936 Gamelin had informed the French Cabinet that no counteraction was possible without extensive mobilization.

Chapter 4

1. Standing or professional armies are composed of volunteer (regular) soldiers serving during peacetime and war; conscript and militia armies are composed of citizen-soldiers who are normally employed in the civilian sector but are liable for military service during a national emergency.

2. The following authors discuss the domestic political origins of the controversy about the length of conscription: Bonnefous, *Histoire politique*, 311; Harvey, "French Concepts of Military Strategy," 41; Monteilhet, *Les institutions militaires*, 221, 235.

3. Classic texts that embody the French Left's political culture about the military include Jaurès, *L'armée nouvelle*; Monteilhet, *Les institutions militaires*; and Nardain, *Vers l'armée de la République*. For a more contemporary statement, see Dabezies, "Milices."

4. Dabezies, "Milices," 1084; Charnay, *Société militaire et suffrage politique*, 148–49. For expressions of the importance of blending the army with the state, see B.A.R., *L'armée nouvelle et le service d'un an*, 80–81; Cabannes, *La nation armée et le Parti socialiste*, 18; Commission militaire du conseil national de la résistance, *Pour une armée nationale*; and Guyot, *Les problèmes de la défense nationale*, 10–11.

5. Léon Blum, "Vers l'armée de métier," *Le populaire*, November 30, 1934.

6. Porch, *The March to the Marne*, 29.

7. Jaurès, "Les officiers et les organisations ouvrières," in *L'armée nouvelle*, vol. 2, 341–75.

8. Cabannes, *La nation armée*, 14–16; On Jaurès's call for premilitary training, see Challener, *Nation in Arms*, 73.

9. Léon Blum, "A bas l'armée de métier!" *Le populaire*, December 1, 1934.

10. Sénéchal, *Droits politiques et liberté d'expression*, 79.

11. Monteilhet, "L'avènement," 33; Vaillant-Couturier, "Obéissance passive et l'armée de métier," *L'humanité*, July 5, 1934, 1.

12. Quoted in Monteilhet, *Les institutions militaires*.

13. Ibid., 166.

14. Quoted in Bonnefous, *Histoire politique*, 311.

15. Casanova, *Nouvelle critique*, June 1959 (from a speech given at the Tenth Party Congress of the French Communist Party, Ivry, June 26–30, 1945).

16. Howorth and Chilton, "Introduction," in *Defence and Dissent in Contemporary France*, 2; Prochasson, "Les grandes dates de l'histoire de la conscription," 67.

17. Monteilhet, *Les institutions militaires*, xxi. On the Left's support for a strong national defense, see MacCearney, *Les lois de recrutement*, 152–304, esp. 304. On the Communist Party and national security, see Racine and Bodin, *Le Parti communiste français*, esp. 90–102. Also note the title of a book by one of the leading military experts in today's French Socialist Party: *Soldat-citoyen*, by Charles Hernu. The Left's participation in the resistance against German occupation and the Vichy regime further reinforced this aspect of its political culture. See, for example, Commission militaire du conseil national de la résistance, *Pour une armée nationale*, esp. 6.

18. Peter Nicols, "Bastille Day Unites Army and Nation," *Times* (London), July 15, 1981.

19. Jaurès, *L'armée nouvelle*; Buffotot, "La politique militaire," 97.

20. On the Left's view of reserves, see Roux, *Gardons le service de deux ans*, 6–7; and Percin, *La guerre*, 7–13.

21. S. Davis, *The French War Machine*, 89–91.

22. On the debate about a unified command, see Cointet, "Gouvernement et haut-commandement," 87–91; Fabry, "La défense nationale," 19–30; Mordacq, *La défense nationale*; Reussner, "La réorganisation du haut-commandement"; Vial, "La défense nationale," 17–18.

23. Blum, "A bas l'armée de métier!" Also see Loge maçonnique, *L'armée cléricale*, 3–4.

24. J. Leferreus, "Naissance et vicissitudes de l'armée nouvelle," *Esprit*, July 1945; Loge maçonnique, *Démocratisation des cadres de l'armée*, 1; Marrane, "Intérêt national," 49; Monteilhet, *Les institutions militaires*, 14. For scholarly discussions, see Katzenbach, "Political Parties and the French Army since Liberation"; and Schumacher, *La politique de sécurité*, 211.

25. Vaillant-Couturier, "Obéissance passive," 1.

26. On the professional army as a threat to democracy, see Cot, *Le procès de la république*, 16; Mysyrowicz, *Anatomie d'une défaite*, 248. Also see a series of articles written by Joseph Paul-Boncour, a leading left-wing politician, in the *Journal* in August 1930. On the militia or reserve forces as compatible with democracy, see Monteilhet, "L'avènement," 8, 17; Monteilhet, *Les institutions militaires*, 121; and Commission militaire du conseil national de la résistance, *Pour une armée nationale*.

27. Monteilhet, "L'avènement," 32; Monteilhet, *Les institutions militaires*, 15–17. For Blum's views, see Conquet, *L'énigme des blindés*.

28. Frankenstein, "A propos des aspects financiers," 8–9.

29. Quoted in Miquel, *La paix de Versailles*, 265.

30. Challener, *Nation in Arms*, 174–76; Debeney, "Armée nationale ou armée de métier?" 250.

31. Marcel Diboux, "Le menace des deux ans: L'état major essaie toujours d'imposer sa doctrine," *Le populaire*, March 7, 1935.

32. "Mobilisons l'opinion publique contre les deux ans: au peuple de mettre en échec les généraux," *Le populaire*, March 3, 1935.

33. "Les deux ans, c'est la guerre," *L'humanité*, March 17, 1935. Also see Cot, "Le service militaire," 77–80.

34. Blum, "A bas l'armée de métier!"

35. Three typical statements of the Right's political culture about the military are Duval, "La crise de notre organisation militaire," 756–96; Lewal, *Contre le service de deux ans*; and Lamy, "L'armée et la démocratie."

36. Lewal, *Contre le service de deux ans*, 46, 51–52, 77; Challener, *Nation in Arms*, 85–87; Croubois, *L'officier français*, 304; Monteilhet, *Les institutions militaires*, 166, 169.

37. Horace de Choiseul, quoted in Monteilhet, *Les institutions militaires*, 166.

38. Gouvion-Saint Cyr, quoted in Sherman, "Le corps des officiers français," 718. On the French system of command that drastically curtailed individual initiative, see Boyer, "De l'aspect social de la profession militaire," 25; Carrias, *La pensée militaire française*, 284–85; Jauffret, "L'officier français," 274; and Kirkland, "Combat Leadership Styles," 62.

39. Carrias, *La pensée militaire française*, 271.

40. Lewal, *Contre le service de deux ans*, 47.

41. Challener, *Nation in Arms*, 76–77.

42. Gibson, "The Maginot Line," 130.

43. De Gaulle to Paul Reynaud, reproduced in Demey, *Paul Reynaud, mon père*, 305.

44. Pertinax [André Géraud], "Le désarmement radical de l'Allemagne est décidé," *L'écho de Paris*, March 11, 1919.

45. Quoted in Miquel, *La paix de Versailles*, 258.

46. On the French revolutionary army, see Bertaud, *La révolution armée*; Bertaud, "Les travaux récents"; and Forrest, *The Soldiers of the French Revolution*.

47. Quoted in Porch, *Army and Revolution*, 3.

48. By 1887 the former war minister, General Boulanger, had become a very popular political figure, and his success aroused fears of a coup d'état. In 1897 the military authorities unjustly accused and convicted Alfred Dreyfus, a Jewish officer on the general staff, of espionage for the Germans. The army's attempt to protect an anti-Semitic and antirepublican officer corps revealed the army's duplicity and incompetence and convinced many on the Left that the republican constitution was in danger.

49. Quoted in Feller, *Le dossier*, 67. The Left won the 1914 elections but the war broke out before the length of service could be modified.

50. A nation-in-arms, or mass army, is made up of short-term military conscripts (in contrast to a professional army, which is generally smaller and made

up of long-serving professional soldiers). On the universal acceptance after World War I of the principle of military service, see Challener, *Nation in Arms*, 166; Dabezies, "Milices," 1080; MacCearney, *Les lois de recrutement*, 165; and Monteilhet, *Les institutions militaires*, 399–401, 408. On the delegitimization of the professional army, see Gibson, "The Maginot Line," 132.

51. Jean Fabry, "Où va notre armée?" *Revue de Paris*, September 15, 1925, 250–51.

52. For example, see Vidéo [pseud.], *L'armée et la politique*.

53. On the Right's call for longer service, see "La loi des cadres devant la chambre," *Le temps*, December 5, 1912; "Le statut militaire devant le parlement," *Le temps*, March 14, 1935; Doutremont, "La loi de recrutement," *L'écho de Paris*, October 8, 1920; and Lewal, *Contre le service de deux ans*, 49–51. On the politicization of the question of reserves, see Challener, *Nation in Arms*, 49.

54. For discussions of recruitment legislation during the 1920s, see Bonnefous, *Histoire politique*, 309–13; Challener, *Nation in Arms*, 147–78; Doughty, *The Seeds of Disaster*, 15–21; S. Davis, *The French War Machine*, 85–94; Feller, *Le dossier*, 175–78; Hughes, *To the Maginot Line*, 112–16, 123–41; and Weigold, "National Security versus Collective Security," 10.

55. For a discussion of the 1928 military legislation as a compromise, see Davis, *The French War Machine*, 72; Hughes, *To the Maginot Line*, 174; MacCearney, *Les lois de recrutement*, 13, 168; and Weigold, "National Security versus Collective Security," 10.

56. Schumacher argues that such compromises were typical of the Radical Party's military policy during the interwar period. Schumacher, *La politique de sécurité*, 209.

57. Davis, *The French War Machine*, 96; Gibson, "The Maginot Line," 134.

58. Hughes, *To the Maginot Line*, 115; Tournoux, *Haut commandement*, 178. For a chronology of the army's repeated demands for the fulfillment of the prior conditions, see Service historique de l'armée de terre (SHAT), 1 N 27, "Avis motive du CSG sur la législation pour l'organisation générale de l'armée" (April 3, 1925).

59. SHAT, 1 N 20, "Résumé succinct des séances du CSG" (April 10, 1925). Also see SHAT, 1 N 20, "Procès verbaux des réunions du CSG" (March 23, 1920, March 31, 1920, and December 13, 1920); SHAT, 1 N 20, "Résumé succinct des séances du CSG" (March 23, 1922, January 15, 1926, and November 8, 1926).

60. *Journal officiel de la République française: débats parlementaires*, Chambre des députés (March 2, 1922), 593; "Le débat militaire," *Le temps*, March 19, 1927, 1.

61. de Jouvenel, "Le service militaire obligatoire." The Right's insistence on the maintenance of a large professional core was expensive. Each additional 1,000 men consumed 10 million francs per year—three times the cost of an equal number of conscripts and equal to the cost of 50 tanks. Lee, "Strategy, Arms, and the Collapse of France," 57.

62. Kirkland, "Professionalism and the Defense of Corporate Interests"; Weigold, "National Security versus Collective Security," 87, 137.

63. Bonnefous, *Histoire politique*, 311; Challener, *Nation in Arms*, 159–62; Gibson, "The Maginot Line," 136.

64. Fabry, "Où va notre armée?" 243–58, esp. 247. Also see Fabry's comments during the debate in the Chamber of Deputies in 1922, *Journal officiel, débats parlementaires*, Chambre des députés, March 2, 1922.

65. SHAT, 1 N 27, file 3, "Lettre de Général Weygand sur la législation sur la organisation de l'armée" (March 5, 1925); SHAT, 1 N 21, comments of Debeney in "Procès verbaux des séances du CSG" (October 12, 1927); SHAT, 1 N 27, file 3, "Rapports de présentation du CSG, lettre de Franchet d'Esperey" (March 6, 1925); SHAT, 1 N 27, file 3, "Rapports de présentation du CSG, lettre de Général Gouraud" (March 4, 1925); SHAT, 1 N 27, file 3, "Rapports de présentation du CSG, lettre de Général Mangin" (March 4, 1925); SHAT, 5 N 581, file lb, Gen. Conquet; SHAT, 1 N 27, file 3, "Lettre de Général Degoutte" (March 5, 1925).

66. Gen. de Castelnau, "Les necessités de la défense nationale exigent le service de deux ans," *L'écho de Paris*, January 11, 1935.

67. Vidéo, *L'armée et la politique*, 52, 73; de Gaulle, *Vers l'armée de métier*, 47.

68. Monteilhet, *Les institutions militaires*, 384–85; Percin, *La guerre*, 14; Weigold, "National Security versus Collective Security," 7.

69. Monteilhet, *Les institutions militaires*, 385.

70. Bonnefous, *Histoire politique*, 427; Doise and Vaisse, *Diplomatie et outil*, 278; Tournoux, *Haut commandement*, 125.

71. On the "dogma" of the inviolability of the frontier, see the interchange between Pétain and Foch and Joffre in SHAT, 1 N 20, "Procès verbaux du CSG" (May 22, 1922). Also see Weygand, *Histoire de l'armée française*, 387.

72. Howard, *The Franco-Prussian War*, 8–9.

73. Monteilhet, *Les institutions militaires*, 28, 235.

74. To compare the British and French understandings of the relationship between conscription and democracy, see Dabezies, "Milices," 1083; de Jouvenel, "La service militaire obligatoire," 8; Dennery, "Democracy and the French Army," 231; Henry Fontanier, "Armée de métier ou nation armée," *Le peuple*, October 15, 1928; Jauffret, "L'image de l'armée britannique," 457; Miquel, *La paix de Versailles*, 277; Pertinax, "Le désarmement radical de l'Allemagne."

75. Beckett, "The Amateur Military Tradition," 408–19; Kennedy, "Great Britain before 1914," 194; Adams and Poirier, *The Conscription Controversy*, 8–42; Bond, *War and Society in Europe*, 74.

76. Chambers, *To Raise an Army*, 74–120.

77. Adams, "The American Democratic Ideal," 230.

78. Quoted in Chambers, *To Raise an Army*, 95.

79. Hacker, "The United States Army as a National Police Force," 259.

80. Quoted in Skowronek, *Building a New American State*, 105.

81. Chambers, "Conscripting for Colossus," 277–81.

82. Quoted in Chambers, *To Raise an Army*, 111.

83. "Pinchot Appeals to Labor: Compulsory Military Service, He Says, Would Destroy Democracy," *New York Times*, March 13, 1917, 4:2.

84. "Universal Training vs. Preparedness," *New Republic*, March 17, 1920, 70–72.

85. For a discussion of French military expenditures and the balance of forces in 1939, see Chapter 3.

86. On Estienne's ideas see Estienne, "Les forces matérielles"; and Ramspacher, *Le général Estienne.*

87. Bond and Alexander, "Liddell Hart and de Gaulle," 603–4; Clarke, "Military Technology," 56–60, 77; Coox, "French Military Doctrine," 92, 185–91; Doughty, *The Seeds of Disaster*, 138. Also see Chapter 3.

88. On Morocco, see Clarke, "Military Technology," 73. On French military exercises, see Conquet, *L'énigme des blindés*, 62; and Coox, "French Military Doctrine," 133, 140.

89. Typical expositions of the lessons derived from the Spanish civil war include Duval, *Les leçons de la guerre d'Espagne*; and Niessel, "Chars, anti-chars et motorisation dans la guerre d'Espagne." Also see Astorkia, "Les leçons aériennes de la guerre d'Espagne," 160–61; Doughty, *The Seeds of Disaster*, 89; Mysyrowicz, *Anatomie d'une défaite*, 141; and Tournoux, *Haut commandement*, 286.

90. Alexander, *The Republic in Danger*, 185.

91. Ibid.

92. See Clarke, "Military Technology," 176–78. Doughty, *The Seeds of Disaster*, 164; Michel, *Le Procès de Riom*, 220. On the lack of parliamentarian control of doctrine, see Dutailly, *Les problèmes de l'armée de terre française*, 139; and Hughes, *To the Maginot Line*, 106–11.

93. Bankwitz, "Maxime Weygand," 173.

94. Hughes, *To the Maginot Line*, 130; Wolfers, *Britain and France between Two Wars*, 95–97. On Maginot's support for offensive capabilities, see Bonnefous, *Histoire politique*, 321.

95. Clarke, "Military Technology," 176–78, 192; Doughty, *The Seeds of Disaster*, 164.

96. *Journal officiel, débats parlementaires*, Chambre des députés, (March 28, 1922), 1181.

97. Although not grounding their argument in the French army's culture, many scholars argue that the reduction in the term of conscription was pivotal to the adoption of a defensive doctrine. Challener, *Nation in Arms*, 218; Doughty, *The Seeds of Disaster*, 33, 52; Feller, *Le dossier*, 64–65; Mandelbaum, *The Fate of Nations*, 63; Weigold, "National Security versus Collective Security," 54.

98. Debeney, "Armée nationale ou armée de métier?" 214.

99. de Castelnau, "Les necessités de la défense nationale exigent le service de deux ans," *L'écho de Paris*, January 11, 1935. Also see SHAT, 1 N 42, file 2, Etat-major Weygand, CSG, "Rapport sur l'état de l'armée" (May 1932); SHAT, 1 N 27, file 3, "Rapports de présentation du CSG, lettre de Maréchal Fayolle au ministre de la guerre, La réduction de la service à un an, et la réorganisation de la défense" (March 9, 1925).

100. Mordacq, *La défense nationale*, 2.

101. de Gaulle, "Vers l'armée de métier," 294; de Gaulle, *Vers l'armée de métier*, 59.

102. France, Ministère des affaires étrangères, *Documents diplomatiques* 1, no. 1, 568.

103. Lewal, *Le danger des milices*, 231.

104. For the argument that modern technology does not require professional soldiers, see Cohen, *Citizens and Soldiers*, 63–66.

105. Duval, "La crise de notre organisation militaire," 575.

106. Debeney, *Sur la sécurité militaire de la France*, esp. 22.

107. Reynaud, *Le problème militaire français*, 45. Also see Vidéo, *L'armée et la politique*, 45.

108. Capt. G, "L'armée nouvelle et le service d'un an," 594. For other examples of French officers arguing that the one-year term of conscription had reduced the army to marginal value, see Souchon, *Feue l'armée française*. Also see SHAT, 1 N 27, file 3, "Rapports de présentation du CSG, lettre de Général Weygand au ministre de la guerre sur les projets pour l'organisation de l'armée" (March 5, 1925); SHAT, 1 N 27, file 3, "Rapports de présentation du CSG, lettre de Général Degoutte au ministre de la guerre" (March 5, 1925); SHAT, 1 N 27, file 3, "Rapports de présentation du CSG, lettre de Maréchal Joffre au ministre de la guerre" (March 1928).

109. SHAT, 1 N 42, file 2, Etat-major Weygand, CSG, "Rapport sur l'état de l'armée" (May 1932).

110. Gunsburg, "Coupable où non?" 149. Many other writers make this connection between conscripts and reduced maneuverability. See Barrows, "L'influence des conquêtes," 136; and Nachin, *Charles de Gaulle*, 66.

111. SHAT, 1 N 21, "Procès verbal de la séance du CSG" (December 14, 1927).

112. Targe, *La garde de nos frontières*, 87, 95–96.

113. SHAT, 1 N 21, "Procès verbal de la séance du CSG" (December 14, 1927).

114. Quoted in Adamthwaite, *France and the Coming of the Second World War*, 228. For other examples of French officers arguing that a short term of conscription precluded an offensive doctrine, see Targe, *La garde de nos frontières*, 87–88, 95–96; also see a report by the chief of staff quoted in Pierre Haxo, "Avant la loi des deux ans: Que vaut l'armée française," *Le populaire*, March 2, 1935. Monteilhet and Blum also discuss this conception within the army. Monteilhet, *Les institutions militaires*, 269–71; Léon Blum, "Soldats de métier et armée de métier," *Le populaire*, November 28, 1934. For an example of this belief before World War I, see SHAT, 1 N 23, file 4, "Modification au régime de recrutement: note de présentation au CSG" (1913). On the association between professional soldiers and offensive operations, see Conquet, *Autour de Maréchal Pétain*, 40.

115. Quoted in Miquel, *La paix de Versailles*, 258. Also see France, Ministère des affaires étrangères, *Documents diplomatiques* 1, no. 1, 569.

116. Quoted in Boggs, *Attempts to Define and Limit "Aggressive" Armament*, 44.

117. "Rapport établi par le ministre de la guerre, chef de la délégation française à la conference du désarmement" (October 14, 1932), France, Ministère des affaires étrangères, *Documents Diplomatiques*, 441; Hughes, *To the Maginot Line*, 236.

118. Some analysts argue that one of the fundamental reasons for the Maginot Line was the reduction in the term of conscription. See Kraehe, "The Motives behind the Maginot Line," 114; and Hughes, *To the Maginot Line*, 204.

119. Quoted in Doughty, *The Seeds of Disaster*, 34.

120. Quoted in Dutailly, *Les problèmes de l'armée de terre française*, 228–30. Also see Doughty, *The Seeds of Disaster*, 31, 182.

121. Clarke, "Military Technology," 108.

122. Hughes, *To the Maginot Line*, 205.

123. Quoted in Howard, *The Franco-Prussian War*, 32.

124. Bond, *War and Society in Europe*, 17.

125. On the French and German use of reserves before 1870, see Howard, *The Franco-Prussian War*, 12–22, 50.

126. Quoted in Feller, *Le dossier*, 65. In his memoirs, Joffre recognizes his mistake. Joffre, *Mémoires de Maréchal Joffre*, vol. 1, 135.

127. Sorb, *La doctrine de défense nationale*, 148–49.

128. Setzen, "The Doctrine of the Offensive," 182.

129. Both statements are quoted in Cole, "Forward with the Bayonet," 35, 42 (emphasis added).

130. Setzen, "The Doctrine of the Offensive," 113.

131. Cole, "Forward with the Bayonet," 41.

132. Setzen, "The Doctrine of the Offensive," 151.

133. On the size of German corps, see McEntree, *Military History of the World War*, 33; Neame, "Appendices I–II," in *German Strategy in the Great War*, 123–27. On the French army's use and opinion of reserves in and before World War I, see Andrew, "France and the German Menace," 128, 142; Monteilhet, *Les institutions militaires*, 346, 393–94; Croubois, *L'officier français*, 306; Pugens, "La guerre de 1870," 5; Tanenbaum, "French Estimates of Germany's Operational War Plans," 151–71; and Weigold, "National Security versus Collective Security," 47–54.

134. Quoted in Sanders, *No Other Law*, 25.

135. After World War I, Paul-Boncour explained that "France's professional army had been beaten by an army consisting of active regiments half filled by reservists, and the Landwehr and Landsturm which were composed exclusively of reservists." *Journal officiel, chambre des députés*, 1181.

136. SHAT, 1 N 22, "Examen des répercussions sur les effectifs à l'armée pouvant résulter du projet de lois, modifiant la loi du 14 juillet, 1932, apportée au Parliament par M. Dernier, député," CSG (December 18, 1933).

137. Duval, "La crise de notre organisation militaire," 775–92.

138. Bennett, *German Rearmament and the West*, 17.

139. Boggs, *Attempts to Define and Limit "Aggressive" Armament*, 45.

140. Levite, *Offense and Defense in Israeli Military Doctrine*.

141. Rothenberg, *The Anatomy of the Israeli Army*, 83; Rolbant, *The Israeli Soldier*, 81–83.

142. Rolbant, *The Israeli Soldier*, 104.

143. Sanders, *No Other Law*. For a discussion of the training of reserves in the French army, see Kiesling, *Arming against Hitler*, 85–115.

144. On de Gaulle's ideas, see de Gaulle, *Vers l'armée de métier*; de Gaulle, "Vers l'armée de métier"; Harvey, "French Concepts of Military Strategy," 187–98; Mysyrowicz, *Anatomie d'une défaite*, 202–13; and Reynaud, *Le problème militaire français*.

145. Debeney, "Encore l'armée de métier," 285–90; Weygand, *La France est-*

elle défendue?, 23; Weygand, "L'unité de l'armée," 18. Also see Hughes, *To the Maginot Line*, 210; Mysyrowicz, *Anatomie d'une défaite*, 262; and Schumacher, *La politique de sécurité*, 211.

146. The following authors argue that de Gaulle lost his campaign primarily because of his call for a professional army: Bond and Alexander, "Liddell Hart and de Gaulle"; Challener, *Nation in Arms*, 251; Christienne, "Le haut commandement," 410; Conquet, *L'énigme des blindés*, 143–48; Doughty, *The Seeds of Disaster*, 186; Feller, *Le dossier*, 218; Girardet, "Opinion et politique," 25; Murray, *The Change in the European Balance of Power*, 102; Nachin, *Charles de Gaulle*, 82–84; and Tournoux, *Haut commandement*, 195.

147. Lefranc and Moulin, "Dialogue sur l'armée," 13.

148. Quoted in Feller, *Le dossier*, 218; For other discussions of the Left's reception to de Gaulle's ideas, see B. Crozier, *De Gaulle*, 63; Duroselle, *La décadence*, 264; and Schumacher, *La politique de sécurité*, 211.

149. Quoted in Hoff, *Les programmes d'armements*, 157. Also see Conquet, *L'énigme des blindés*, 155; and Reynaud, *Mémoires*, 144–45.

150. Conquet, *L'énigme des blindés*, 62; Hoff, *Les programmes d'armement*, 141; Mysyrowicz, *Anatomie d'une défaite*, 237–38, 248; Schumacher, *La politique de sécurité*, 213; and SHAT, 5 N 581, "Journal de marché, Ministère de la guerre, Jean Fabry" (December 26, 1935).

151. Quoted in Paillat, *Dossiers secrets de la France contemporaine*, vol. 3, 205. Also see de Gaulle, *France et son armée*, 195.

152. Quoted in Alexander, *The Republic in Danger*, 39.

153. Clarke, "Military Technology," 60; Mysyrowicz, *Anatomie d'une défaite*, 50.

154. On the domestic politics of the Third Republic generally, see Bonnefous, *Histoire politique*; Goguel, *La politique des partis*; and Mayeur, *La vie politique*. On the Right, see Rémond, *La droite en France*; and Weber, *Action Française*. On the Left, see Berstein, *Histoire du Parti radical*; Marmour, *The French Radical Party in the 1930s*; Lefranc, *Le mouvement socialiste*; and Brunet, *Histoire du Parti communiste français*.

155. On the Popular Front, see Lefranc, *Histoire du front populaire*; and Lacouture, *Léon Blum*.

156. Alexander, "Soldiers and Socialists," 62.

157. For example, the CSG met five times in 1933, twice in 1934, four times in 1935, twice in 1936, once in 1937, and once in 1938 (compiled from index of CSG at SHAT). Also see Adamthwaite, *France and the Coming of the Second World War*, 170–71; Bankwitz, *Maxime Weygand*; and Hoff, *Les programmes d'armement*, 113–16.

158. Adamthwaite, *France and the Coming of the Second World War*, 168.

159. Benoist-Méchin, *1905–1940*, vol. 1 of *A l'épreuve du temps, 1905–1940*, 295. For a discussion of the growing split between the French army and state in the 1930s, see Bankwitz, "Maxime Weygand," 161–64.

160. Adamthwaite, *France and the Coming of the Second World War*, 168; Dutailly, *Les problèmes de l'armée de terre française*, 277.

161. Clayton, *France, Soldiers, and Africa*, 38.

162. Hughes, *To the Maginot Line*, 35–38; Nobecourt, *Une histoire politique de l'armée*, 71.

163. See for example SHAT, 5 N 601, file 5, "Note de Directeur de Contentieux et de la Justice Militaire: au point de vue de la discipline dans l'armée, la campagne de propagande antimilitariste menée par la presse communiste, poursuites contre les journaux 1924–27"; SHAT, 5 N 601, file 4, "Liste des publications interdites au militaires: file 5, Poursuites contre les journaux antimilitaristes, presse communiste (1924–27)"; SHAT, 5 N 601, "Circulaires relative à la repression de la propagande révolutionnaire, 1921–1939." The Communist Party tried to penetrate the army, publishing the newspaper *Le conscript* to encourage insubordination among the draftees. The words of leading Communist figures heightened the army's anxiety: "We insist that our members penetrate the army in order to accomplish the needs of the working class, which is to break up this army. . . . Our party is the invisible enemy of national defense." Quoted in Bourdrel, *La Cagoule*, 179–80.

164. Bourdrel, *La Cagoule*, 190–93; Dutailly, *Les problèmes de l'armée de terre française*, 279; Feller, *Le dossier*, 241–42; Paillat, *Dossiers secrets*, vol. 3, 341–42. The archives concerning these organizations were completely destroyed upon their discovery in 1938. Most knowledge of these secret networks is based on the memoirs of their founder, General Georges Loustaunau-Lacau.

165. Quoted in Tournoux, *Haut commandement*, 253.

166. SHAT, 7 N 4034, "Analyses des rapport sur le morale et l'état d'esprit dans l'armée, lettre de ministre de la guerre, Général Louis Maurin" (April 1937).

167. Laure, *Pétain*, 381–82.

168. The strength of pacifist sentiment declined from 1936 to 1938 and dropped precipitously after Munich. Vaisse, "Le pacifisme français," 38–49.

169. Mysyrowicz, *Anatomie d'une défaite*, 279–302.

170. Quoted in Murray, *The Change in the European Balance of Power*, 104; Weigold, "National Security versus Collective Security," 248.

171. Mysyrowicz, *Anatomie d'une défaite*, 303; Nachin, *Charles de Gaulle*, 83.

172. Kirkland, "Anti-Military Group Fantasies," 15.

173. Kirkland, "Governmental Policy and Combat Effectiveness," 175–91.

174. Coox, "French Military Doctrine," 153. For a reappraisal of the rigidity of French army thought see Kiesling, *Arming against Hitler*, 125–30.

175. Snyder, *The Ideology of the Offensive*, 41–106; also see Ralston, *The Army of the Republic*, 203–315.

Chapter 5

1. Reid, "Introduction," in Mackenzie and Reid, eds., *The British Army*, 7–11.

2. Note the distinction between mechanization and motorization. Both are innovations, the first doctrinal and the other technological. Mechanization does not mean transportation alone; mechanized units fight while in their vehicles. Motorization is simply a way to transport troops quickly from one location to another; the troops still fight on foot. The technology was not controversial and spread rapidly within the British army, while the doctrine met insurmountable opposition. Hacker, "The Military and the Machine," 15–19.

3. War Office, *Infantry Training*, vol. 1, *Training*, 12 (emphasis in original). Also see War Office, *Field Service Regulations*, vol. 2, *Operations*, 161.

4. War Office, *Infantry Training*, vol. 2, *War*, 13, 32–39.

5. War Office, *Infantry Training: Training and War*, 122.

6. War Office, *Cavalry Training, Mechanized*, pamphlet no. 1, *Armoured Cars*, 1.

7. Director of staff duties quoted in Macksey, *Armoured Crusader*, 131. War Office, *Mobile Division*, 2.

8. On air control in the RAF, see Hyde, *British Air Policy*, 90, 148; and Jackson, *Before the Storm*, 31. On the RAF and strategic bombing, see Frankland, *The Bombing Offensive*, 39–47; Jones, *The Origins of Strategic Bombing*; and M. Smith, *British Air Strategy*. On the RAF and air defense, see R. Clark, *Tizard*; Ferte, *The Fated Sky*; Price, *Blitz on Britain*; Wood and Dempster, *The Narrow Margin*; and Wykeham, *Fighter Command*.

9. Kupchan, *The Vulnerability of Empire*, 105–84; Friedberg, *The Weary Titan*.

10. Bond, *British Military Policy*, 10–17, 73–74, 82; Dennis, *Decision by Default*, 14; Gibbs, *Grand Strategy*, vol. 1, *History of the Second World War*, 827; Howard, *The Continental Commitment*, 105.

11. Warren Fisher quoted in Wark, *The Ultimate Enemy*, 17–18. Chamberlain quoted in Charmley, *Chamberlain and the Lost Peace*, 24. The War Office disagreed about aspects of German army doctrine, but they knew that the German army would fight a quick war of movement. Hyde, *British Air Policy*, 363–64; Wark, *The Ultimate Enemy*, 81, 93–99, 193. Baldwin quoted in Gibbs, *Grand Strategy*, vol. 1, 107.

12. Posen, *The Sources of Military Doctrine*, 142.

13. Many scholars argue that the lack of a continental commitment was an important factor in the British army's failure to mechanize. See, for example, Bond, *British Military Policy*, 8, 187; Carver, *The Apostles of Mobility*, 52; Larson, *The British Army*, 124; Postan, Postan, and Scott, *Design and Development of Weapons*, 306, 309–11; Willcocks, "Air Mobility and the Armoured Experience," 119; and Winton, *To Change an Army*, 229–31.

14. Bond, *British Military Policy*, 24.

15. Dennis, *Decision by Default*, 81–99.

16. Quoted in Feiling, *The Life of Neville Chamberlain*, 314.

17. Bond, *British Military Policy*, 257–61; Dennis, *Decision by Default*, 64–65, 115–21; Dilks, "The Unnecessary War?" 122; Gibbs, "British Strategic Doctrine," 209.

18. Quoted in Howard, *The Continental Commitment*, 116.

19. Bond, *British Military Policy*, 299–301.

20. Bird, "A Note on British National Strategy," 244; Kennedy, *The Realities behind Diplomacy*, 129.

21. M. Smith, *British Air Strategy*, 84.

22. Quoted in Cairns, "A Nation of Shopkeepers," 728.

23. Chamberlain quoted in Gibbs, *Grand Strategy*, vol. 1, 37. Hankey quoted in Wark, *The Ultimate Enemy*, 191, also see 193. Also see Bond, *British Military Policy*, 196; and Gibbs, *Grand Strategy*, vol. 1, 113.

24. General Staff quoted in Gibbs, *Grand Strategy*, vol. 1, 41. Also see Dilks, "The Unnecessary War?" 103.

25. Liddell Hart, *Memoirs*, vol. 1 , 264. For example, see *Army Quarterly* 32 (April 1936); 27 (April 1934); and 33 (January 1937).

26. Pownall quoted in Dunbabin, "The British Military Establishment," 188 (emphasis in original). Chiefs of staff quoted in Bond, *British Military Policy*, 214. See also Bond, *Chief of Staff*, vol. 1, *1933–40*, 127; Charmley, *Duff Cooper*, 99; Winton, *To Change an Army*, 199; Douglas, *In the Year of Munich*, 102.

27. The Battle of Passchendaele symbolized the horror of trench warfare in World War I; British and Allied forces suffered 300,000 casualties, and the German army used mustard gas for the first time. Bond, *British Military Policy*, 209, 216–17; Bond and Alexander, "Liddell Hart and de Gaulle," 611.

28. On DRC discussions about a continental commitment, see Bond, *British Military Policy*, 194–255; Charmley, *Duff-Cooper*, 86–87, 97–99; Dennis, *Decision by Default*, 35–99; Gibbs, *Grand Strategy*, vol. 1, 110–13, 208–9, 254–66; Howard, *The Continental Commitment*, 105–17; Post, "Mad Dogs and Englishmen," 333–37; and Shay, *British Rearmament*, 23–189.

29. On Chamberlain and a continental commitment, see Bond, *British Military Policy*, 205–6; Bond, *Chief of Staff*, 126–28; Dennis, *Decision by Default*, 39–44, 81–82; and Shay, *British Rearmament*, 35–39, 88.

30. Bond, "The Late Victorian Army," 199; Ehrman, *Cabinet Government and War*, 37; Kennedy, *The Realities behind Diplomacy*, 132; and Spiers, *The Army and Society*, 268–69.

31. Barnett, *Britain and Her Army*, 363, 371, 423; Kennedy, *The Realities behind Diplomacy*, 131.

32. Barnett, *Britain and Her Army*, 419.

33. Although Britain's relative position worsened during the interwar period, Britain was also relatively weak before World War I. British economic power had peaked in 1865 and declined in the decades preceding World War I. Kennedy, *The Realities behind Diplomacy*, 21–22.

34. Posen, *The Sources of Military Doctrine*, 175.

35. In addition, the celebrated switch from bombers to fighters in 1937 may not be as fundamental as many analysts imply. Robert W. Krauskopf explains that "ultimately the greatest emphasis was still placed on the offensive arm, Bomber Command, which by March 1942 was to have not only 1,360 first-line aircraft, but behind this fully 300% reserves." Krauskopf, "French Air Power Policy," 338.

36. Howard, *The Continental Commitment*, 81–84; Powers, "The Development of British Air Defense," 269.

37. Wark, *The Ultimate Enemy*, 39–56.

38. Bond, *British Military Policy*, 195–213, esp. 205; Dennis, *Decision by Default*, 35–62; Gibbs, "British Strategic Doctrine," 105–16, and esp. 203; Hyde, *British Air Policy*, 364; Post, "Mad Dogs and Englishmen," 333–37; Wark, *The Ultimate Enemy*, 31.

39. See Fridenson and Lecuir, *La France et la Grande-Bretagne*, 24; Kennedy, *The Realities behind Diplomacy*, 274; and Powers, "The Development of British

Air Defense," 274. Baldwin quoted in Wark, *The Ultimate Enemy*, 27–28 (emphasis in original).

40. See Taylor, *English History*, 392. Tizard quoted in R. Clark, *Tizard*, 168.

41. Hyde, *British Air Policy*, 338–41.

42. R. Clark, *Tizard*, 155.

43. Quoted in Hyde, *British Air Policy*, 406–7.

44. Rosen, *Winning the Next War*, 14–18.

45. Collier, *Leader of the Few*, 22; Hyde, *British Air Policy*, 329; Wright, *Dowding*, 56.

46. Quoted in Wright, *Dowding*, 53; Also see Postan, Postan, and Scott, *Design and Development of Weapons*; Wykeham, *Fighter Command*, 62.

47. Rosen, *Winning the Next War*, 14–15.

48. On the development of radar, see Burns and Stalker, *The Management of Innovation*, 37–42; R. Clark, *Tizard*, 106–31, 155–56; Hartcup, *The Challenge of War*, 93–99; Watson-Watt, *Three Steps to Victory*; Wood and Dempster, *The Narrow Margin*, 55–57; and Wykeham, *Fighter Command*, 36–41.

49. R. Clark, *Tizard*, 168; Frankland, *The Bombing Offensive*, 45; Wykeham, *Fighter Command*, 41.

50. Rosen, *Winning the Next War*, 15.

51. Trenchard quoted in Hyde, *British Air Policy*, 496. See also Powers, "The Development of British Air Defense," 281.

52. Chaired by Sir Eric Geddes, the Committee on National Expenditure of 1921–22 established the precedent of low military expenditures for the next decade. Larson, *The British Army*, 34. Also see Bond, *British Military Policy*, 24–25, 30–33; Dennis, *Decision by Default*, 12; Gibbs, "British Strategic Doctrine," 194; Kennedy, *The Realities behind Diplomacy*, 231; and Silverman, "The Ten Year Rule."

53. Murray, *The Change in the European Balance of Power*, 54.

54. Shay, *British Rearmament*, 79.

55. Hankey quoted in Douglas, *In the Year of Munich*, 80. On rearmament, see Gibbs, *Grand Strategy*; Shay, *British Rearmament*. On the priorities among the services, see Gibbs, *Grand Strategy*, vol. 1, 103, 127; Kennedy, *The Realities behind Diplomacy*, 232; M. Smith, *British Air Strategy*, 132–35; and Wark, *The Ultimate Enemy*, 40.

56. Macksey, *A History of the Royal Armoured Corps*, 14–39; Bond, *British Military Policy*, 128, 134–38; Hacker, "The Military and the Machine," 31–32; Luvass, *The Education of an Army*, 331–424; Ogorkiewicz, *Armour*, 57–59.

57. On Liddell Hart, see Bond and Alexander, "Liddell Hart and de Gaulle," 598–623; Howard, "The Liddell Hart Memoirs"; Pile, "Liddell Hart and the British Army"; Mearsheimer, *Liddell Hart and the Weight of History*.

58. Broad, "A Mechanized Formation"; Carver, *The Apostles of Mobility*; Larson, *The British Army*, 72–82.

59. Murray, *The Change in the European Balance of Power*, 90.

60. Bond, *British Military Policy*, 53.

61. Winton, *To Change an Army*, 79.

62. Macksey, *Armoured Crusader*, 141–47.

63. Bond, *British Military Policy*, 181–87; Macksey, *Armoured Crusader*, 135, 141–47, 152–53, 178.

64. Hacker, "The Military and the Machine," 61; Liddell Hart, *Memoirs*, vol. 1, 116.

65. Liddell Hart's article "An Army Mystery—Is There a Mechanical Force?" is quoted in Winton, *To Change an Army*, 77–78.

66. Bond, *British Military Policy*, 150; Hacker, "The Military and the Machine," 44.

67. Macksey, *Armoured Crusader*, 111–12.

68. Macksey, *A History of the Royal Armoured Corps*, 55.

69. Alexander, *The Republic in Danger*, 202, 252–53, 266.

70. Both quotations are from Gibbs, *Grand Strategy*, vol. 1, 62.

71. Bialer, *The Shadow of the Bomber*, 68.

72. Bond, *Liddell Hart*, 67; Bond and Murray, "The British Armed Forces"; Howard, *The Continental Commitment*, 105–6; Wark, *The Ultimate Enemy*, 30. Also see Bialer, *The Shadow of the Bomber*, 54–68.

73. Quoted in Howard, *The Continental Commitment*, 106.

74. Quoted in Wark, *The Ultimate Enemy*, 28–29. For a discussion of the RAF's reluctance to accept the Foreign Office's preferred pace of rearmament, see Gibbs, *Grand Strategy*, vol. 1, 108; Slessor, *The Central Blue*, 169–72; M. Smith, *British Air Strategy*, 127; and Wark, *The Ultimate Enemy*, 33–34.

75. Wark, *The Ultimate Enemy*, 28–31, 192.

76. Bond, *British Military Policy*, 93; Wark, *The Ultimate Enemy*, 87–89.

77. Bialer, *The Shadow of the Bomber*, 56. Also see Wark, *The Ultimate Enemy*, 37–51, 77.

78. Quoted in M. Smith, "The Royal Air Force," 162.

79. Ellington quoted in Watt, "British Intelligence and the Coming of the Second World War," 256, see also 258.

80. Posen, *The Sources of Military Doctrine*, 159–63.

81. Lloyd George quoted in Powers, "The Development of British Air Defense," 241. On the organizational development of the RAF, see Hyde, *British Air Policy*, 25, 83; Powers, *Strategy without Slide-rule*; Powers, "The Development of British Air Defense," 54–57, 89, 111, 148, 234–41; and Wykeham, *Fighter Command*, 25.

82. Hyde, *British Air Policy*, 100.

83. Bialer, *The Shadow of the Bomber*, 57, 128–33. Also see Price, *Blitz on Britain*, 12, 21–22; Wark, *The Ultimate Enemy*, 36–55.

84. Frankland, *The Bombing Offensive*, 56.

85. Bond and Murray, "The British Armed Forces," 113.

86. Fridenson and Lecuir, *La France et la Grande-Bretagne*; Watt, *Too Serious a Business*, 76.

87. See Howard, *The Continental Commitment*, 111; and R. Clark, *Tizard*, 161.

88. Frankland, *The Bombing Offensive*, 36; Powers, "The Development of British Air Defense," 241; M. Smith, *British Air Strategy*, 21.

89. P. Smith, "The Role of Doctrine," 403–10.

90. SHAA, 1 B 1 (March 16, 1933).

91. For the army's position, see Christienne, "La résistance au changement," 84–86; Langeron, *Misère et grandeur*, 21; SHAA, 1 B 1, Le ministre de la guerre (March 17, 1933); SHAA, 1 B 2, General Georges, "Note sur le Plan II de l'ar-

mée de l'air," CSG (November 24, 1936). For Gamelin's position on strategic bombing, see SHAA, 1 B l, "Note relative au projets de réorganisation des forces aériennes, point de vue du Général Gamelin" (March 25, 1933). However, Pétain supported strategic bombing. See SHAA, 1 B l, "Note au sujet des forces aériennes de cooperation de l'armée de terre," Etat-major de l'armée (January 8, 1937).

92. For a detailed exposition of the army and air force positions, see SHAA, 1 B l, "Questions soulevées par le ministre de l'air" (March 19, 1933). Also see SHAA, 1 B l, "Note pour M. le ministre de l'air, Etude d'une lettre no. 1061 S" (March 16, 1933); SHAA, 1 B 1, "Projet de loi de création de l'armée de l'air, exposé des motifs" (January 11, 1929). On interservice rivalry, see Buffotot, "La doctrine aérienne," 169–81; Christienne and Lissarrague, *Histoire de l'aviation militaire*, 271–72; Masson, "De Douhet et de quelques marins," 19.

93. Ferris, *Men, Money and Diplomacy*, 7.

94. On the organizational development of the French air force, see Christienne and Lissarrague, *Histoire de l'aviation militaire*, 255–62; Doise and Vaisse, *Diplomatie et outil*, 291; Jauneaud, *De Verdun à Dien-Bien-Phu*, 15–36; Krauskopf, "French Air Power Policy," 31–37; Mysyrowicz, *Anatomie d'une défaite*, 168–69; and Vennesson, *L'institutionalisation de l'armée de l'air.*

95. Christienne and Buffotot, "L'armée de l'air française," 56; Hébrard, *Vingt-cinq années d'aviation militaire*, 143–53; Danel and Cuny, *L'aviation française*, 134; Fridenson and Lecuir, *La France et la Grand Bretagne*, 31–32; Krauskopf, "French Air Power Policy," 100–102; SHAA, 1 B 1, Pierre Cot, "Conception d'emploi et organisation des forces aériennes" (February 27, 1933).

96. On French air force doctrine from 1919 to 1933, see Buffotot, "La doctrine aérienne"; Goyet, "Evolution de la doctrine," 4–7; Teyssier, "L'appui au forces," 249–53.

97. On the French air force and strategic bombing, see Astorkia, "Les leçons aériennes," 166–68; Goyet, "Evolution de la doctrine," 13–15; Hébrard, *Vingt-cinq années d'aviation militaire*, 127–30; Krauskopf, "French Air Power Policy," 63–72; and Mysyrowicz, *Anatomie d'une défaite*, 171–80.

98. Vennesson, "La fabrication de l'armée de l'air," 70, 75–77, and esp. 80. Also see Vennesson, *L'institutionalisation de l'armée de l'air.*

99. Quoted in Astorkia, "Les leçons aériennes," 166.

100. Boussard, *Un problème de défense nationale*, 95–96, 109–10; Christienne, "L'armée de l'air française," 181–83; SHAA, 1 B 1, Pierre Cot, "Conception d'emploi et organisation des forces aeriénnes" (February 27, 1933); Teyssier, "L'appui aux forces," 257–60.

101. On Cot's change to ground support in 1937, see Teyssier, "L'appui au forces," 261–62; and Astorkia, "L'aviation et la guerre d'Espagne," 154.

Chapter 6

1. Friedman, "Conscription and the Constitution," 238; Johnson, *Defence by Committee*, 15; Ritter, *The European Powers*, vol. 2, *The Sword and the Scepter*, 34–35.

2. Barnett, *Britain and Her Army*, viii, also see 79–118.

3. Schwoerer, *"No Standing Armies!"* 51–71, 137, 188–95.

4. Preston, "Introduction," in Preston and Dennis, eds., *Soldiers as Statesmen*, 21; Ritter, *The Sword and the Scepter*, 38–43; Vagts, *A History of Militarism*, 226.

5. Barnett, *Britain and Her Army*, 166, also see 288–91.

6. Preston, "Introduction," 22; also see Ritter, *The Sword and the Scepter*, 37.

7. Quoted in Ehrman, *Cabinet Government*, 17–18.

8. Howard, *War in European History*, 88.

9. Barnett, *Britain and Her Army*, 333–67; Ehrman, *Cabinet Government*, 7–24; Harries-Jenkins, *The Army in Victorian Society*; Poe, "British Army Reforms."

10. Bond, *The Victorian Army*, 33, 44, 120, 146, 212, 239; Dreyer, "The Birth of a Staff System."

11. "Report of the Commissioners Appointed to Enquire into the Purchase of Commissions in the Army, Evidence," *Parliamentary Papers*, 2d sess., 1857, vol. 18, 49, 79–80, 177, 254, 333. Quoted at length in Guttsman, ed., *The English Ruling Class*, 268–70.

12. Preston, "Introduction," 23.

13. van Doorn, "The Officer Corps," 270. Also see Bidwell, "Five Armies," 171; Ellison, "Army Administration," 9–13.

14. Editorial, *Army Quarterly* 27, no. 1 (1934), 195.

15. After World War II, the British again rejected the consolidation of the three services and the creation of a combined general staff. Broadbent, *The Military and Government*, 16.

16. See Blanco, "Reform and Wellington's Post-Waterloo Army," 126, 127. Also see Ritter, *The Sword and the Scepter*, 35–36.

17. Ritter, *The Sword and the Scepter*, 35.

18. Cohen, *Citizens and Soldiers*, 26.

19. *Defence Expenditure in Future Years. Interim Report by the Minister for Coordination of Defence*, C.P.316(37), December 15, 1937, Cab.24/273; Kennedy, *The Realities behind Diplomacy*, 19.

20. Quoted in Gibbs, *Grand Strategy*, vol. 1, *History of the Second World War*, 301.

21. Quoted in Shay, *British Rearmament*, 163.

22. See Shay, *British Rearmament*, 163; and Schmidt, *The Politics and Economics of Appeasement*, 254. Michael Howard also notes that fear of social revolution blinded many civilians to the German threat. Howard, *War in European History*, 119.

23. Steiner, "Review of Gustav Schmidt," 1334.

24. Schmidt, *The Politics and Economics of Appeasement*, 252.

25. Baldwin, March 9, 1936, House of Commons, ser. 5, vol. 309, col. 1832. Quoted in Schmidt, *The Politics and Economics of Appeasement*, 228.

26. Quoted in Charmley, *Duff-Cooper*, 111.

27. Bialer, *The Shadow of the Bomber*, 9, 18, 42, 47; Howard, *The Continental Commitment*, 79; Wolfers, *Britain and France*, 223, 359.

28. Kennedy, *The Realities behind Diplomacy*, 231.

29. Murray, *The Change in the European Balance of Power*, 54.

30. Treasury statement quoted in Shay, *British Rearmament*, 24, see also 23–27. On the Treasury's influence on strategic policy, see Bond, *British Military Policy*, 135, 248–50; and Ferris, *Men, Money, and Diplomacy*.

31. Gibbs, "British Strategic Doctrine," 204.

32. See Bond, *British Military Policy*, 249; Dennis, *Decision by Default*, 165–71; Shay, *British Rearmament*, 4, 291–92.

33. Gibbs, *Grand Strategy*, 127; Kennedy, *The Realities behind Diplomacy*, 274; Shay, *British Rearmament*, 90. The cost effectiveness of policing the empire with the air force guaranteed the permanent establishment of the third service. M. Smith, "The RAF and Counter-force Strategy," 70.

34. Most analysts argue that the switch to fighters stemmed from financial considerations. See Frankland, *Bombing Offensive*, 45; Hyde, *British Air Policy*, 206; Rosen, *Winning the Next War*, 14; Shay, *British Rearmament*, 164–73; M. Smith, "The Royal Air Force," 167, 170; and Taylor, *English History*, 391.

35. *Defence Expenditure in Future Years*.

36. Shay, *British Rearmament*, 168.

37. Douglas, *In the Year of Munich*, 80–81.

38. Liddell Hart, *The British Way in Warfare*. Also see Bond, *Liddell Hart*, 67–75, 90–114; Bird, "A Note on British National Strategy."

39. Barnett, *Britain and Her Army*, 147, 185; Johnson, *Defence by Committee*, 25–38.

40. Baylis, *British Defence Policy*, 8–9; Bird, "A Note on British National Strategy," 244–47; Kennedy, *The Realities behind Diplomacy*, 180–81; Murray, *The Change in the European Balance of Power*, 86.

41. Liddell Hart, *Memoirs*, vol. 1, 281.

42. Quoted in Baylis, *British Defence Policy*, 9.

43. Strachan, "The British Way in Warfare," 417.

44. Bialer, *The Shadow of the Bomber*, 142; Howard, *The Continental Commitment*, 79, 108, 114; Wark, *The Ultimate Enemy*, 31.

45. Dennis, *Decision by Default*, 45.

46. Quoted in Gibbs, *Grand Strategy*, 107.

47. Many historians argue that financial considerations were foremost in the decision not to adopt a continental commitment. See Bialer, *The Shadow of the Bomber*, 138; Bond, *Liddell Hart*, 108; Larson, *The British Army*, 34–36; Howard, *The Continental Commitment*, 125; and Wark, *The Ultimate Enemy*, 31.

48. Charmley, *Duff-Cooper*, 86. Also see Dunbabin, "British Rearmament," 590, 597.

49. Bond, "Leslie Hore-Belishe," 116; Murray, *The Change in the European Balance of Power*; Peden, "The Burden of Imperial Defense," 411.

50. Quoted in Bond, *Liddell Hart*, 107.

51. Bond and Murray, "The British Armed Forces," in *Military Effectiveness*, vol. 2, *The Interwar Period*, 107; Winton, *To Change an Army*, 230.

52. On the Cardwell system, see Appleton, "The Cardwell System"; Bond, *British Military Policy*, 97–100; Winton, *To Change an Army*, 9.

53. Quoted in Bond, *British Military Policy*, 80, 101.

54. Shay, *British Rearmament*, 230.

55. Gibbs, "British Strategic Doctrine," 187.

56. Bond, *British Military Policy*, 41; Johnson, *Defence by Committee*, 12–13.

57. Quoted in Poe, "British Army Reforms," 132.

58. Liddell Hart, *Memoirs*, vol. 2, 6–7, 57, 83.

59. Macksey, *A History of the Royal Armoured Corps*, 41–53; Winton, *To Change an Army*, 230.

60. Howard, "The Liddell Hart Memoirs," 60. Also see Bond and Murray, "The British Armed Forces," 115; Martel, *Our Armoured Forces*, 6; Peden, *British Rearmament and the Treasury*. Some analysts argue that the lack of resources hindered efforts at mechanization. Barnett, *Britain and Her Army*; Bond, *British Military Policy*, 135, 161, 187; Carver, *Apostles of Mobility*, 52; Shay, *British Rearmament*, 95–106, 125–32, 148–63, 207, 247–49, 276–77, 286–95; Macksey, *A History of the Royal Armoured Corps*, 54.

61. For a fascinating account of Liddell Hart's reconstruction of history and especially his role in it, see Mearsheimer, *Liddell Hart and the Weight of History*.

62. Bond, *British Military Policy*, 187.

63. Many analysts at least partially attribute the British army's defensive doctrine to the conservatism of the officer corps. See Barnett, *The Desert Generals*, 98–103; Bidwell and Graham, *Fire-power*; Bond, *British Military Policy*, 187; and Macksey, *A History of the Royal Armoured Corps*, 43–44. Many of the British armored advocates agree. See Broad, "A Mechanized Formation," 15; Fuller, *Memoirs of an Unconventional Soldier*; and Liddell Hart, *Memoirs*, vol. 1, 274–75. Others downplay the importance of the army's conservatism (Larson, *The British Army*, 31; Winton, *To Change an Army*, 225–26) or blame the parochialism of the regimental system (Bidwell, "Five Armies," 172; Bond and Murray, "The British Armed Forces," 110–12; Howard, "Soldiers in Politics," 81).

64. Quoted in Blanco, "Reform and Wellington's Post-Waterloo Army," 128. For discussion about the nineteenth-century British officer, see Barnett, *Britain and Her Army*, 312–421; Bond, "The Late Victorian Army," 624; Bond, *The Victorian Army*, 17–24; Harries-Jenkins, *The Army in Victorian Society*; and Winton, *To Change an Army*, 8–13.

65. See *Report of the Select Committee on Military Education*, 1901, *Parliamentary Papers 1902*, vol. 10, quoted in Guttsman, ed., *The English Ruling Class*, 283; Reader, *Professional Men*, 98; and Spiers, *The Army and Society*, 23–24.

66. Farwell, *For Queen and Country*, 61.

67. Apparently, little changed in the post–World War II period. See Abrams, "The Late Profession of Arms"; and Stanhope, *The Soldiers*, 181–82.

68. On the development of professional armies in Europe, see Harries-Jenkins, *The Army in Victorian Society*, 3–4; and van Doorn, "The Officer Corps."

69. Slessor, *The Central Blue*, 83–84.

70. Quoted in Dickinson, *Officers' Mess Life*, 5.

71. Slessor, *The Central Blue*, 84. On the French army's indifference to team sports, see Clayton, *France, Soldiers, and Africa*, 12–14.

72. Harries-Jenkins, *The Army in Victorian Society*, 85; Barnett, *Desert Generals*, 105; Farwell, *For Queen and Country*, 58.

73. Macksey, *Armoured Crusader*, 71.

74. Wavell, "The Training of the Army for War," 259.

75. Masters, *Bugles and a Tiger*, 39.

76. Barnett, *Britain and Her Army*, 411; Bond, *British Military Policy*, 64.

77. Bidwell, "Five Armies," 173; Bond and Murray, "The British Armed Forces," 100.

78. Wavell, "The Higher Commander," 22. The ideal of the gentleman-officer impeded the development of intelligence within the army because espionage was considered ungentlemanly conduct. Wark, *The Ultimate Enemy*, 23.

79. Quoted in Abrams, "Democracy, Technology, and the Retired British Officer," 150.

80. Wykeham, *Fighter Command*, 73.

81. E. S. Turner, *Gallant Gentlemen*, 317. As late as 1955, the Labour Party was unable to remove the phrase "unbecoming to the character of an officer and gentleman" from the *Queen's Regulations*. See Abrams, "Democracy, Technology, and the Retired British Officer," 145.

82. War Office, *Field Service Regulations, Provisional*, vol. 2, *Operations*, 13.

83. War Office, *Infantry Training*, vol. 2, *War*, 5.

84. "Mechanized Forces," *Cavalry Journal* (April 1934), 227.

85. War Office, *Infantry Training*, vol. 1, *Training*, 14.

86. Masters, *Bugles and a Tiger*, 32.

87. *Cavalry Journal* (January 1922).

88. Blanco, "Reform and Wellington's Post-Waterloo Army," 128; Bond, *British Military Policy*, 69; Farwell, *For Queen and Country*, 62.

89. Dickinson, *Officers' Mess Life*, 12.

90. Harries-Jenkins, *The Army in Victorian Society*, 103, 162.

91. McNair, "The Study of War by Junior Officers," 245.

92. Quoted in Larson, *The British Army*, 21.

93. Slessor, *The Central Blue*, 85.

94. Ironside, "The Modern Staff Officer," 436.

95. Wavell, "The Higher Commander," 19–20.

96. Winton, *To Change an Army*, 30.

97. Barnett, "The Education of Military Elites," 203. Also see Fisher, "The Training of the Regimental Officer."

98. War Office, *Infantry Training*, vol. 1, *Training*.

99. War Office, *Infantry Training: Training and War*, 13.

100. Festing, "The Value of Close Order Drill," 115.

101. Masters, *Bugles and a Tiger*, 17.

102. See War Office, *Operations*, 12.

103. Hamilton, "The Re-forming Army," 145–46.

104. Brighten, "The Senior Officers' School"; Burrow, "Junior Officers' Schools"; Fisher, "The Training of the Regimental Officer"; Milling, "The Training of the Army Officer."

105. Mahony, "A Junior School of Tactics and Leadership," 360–66.

106. War Office, *Cavalry Training*, vol. 1, *Training*.

107. For example, see War Office, *Training Manual*.

108. The quotations in this paragraph are taken from, in order: Ferte, *The*

Third Service, 87; Lawrence, *The Mint*, 231; and Wykeham, *Fighter Command*, 73. See also E. S. Turner, *Gallant Gentlemen*, 324–25.

109. Air force officer quoted in Moolgavkar, "AF and Professionals," 5. See also Lawrence, *The Mint*, 95.

110. Quoted in Blanco, "Reform and Wellington's Post-Waterloo Army," 128.

111. Ironside, "The Modern Staff Officer," 436.

112. Wavell, "The Higher Commander," 22.

113. de Watteville, "A Hundred Years of the British Army," 295.

114. War Office, *Cavalry Training*, vol. 1, *Training*, 37–38.

115. Westmorland, "The Training of the Army Officer," 584.

116. Quoted in Macksey, *Armoured Crusader*, 159.

117. Quoted in Larson, *The British Army*, 21.

118. Wykeham, *Fighter Command*, 29.

119. Sherbrooke-Walker, *Khaki and Blue*, 7.

120. Liddell Hart, *Memoirs*, vol. 1, 79.

121. "The Royal Horse Artillery with Cavalry," 238, and "The Tank Corps," 308.

122. Quoted in War Office, *Report on War Office Exercises No. 2*.

123. Quoted in Liddell Hart, *Memoirs*, vol. 1, 277.

124. Stanhope, *The Soldiers*, 169–70.

125. Maclean, "The Royal Air Force Training Year," 54.

126. Wykeham, *Fighter Command*, 28.

127. For example, see Game, "Service in the Royal Air Force," 7.

128. Kirkland, "Combat Leadership Styles," 65.

129. Collier, *Leader of the Few*, 81; Allen, ed., *Plain Tales from the Raj*, 178.

130. Quotations in this paragraph are from War Office, *Cavalry Training*, vol. 1, *Training*, 39; and "A Horse! A Horse! My Kingdom for a Horse!" 152.

131. Raleigh, *The War in the Air*, 441. Also see Ferte, *Fated Sky*, 103.

132. Lawrence, *The Mint*, 110.

133. Gordon-Dean, "The Development of Leadership," 23.

134. Lawrence, *The Mint*, 206.

135. Sherbrooke-Walker, *Khaki and Blue*, 4.

136. Ibid., 6.

137. *Royal Air Force Quarterly* 8, no. 1 (January 1937).

138. Bond, *British Military Policy*, 35; Howard, "The Liddell Hart Memoirs," 61.

139. Barnett, *The Desert Generals*, 103. Also see Howard, "The Liddell Hart Memoirs," 61; Macksey, *Armoured Crusader*, 71.

140. Winton, *To Change an Army*, 127.

141. Howard, "The Liddell Hart Memoirs," 61.

142. Bond, *British Military Policy*, 42–43, 58; Bond and Murray, "The British Armed Forces," 110–11; Garnier, "Technology, Organizational Culture, and Recruitment," 83; Winton, *To Change an Army*, 10.

143. Bidwell, "Five Armies," 171.

144. "Infantry Reorganization: A Reply," 564, 569. Also see Barnett, *The Desert Generals*, 106. Without the regimental system and the attendant mess and particular traditions and customs, the airmen developed a servicewide culture.

See Braithwaite, "A Regimental System for the RAF," 368–69; Ferte, *The Third Service*, 86; Raleigh, *War in the Air*, 230; and Sherbrooke-Walker, *Khaki and Blue*, 8.

145. For a discussion of organizational subcultures, see Sackmann, "Culture and Subcultures," 140–61.

146. The army preferred the regimental system because it believed it fostered morale. Bond, *British Military Policy*, 62; Garnier, "Technology, Organizational Culture, and Recruitment," 83; Stanhope, *The Soldiers*, 322; "Infantry Reorganization," 569.

147. Quoted in Keegan, "Regimental Ideology," 15.

148. Garnier, "Technology, Organizational Culture, and Recruitment," 83–89.

149. *Cavalry Journal* (April 1922).

150. *Cavalry Journal* (April 1929).

151. *Royal Engineers Journal* 43 (June 1929).

152. Hacker, "The Military and the Machine," 86–87.

153. The Guards and Household Cavalry were the most prestigious, the technical units the least. Only infantry and cavalry were part of the regimental system. The rest of the army—artillery, engineers, supply, and technical services—formed branches as in other armies. On the "class structure" of the British army, see Barnett, *The Desert Generals*, 108; Garnier, "Technology, Organizational Culture, and Recruitment," 83; and Stanhope, *The Soldiers*, 322.

154. On the cautious movement toward mechanization, see Bond, *British Military Policy*, esp. 144–45, 152.

155. The quotations in this paragraph are taken from, in order: Winton, *To Change an Army*, 97; Bond, *British Military Policy*, 166; Macksey, *Armoured Crusader*, 154; and Bond and Murray, "The British Armed Forces," 112.

156. Quoted in Liddell Hart, *Memoirs*, vol. 2, 8.

157. *Memorandum on Army Training: Collective Training Period*, para. 6 (London: HMSO, 1927). Quoted in Willcocks, "Air Mobility and the Armoured Experience," 111.

158. Jeffery, "The Post-War Army," 217.

Chapter 7

1. Quoted in B. Crozier, *De Gaulle*, 97.

2. Hall, "Introduction," 5, also see 367.

3. Quoted in Miquel, *La paix de Versailles*, 258. Also see France, Ministère des affaires étrangères, *Documents diplomatiques français* 1, no. 1, 569.

4. Quoted in Miquel, *La paix de Versailles*, 256.

5. de Jouvenel, "Le service militaire obligatoire," 8; Pertinax [André Géraud], "Le désarmement radical de l'Allemagne est décidé," *L'écho de Paris*, March 11, 1919.

6. Temperley, *The Settlement with Germany*, vol. 2, 128.

7. Swidler, "Culture in Action," 276.

8. Travers, *The Killing Ground*.

9. Vlahos, "Military Reform," 248.

10. Nicholson and Johns, "The Absence Culture," 397–407. Also see Ouchi, *The M-form Society*.

11. M. Crozier, *The Bureaucratic Phenomenon*; Stinchcombe, "Social Structure and Organizations," 141–43, 153–59. Also see Hofstede, *Culture's Consequences*; Lammers and Hickson, "A Cross-National and Cross-Institutional Typology," 420–34.

12. Sheppard, *A Short History of the British Army*, 476; Kirkland, "Combat Leadership Styles," 65.

13. Wolsely, "The Army," 167. On the persistence of feudalistic interaction within the British army, see Barnett, "The Education of Military Elites," 204; Blanco, "Reform and Wellington's Post-Waterloo Army," 128; and Sheppard, *A Short History of the British Army*, 476.

14. Blanco, "Reform and Wellington's Post–Waterloo Army," 128.

15. Raven, *The English Gentleman*, 141–43.

16. Ibid., 145.

17. On the paternalistic relationship between the officer and the rank, see Bond, *British Military Policy*, 62; Sheppard, *A Short History of the British Army*, 476; and Stanhope, *The Soldiers*, 322.

18. Carrias, *La pensée militaire allemande*, 268–72; Elliott-Bateman, "Vocabulary," 265–66; Vial, "Les doctrines militaires," 124–25.

19. Quoted in Dupuy, *A Genius for War*, 116.

20. Quoted in Abenheim, *Reforging the Iron Cross*, 18.

21. Herwig, *The German Naval Officer Corps*, 59, 69.

22. For example, see Larson, *The British Army*, 17.

23. Barnett, "The Education of Military Elites," 205.

24. Barker, *Soldiering On*, 126.

25. Janowitz, *The Professional Soldier*, 292. On the dominance of the organization over social origins, see Feller, *Le dossier de l'armée française*, 166.

26. Rose, "The Social Structure of the Army," esp. 361–62.

27. Kets de Vries and Miller, "Personality, Culture, and Organization"; Schein, *Organizational Culture and Leadership*; Selznick, *Leadership in Administration*. Some organizational theorists argue that founders do not play an important role in creating an organization's culture. Sergiovanni, "Cultural and Competing Perspectives"; Rowlinson and Hassard, "The Invention of Corporate Culture," 304–23.

28. Watson, *A Business and Its Beliefs*.

29. B. Clark, *The Distinctive College*.

30. Setear, Builder, Baccus, and Madewell, *The Army in a Changing World*, 71.

31. "Career Opportunities," *Economist*, July 8, 1995, 59.

32. Bond, "Leslie Hore-Belisha," 113–14.

33. Floyd Norris, "Looking Out for No. 1," *New York Times*, August 19, 1991, D1, D5.

34. Maurice, Sorge, and Warner, "Societal Differences in Organizing Manufacturing Units," 59–86.

35. Solomon, "Transplanting Corporate Cultures Globally," 80–81.

36. Quoted in Doren P. Levin, "Adjusting to Japan's Car Culture," *New York Times*, March 4, 1992, D6.

37. Lawrence, *The Mint*, 95.

38. Quoted in Carrias, *La pensée militaire allemande*, 272.

39. Quoted in van Creveld, *Fighting Power*, 29, also see 35–40, 165; Dupuy, *A Genius for War*, 116, 133–34; and Murray, "The German Response to Victory in Poland," 286–87.

40. Alain Rouquie argues that the traditional aspects of the army's "military mind" are not functional. See Rouquie, "Les processus politiques," 26.

41. Mitroff and Kilmann, *Corporate Tragedies*, 68–69. For an argument that organizational cultures are more adaptive than is currently thought, see Wilkins and Ouchi, "Efficient Cultures," esp. 478–80.

42. Wilms, Hardcastle, and Zell, "Cultural Transformation at NUMMI," 100.

43. Ott, *The Organizational Culture Perspective*, 4, 12–13, 43–44.

44. Keller, *Rude Awakening*, 11. Journalistic accounts provide numerous examples of cultural rigidity in both the government and private industry. See, for example, Tim Weiner, "The C.I.A.'s 'Old-Boy' Camaraderie," *New York Times*, October 16, 1994, 30L; and "Corporate Culture: Those hard-to-change values that spell success for failure," *Business Week*, October 27, 1980, 148–60.

45. On selection processes in an economic realm, see Alchian, "Uncertainty, Evolution, and Economic Theory," 213–14.

46. Avant, *Political Institutions and Military Change*, 12.

47. Hovland, Janis, and Kelley, *Communication and Persuasion*, 215–22; Zimbardo and Ebbesen, *Influencing Attitudes and Changing Behavior*, 30–31.

48. For an important study of wartime (and peacetime) innovation, see Rosen, *Winning the Next War*.

49. Janowitz, *The Professional Soldier*, 8–15; Janowitz, *Sociology and the Military Establishment*, 33–37.

50. Stewart, *Mates and Muchachos*, 35.

51. Nathaniel C. Nash, "In Peru, a 'Second Coup' Reveals the Upper Hand," *New York Times*, May 2, 1993, E6.

52. Snyder, *Myths of Empire*, 317.

53. Ibid., 317–18. Also see Katzenstein, *Small States in World Markets*. Miriam Fendius Elman challenges the argument that international factors are more likely to explain the foreign policies of small states. See Elman, "The Foreign Policies of Small States," 171–217.

54. Legro, *Cooperation under Fire*.

55. Krepinevich, *The Army and Vietnam*; Paret, *French Revolutionary Warfare from Indochina to Algeria*.

56. Steven A. Holmes, "Time and Money Producing Racial Harmony in Military," *New York Times*, April 5, 1995, A1, A12.

57. For discussions of organizational culture and change, see Brunsson, "The Irrationality of Action"; Dunbar, "Crossing Mother"; Normann, "Developing Capabilities for Organizational Learning"; Starbuck, Greve and Hedberg, "Responding to Crisis"; and Pettigrew, "Examining Change."

58. Quoted in Steve Lohr, "Pulling One's Own Weight at the New I.B.M.," *New York Times*, F6.

59. Lundberg, "On the Feasibility of Cultural Intervention in Organizations," 169–86.

60. Porch, *The March to the Marne*, 77–80.

61. *New York Times*, April 5, 1995, A13.

62. Rosen, *Winning the Next War*; Zisk, *Engaging the Enemy*; Avant, *Political Institutions and Military Change*.

63. For example, Keohane, *After Hegemony*; and Waltz, *Theory of International Politics*.

64. For example, Eden, *Constructing Destruction*; Katzenstein, ed., *The Culture of National Security*; Risse-Kappen, *Cooperation among Democracies*, and Wendt, "Anarchy Is What States Make of It."

Works Cited

Abenheim, Donald. *Reforging the Iron Cross: The Search for Tradition in the West German Armed Forces*. Princeton, N.J.: Princeton University Press, 1988.

Abrams, Philip. "Democracy, Technology, and the Retired British Officer." In *Changing Patterns of Military Politics*, edited by Samuel Huntington. New York: Free Press of Glencoe, 1962.

———. "The Late Profession of Arms: Ambiguous Goals and Deteriorating Means in Britain." *Archives européennes de sociologie* 4, no. 2 (1965).

Adams, Brooks. "The American Democratic Ideal." *Yale Review* 5 (January 1916).

Adams, Ralph James Q., and Philip P. Poirier. *The Conscription Controversy in Great Britain, 1900–18*. Basingstoke, Eng.: Macmillan, 1987.

Adams, Richard. "Energy and the Regulation of the Nation-State." *Cultural Dynamics* 1 (1988).

Adamthwaite, Anthony. *France and the Coming of the Second World War, 1936–39*. London: Frank Cass, 1977.

———. "France and the Coming of War." In *The Fascist Challenge and the Policy of Appeasement*, edited by Wolfgang J. Mommsen and Lothar Kettenecker. London: George Allen and Unwin, 1983.

———. "Reaction to the Munich Crisis." In *Troubled Neighbours: Franco-British Relations in the Twentieth Century*, edited by Neville Waites. London: Weidenfeld and Nicolson, 1971.

Alchian, Armen A. "Uncertainty, Evolution, and Economic Theory." *Journal of Political Economy* 58, no. 3 (1950).

Alerme, Colonel Marie. *Les causes militaires de notre défaite*. Paris: Centre d'études de l'agence "Inter-France," 1941.

Alexander, Arthur J. *Decision-Making in Soviet Weapons Procurement*. Adelphi Paper, no. 147–8. London: International Institute for Strategic Studies, 1978.

Alexander, Don W. "Repercussions of the Breda Variant." *French Historical Studies* 8, no. 3 (1974).

Alexander, Jeffrey. "Analytic Debates: Understanding the Relative Autonomy of Culture." In *Culture and Society: Contemporary Debates*, edited by Jeffrey C. Alexander and Steven Seidman. Cambridge, Eng.: Cambridge University Press, 1990.

Alexander, Martin S. "The Fall of France, 1940." *Journal of Strategic Studies* 13, no. 1 (1990).

———. *The Republic in Danger: General Maurice Gamelin and the Politics of French Defence, 1933–1940*. Cambridge, Eng.: Cambridge University Press, 1992.

———. "Soldiers and Socialists: The French Officer Corps and Leftist Governments, 1935–7." In *The French and Spanish Popular Fronts*, edited by Martin S. Alexander and Helen Graham. Cambridge, Eng.: Cambridge University Press, 1985.

Allen, Charles, ed. *Plain Tales from the Raj: Images of British India in the Twentieth Century*. London: Andre Deutsch, 1975.

Almond, Gabriel, and Sidney Verba. *The Civic Culture: Political Attitudes and Democracy in Five Nations*. Princeton, N.J.: Princeton University Press, 1963.

Andrew, Christopher M. "France and the German Menace." In *Knowing One's Enemies: Intelligence Assessment before the Two World Wars*, edited by Ernest R. May. Princeton, N.J.: Princeton University Press, 1986.

Applegate, Major R.A.D., and J. R. Moore. "The Nature of Military Culture." *Defense Analysis* 6, no. 3 (1990).

Appleton, Captain G. L. "The Cardwell System: A Criticism." *Journal of the Royal United Service Institution* 72, no. 487 (1927).

Armengaud, General Paul François Marie. *Batailles politiques et militaires sur l'Europe*. Paris: Editions du Myrte, 1948.

Astorkia, Madelin. "L'aviation et la guerre d'Espagne: la cinquième arme face aux exigences de la guerre moderne." In *Recueil d'articles et études, 1976–1978*. Vincennes: Service historique de l'armée de l'air, 1984.

———. "Les leçons aériennes de la guerre d'Espagne." *Revue historique des armées* 4, no. 2 (1977).

Avant, Deborah D. *Political Institutions and Military Change: Lessons from Peripheral Wars*. Ithaca, N.Y.: Cornell University Press, 1994.

B.A.R. *L'armée nouvelle et le service d'un an*. Paris: Librairie Plon, 1921.

Bankwitz, Philip C. F. *Maxime Weygand and Civil-Military Relations in Modern France*. Cambridge, Mass.: Harvard University Press, 1967.

———. "Maxime Weygand and the Army-Nation Concept in the Modern French Army." *French Historical Studies* 2, no. 2 (1961).

Bardies, Colonel Raphael de. *La campagne, 1939–40*. Paris: Fayard, 1947.

Barker, Dennis. *Soldiering On: An Unofficial Portrait of the British Army*. London: Andre Deutsch, 1981.

Barnett, Correlli. *Britain and Her Army, 1509–1970: A Military, Political, and Social Survey*. London: Allen Lane, 1970.

———. *The Desert Generals*. London: Pan Books, 1960.

———. "The Education of Military Elites." In *Governing Elites: Studies in Training and Selection*, edited by Rupert Wilkinson. New York: Oxford University Press, 1969.

Barrows, Leland Conley. "L'influence des conquêtes coloniales sur l'armée française, 1830–1919." *Le mois en Afrique* (December 1981–January 1982).

Baylis, John. *British Defence Policy*. London: Macmillan, 1989.

Beckett, Ian. "The Amateur Military Tradition." In *The Oxford Illustrated History of the British Army*, edited by David G. Chandler. Oxford, Eng.: Oxford University Press, 1994.

Bennett, Edward W. *German Rearmament and the West, 1923–1933*. Princeton, N.J.: Princeton University Press, 1979.

Benoist-Mechin, Jacques. *A l'épreuve du temps*. Vol. 1, *1905–1940*. Paris: Julliard, 1989.

Berger, Peter L., and Thomas Luckmann. *The Social Construction of Reality: A Treatise in the Sociology of Knowledge*. Garden City, N.Y.: Doubleday, 1966.

Berstein, Serge. *Histoire du Parti radical.* 2 vols. Paris: Presses de la fondation nationale des sciences politiques, 1980–1982.

———. *La France des années 30.* Paris: Armand Colin, 1988.

Bertaud, Jean-Paul. *La révolution armée: Les soldats-citoyens et la révolution française.* Paris: Editions Robert Laffont, 1979.

———. "Les travaux récents sur l'armée de la Révolution et de l'Empire." *Revue internationale d'histoire militaire* 61 (1985).

Betts, Richard. *Cruise Missiles: Technology, Strategy, and Politics.* Washington D.C.: Brookings Institution, 1981.

Bialer, Uri. *The Shadow of the Bomber: The Fear of Air Attack and British Politics, 1932–1939.* London: Royal Historical Society, 1980.

Bidwell, Shelford. "Five Armies, 1920–1970." *Army Quarterly* 100, no. 2 (1970).

Bidwell, Shelford, and Dominick Graham. *Fire-power: British Army Weapons and the Theories of War, 1904–1945.* London: Allen and Unwin, 1982.

Bird, Major General Sir W. D. "A Note on British National Strategy, Past and Future, as Regards the Use of Land Force in Time of War." *Army Quarterly* 3, no. 2 (1937).

Blanco, Richard L. "Reform and Wellington's Post-Waterloo Army, 1815–1854." *Military Affairs* 29, no. 3 (1965).

Bloch, Marc. *Strange Defeat.* Trans. Gerald Hopkins. New York: Norton, 1968.

Boggs, Marion William. *Attempts to Define and Limit "Aggressive" Armament in Diplomacy and Strategy.* Columbia: University of Missouri Press, 1941.

Bois, Jacques. "Procès de la conscription." *Esprit* 3, no. 32 (May 1, 1935).

Bond, Brian. *British Military Policy between the Two World Wars.* Oxford, Eng.: Clarendon, 1980.

———. *Chief of Staff: The Diaries of Lieutenant-General Sir Henry Pownall.* Vol. 1, *1933–40.* London: Leo Cooper, 1972.

———. "The Late Victorian Army." *History Today,* September 1961.

———. "Leslie Hore-Belisha at the War Office." In *Politicians and Defence: Studies in the Formulation of British Defence Policy, 1845–1970,* edited by Ian Beckett and John Gooch. Manchester, Eng.: Manchester University Press, 1981.

———. *Liddell Hart: A Study of His Military Thought.* New Brunswick, N.J.: Rutgers University Press, 1977.

———. *The Victorian Army and the Staff College.* London: Eyre Methuen, 1972.

———. *War and Society in Europe, 1870–1970.* Leicester, Eng.: Leicester University Press, in association with Fontana Paperbacks, 1983.

Bond, Brian, and Martin Alexander. "Liddell Hart and de Gaulle: The Doctrines of Limited Liability and Mobile Defense." In *Makers of Modern Strategy from Machiavelli to the Nuclear Age,* edited by Peter Paret. Oxford, Eng.: Clarendon, 1986.

Bond, Brian, and Williamson Murray. "The British Armed Forces, 1918–39." In *Military Effectiveness.* Vol. 2, *The Interwar Period,* edited by Allan R. Millett and Williamson Murray. Boston: Allen and Unwin, 1988.

Bonnefous, Edouard. *L'après-guerre.* Vol. 3, *Histoire politique de la troisième République.* Paris: Presses Universitaires de France, 1968.

Bourdrel, Philippe. *La Cagoule: 30 ans de complots*. Paris: Editions j'ai lu, 1973.

Boussard, Dominique. *Un problème de défense nationale: l'aéronautique militaire au parlement, 1928–1940*. Vincennes: Service historique d'armée de l'air, 1983.

Boyer, Captain. "De l'aspect social de la profession militaire." *Revue militaire d'information*, April 10, 1951.

Braithwaite, Flight Lieutenant F. J. "A Regimental System for the RAF." *Royal Air Force Quarterly* 8, no. 4 (1937).

Bridge, F. R. *From Sadowa to Sarajevo: the Foreign Policy of Austria-Hungary, 1866–1914*. London: Routledge and Kegan Paul, 1972.

Brighten, Brevet Lieutenant Colonel E. W. "The Senior Officers' School: The Case for a College of Tactics." *Journal of the Royal United Service Institution* 73, no. 489 (1928).

Broad, Colonel C.N.F. "A Mechanized Formation." *Journal of the Royal United Service Institution* 73, no. 489 (1928).

Broadbent, Sir Ewen. *The Military and Government: From Macmillan to Heseltine*. London: Macmillan, 1988.

Brotz, Howard, and Everett Wilson. "Characteristics of Military Society." *American Journal of Sociology* 51, no. 5 (1946).

Brown, Michael. *Flying Blind: The Politics of the U.S. Strategic Bomber Program*. Ithaca, N.Y.: Cornell University Press, 1992.

Brunet, Jean Paul. *Histoire du Parti communiste français, 1920–1982*. Paris: Presses Universitaires de France, 1982.

Brunsson, Nils. "The Irrationality of Action and Action Rationality: Decisions, Ideologies, and Organizational Actions." *Journal of Management Studies* 19, no. 1 (1982).

Buffotot, Patrice. "La doctrine aérienne du commandement français pendant l'entre-deux guerres. *Revue internationale d'histoire militaire*, no. 55 (1983).

———. "The French High Command and the Franco-Soviet Alliance, 1933–1939." *Journal of Strategic Studies* 5, no. 4 (1982).

———. "La perception du réarmement allemand par les organismes de renseignement français de 1936 à 1939." *Revue historique des armées*, no. 3 (special issue, 1979).

———. "La politique militaire du Parti socialiste SFIO aux lendemains de la libération." *Revue d'histoire de la deuxième guerre mondiale* 28, no. 110 (1978).

Builder, Carl H. *The Masks of War: American Military Styles in Strategy and Analysis*. Baltimore, Md.: Johns Hopkins University Press, 1989.

Burns, Tom, and G. M. Stalker. *The Management of Innovation*. London: Tavistock, 1961.

Burrow, Brevet Lieutenant Colonel H. M. "Junior Officers' Schools." *Journal of the Royal United Service Institution* 73, no. 490 (1928).

Cabannes, René. *La nation armée et le Parti socialiste*. Paris: Les publications sociales, 1928.

Cairns, John C. "A Nation of Shopkeepers in Search of a Suitable France, 1919–1940." *American Historical Review* 79, no. 3 (1974).

Carr, Edward H. *International Relations between the Two World Wars, 1919–1939.* London: Macmillan, 1947.

Carrias, Eugène. *La pensée militaire allemande.* Paris: Presses Universitaires de France, 1948.

———. *La pensée militaire française.* Paris: Presses Universitaires de France, 1960.

Carver, Field Marshal Michael. *The Apostles of Mobility: The Theory and Practice of Armoured Warfare.* London: Weidenfeld and Nicolson, 1979.

Challener, Richard D. *The French Theory of the Nation in Arms, 1988–1939.* New York: Columbia University Press, 1955.

Chambers, John Whiteclay. "Conscripting for Colossus: The Progressive Era and the Origins of the Modern Military Draft in the United States in World War I." In *The Military in America: From the Colonial Era to the Present*, edited by Peter Karsten. New York: Free Press, 1980.

———. *To Raise an Army: The Draft Comes to Modern America.* New York: Free Press, 1987.

Chandessais, Colonel Charles. *La psychologie dans l'armée.* Paris: Presses Universitaires de France, 1956.

Charmley, John. *Chamberlain and the Lost Peace.* Chicago, Ill.: Ivan R. Dee, 1989.

———. *Duff-Cooper: The Authorized Biography.* London: Weidenfeld and Nicolson, 1986.

Charnay, Jean-Paul. *Société militaire et suffrage politique en France depuis 1789.* Paris: SEVPEN, 1964.

Chita [pseud.] "The Officers' Training Corps." *Journal of the Royal United Service Institution* 80, no. 519 (1935).

Christienne, General Charles. "L'armée de l'air française de mars 1936 à septembre 1939." *Recueil d'articles et études, 1976–1978.* Vincennes: Service historique de l'armée de l'air, 1984.

———. "Le haut commandement français face au progrès technique entre les deux guerres." *Acta No. 5, Bucarest 10–17 VIII, 1980.* Bucharest: Commission internationale d'histoire militaire, 1981.

———. "La résistance au changement dans l'armée française entre les deux guerres. Un exemple: l'attitude de l'état-major de l'armée face aux problèmes posés par l'aviation militaire." *Recueil d'articles et études, 1976–1978.* Vincennes: Service historique de l'armée de l'air, 1984.

Christienne, General Charles, and Patrice Buffotot. "L'armée de l'air française et la crise du 7 mars 1936." *Recueil d'articles et études, 1976–1978.* Vincennes: Service historique de l'armée de l'air, 1984.

Christienne, General Charles, and General Pierre Lissarrague. *Histoire de l'aviation militaire française.* Paris: Charles Lavauzelle, 1980.

Clark, Burton R. *The Distinctive College: Antioch, Reed and Swarthmore.* Chicago, Ill.: Aldine, 1970.

Clark, Ronald W. *Tizard.* London: Methuen, 1965.

Clarke, Jeffrey Johnstone. "Military Technology in Republican France: The Evolution of the French Armored Force, 1917–1940." Ph.D. diss., Duke University, 1968.

Clayton, Anthony. *France, Soldiers, and Africa*. London: Brassey's Defence Publishers, 1988.

Cohen, Eliot A. *Citizens and Soldiers: The Dilemmas of Military Service*. Ithaca, N.Y.: Cornell University Press, 1985.

Cohen, Eliot A., and John Gooch. *Military Misfortune: The Anatomy of Failure in War*. New York: Free Press, 1990.

Cointet, Jean-Paul. "Gouvernement et haut-commandement en France entre les deux guerres." *La défense nationale* 33 (April 1977).

Cole, Ronald H. "Forward with the Bayonet: The French Army Prepares for Offensive Warfare." Ph.D. diss., University of Maryland, 1975.

Collier, Basil. *Leader of the Few: The Authorized Biography of Air Chief Marshal the Lord Dowding of Bentley Pirory*. London: Jarrolds, 1957.

Commission militaire du conseil national de la résistance. *Pour une armée nationale contre une armée de caste*. Paris: ATU Imprimeur, 1945.

Conquet, General Alfred. *Autour de maréchal Pétain*. Paris: Nouvelles éditions Latines, 1963.

———. *L'énigme des blindés, 1932–1940*. Paris: Nouvelles éditions Latines, 1956.

Coox, Alvin David. "French Military Doctrine, 1919–1939: Concepts of Ground and Aerial Warfare." Ph.D. diss., Harvard University, 1951.

Corse, Sarah M., and Marian A. Robinson. "Cross-cultural Measurement and New Conceptions of Culture: Measuring Cultural Capacities in Japanese and American Preschools." *Poetics* 22, no. 4 (1994).

Cossé-Brissac, Lieutenant Colonel Charles de. "L'armée allemande dans la campagne de France de 1940." *Revue d'histoire de la deuxième guerre mondiale* 53 (January 1964).

Cot, Pierre. "The Defeat of the French Air Force." *Foreign Affairs* 19, no. 4 (1941).

———. *Le procès de la république*. New York: Editions de la maison française, 1944.

———."Le service militaire de deux ans et la défense nationale." *Cahiers des droits de l'homme*, February 10, 1935.

Cotton, Charles A. "Institutional and Occupational Values in Canada's Army." *Armed Forces and Society* 8 (fall 1981).

Croubois, Claude, ed. *L'officier français des origines à nos jours*. St-Jean-d'Angely: Editions Bordessoules, 1987.

Crozier, Brian. *De Gaulle: The Warrior*. London: Eyre Methuen, 1973.

Crozier, Michel. *The Bureaucratic Phenomenon*. Chicago, Ill.: University of Chicago Press, 1964.

Dabezies, Pierre. "Milices, conscription, armée de métier." *Projet* 79 (November 1973).

Danel, Raymond. "L'armée de l'air française à l'entrée en guerre." *Revue d'histoire de la deuxième guerre mondiale* 73, no. 19 (1969).

———. "En mai–juin 1940, ils étaient les plus forts." *Icare* 54 (summer 1970).

Danel, Raymond, and Jean Cuny. *L'aviation française de bombardement et de renseignement, 1918–1940*. Paris: Editions Larivière, 1978.

Darcy, Robert. *Oraison funèbre pour la vieille armée.* Paris: Boivin, 1947.

Davis, A. W. "The Tank Driver." *Royal Tank Corps Journal* 15, no. 175 (1933).

Davis, Shelby Cullom. *The French War Machine.* London: George Allen and Unwin, 1937.

De Gaulle, Charles. *La France et son armée.* Paris: Librairie Plon, 1938.

———. "Philosophie du recrutement." *Revue de l'infanterie,* April 1929.

———. "Vers l'armée de métier." *Revue politique et parlementaire,* May 10, 1933.

———. *Vers l'armée de métier.* Paris: Editions Berger-Levrault, 1944.

Debeney, General Eugène. "Armée nationale ou armée de métier?" *Revue des deux mondes,* September 15, 1929.

———. "Encore l'armée de métier." *Revue des deux mondes,* July 15, 1935.

———. *Sur la sécurité militaire de la France.* Paris: Payot, 1930.

Delaunay, Jean. "Chars de combat et cavalerie, 1917–1942: la naissance de l'arme blindée." *Revue historique des armées* 155 (June 1984).

Demey, Evelyne. *Paul Reynaud, mon père.* Paris: Librairie Plon, 1980.

Dennery, Etienne. "Democracy and the French Army." *Military Affairs* 4, no. 4 (1941).

Dennis, Peter. *Decision by Default: Peacetime Conscription and British Defense, 1919–1939.* Durham, N.C.: Duke University Press, 1972.

Destremau, Christian, and Jérôme Hélie. *Les militaires: être officier aujourd'hui.* Paris: Olivier Orban, 1990.

Dickinson, Richard John. *Officers' Mess Life and Customs in the Regiments.* Tunbridge Wells, Eng., 1977.

Dilks, David. "The Unnecessary War? Military Advice and Foreign Policy in Great Britain, 1931–1939." In *General Staffs and Diplomacy before the Second World War,* edited by Adrian Preston. London: Croom Helm, 1978.

Dobbin, Frank. *Forging Industrial Policy: The United States, Britain, and France in the Railway Age.* Cambridge, Eng.: Cambridge University Press, 1994.

Doise, Jean, and Maurice Vaisse. *Diplomatie et outil militaire, 1871–1968.* Paris: Imprimerie Nationale, 1987.

Dornbusch, Sanford. "The Military Academy as an Assimilating Institution." *Social Forces* 33 (May 1955).

Doughty, Robert A. "The Illusion of Security: France, 1919–1940." In *The Making of Strategy: Rulers, States, and War,* edited by Williamson Murray, MacGregor Knox, and Alvin Bernstein. Cambridge, Eng.: Cambridge University Press, 1994.

———. *The Seeds of Disaster: The Development of French Army Doctrine, 1919–1939.* Hamden, Conn.: Archon Books, 1985.

Douglas, Roy. *In the Year of Munich.* London: Macmillan, 1977.

Doumenc, Major Joseph Edouard Aimé. "Puissance et mobilité." *Revue militaire française* 9 (January–March 1923).

Dournel, Jean-Pierre. "L'armée de l'air en 1946." *Recueil d'articles et études, 1974–1975.* Vincennes: Service historique de l'armée de l'air, 1977.

Dreyer, Rear Admiral. "The Birth of a Staff System." *Journal of the Royal United Service Institution* 73, no. 489 (1928).

Dunbabin, John. "The British Military Establishment and the Policy of Appeasement." In *The Fascist Challenge and the Policy of Appeasement*, edited by Wolfgang J. Mommsen and Lothar Kettenacker. London: George Allen and Unwin, 1983.

———. "British Rearmament in the 1930s: A Chronology and Review." *Historical Journal* 18, no. 3 (1975).

Dunbar, Roger L. M. "Crossing Mother: Ideological Constraints on Organizational Improvements." *Journal of Management Studies* 19 (January 1982).

Dupuy, Trevor N. *A Genius for War: The German Army and General Staff, 1807–1945*. Englewood Cliffs, N.J.: Prentice-Hall, 1977.

Duroselle, Jean-Baptiste. *La décadence, 1932–39*. Paris: Imprimerie Nationale, 1979.

Dutailly, Lieutenant-Colonel Henry. "Faiblesses et potentialités de l'armée de terre, 1939–1940." In *Les armées françaises pendant la seconde guerre mondiale, 1939–1945*, edited by La Fondation pour les études de défense nationale. Paris: Ecole nationale supérieure de techniques avancées, 1985.

———. "Motorisation et mécanisation dans l'armée de terre française." *Revue internationale d'histoire militaire*, no. 55 (1983).

———. *Les problèmes de l'armée de terre française, 1935–39*. Vincennes: Service historique de l'armée de terre, 1980.

———. "La puissance militaire de la France en 1938." *Revue historique des armées* 152, no. 3 (1983).

Dutourd, Jean. *Les taxis de la Marne*. Paris: Gallimard, 1956.

Duval, General Maurice. "La crise de notre organisation militaire." *Revue de Paris* 32, no. 8 (1926).

———. *Les leçons de la guerre d'Espagne*. Paris: Librairie Plon, 1938.

Eden, Lynn. "Constructing Destruction: Knowledge, Organizations, and U.S. Nuclear Weapons Effects." Stanford University, 1996.

Ehrman, John. *Cabinet Government and War, 1890–1940*. Cambridge, Eng.: Cambridge University Press, 1958.

Elkins, Frederick. "The Soldier's Language." *American Journal of Sociology* 51, no. 5 (1946).

Elliott-Bateman, Michael. "Vocabulary: The Second Problem of Military Reform." *Defense Analysis* 6, no. 4 (1990).

Ellison, Major General. "Army Administration." *Army Quarterly* 3, no. 1 (1921).

Elman, Miriam Fendius. "The Foreign Policies of Small States: Challenging Neorealism in Its Own Backyard." *British Journal of Political Science* 25 (April 1995).

Ely, General Paul. *L'armée dans la nation*. Paris: Fayard, 1961.

Estienne, General Jean-Baptiste. "Les forces matérielles à la guerre." *Revue de Paris* 29 (January 15, 1922).

Evans, General William J. "The Impact of Technology on U.S. Deterrent Forces." *Strategic Review* 4, no. 3 (1976).

Fabry, Jean. "La défense nationale." *Revue militaire générale*, January 1938.

———. "Où va notre armée?" *Revue de Paris*, September 15, 1925.

Facon, Patrick. "Les leçons de la campagne de Pologne vu par l'état major aérien français." *Revue historique des armées* 161 (December 1985).

Farwell, Byron. *For Queen and Country*. London: Allen Lane, 1981.

Feiling, Keith. *The Life of Neville Chamberlain*. London: Macmillan, 1946.

Feller, Jean. *Le dossier de l'armée française: la guerre de "cinquante ans."* Paris: Librairie Academique Perrin, 1966.

Ferré, Colonel Georges. *Le défaut de l'armure: nos chars pouvaient-ils vaincre en 1940?* Paris: Charles Lavauzelle, 1948.

Ferris, John Robert. *Men, Money, and Diplomacy: The Evolution of British Strategic Policy, 1919–26*. Ithaca, N.Y.: Cornell University Press, 1989.

Ferte, Air Chief Marshal Sir Philip Joubert de la. *The Fated Sky*. London: Hutchinson, 1952.

———. *The Third Service: The Story behind the Royal Air Force*. London: Thames and Hudson, 1955.

Festing, Major M. C. "The Value of Close Order Drill in Training the Soldier for War." *Journal of the Royal United Service Institution* 66, no. 461 (1921).

Finer, Samuel. *The Man on Horseback: The Role of the Military in Politics*. Boulder, Colo.: Westview, 1988.

Fisher, Brigadier B. D. "The Training of the Regimental Officer." *Journal of the Royal United Service Institution* 74, no. 494 (1929).

Flavigny, Colonel Jean Alphonse Louis. "Manoeuvres de la 4e division de cavalerie en Rhénanie en 1928." *Revue de Cavalerie* 9, no. 2 (1929).

[Foch, Marshal Ferdinand]. "L'armée qu'il nous faut." *Revue des deux mondes*, January 1, 1921.

Forrest, Alan. *The Soldiers of the French Revolution*. Durham, N.C.: Duke University Press, 1990.

France, Ministère des affaires étrangères. *Documents diplomatiques français, 1932–1939*. Paris: Imprimerie Nationale, 1964.

Frankenstein, Robert. "A propos des aspects financiers du réarmement français, 1935–39." *Revue d'histoire de la deuxième guerre mondiale* 102 (April 1976).

———. *Le prix du réarmement français, 1935–1939*. Paris: Publications de la Sorbonne, 1982.

Frankland, Noble. *The Bombing Offensive against Germany*. London: Faber and Faber, 1965.

Frazer, Jendayi. "Sustaining Civilian Control: Armed Counterweights in Regime Stability in Africa." Ph.D. diss., Stanford University, 1992.

Fridenson, Patrick, and Jean Lecuir. *La France et la Grande-Bretagne face aux problèmes aériens*. Vincennes: Service historique de l'armée de l'air, 1976.

Friedberg, Aaron L. *The Weary Titan: Britain and the Experience of Relative Decline, 1895–1905*. Princeton, N.J.: Princeton University Press, 1988.

Friedman, Leon. "Conscription and the Constitution: The Original Understanding." In *The Military Draft: Selected Readings on Conscription*, edited by Martin Anderson. Stanford, Calif.: Hoover Institution Press, 1982.

Fuller, J.F.C. *The Decisive Battles of the Western World*. Vol. 3. London: Eyre and Spottiswoode, 1956.

———. *Memoirs of an Unconventional Soldier*. London: Nicholson and Watson, 1936.

G., Captain. "L'armée nouvelle et le service d'un an." *Revue militaire générale*, August 1921.

Game, Air Vice Marshal Sir Philip. "Service in the Royal Air Force." *Royal Air Force Quarterly* 1, no. 1 (1930).

Gamelin, General Maurice. *Servir: les armées françaises de 1940*. Paris: Librairie Plon, 1946.

Garnier, Maurice. "Technology, Organizational Culture, and Recruitment in the British Military Academy." In *World Perspectives in the Sociology of the Military*, edited by George A. Kourvetaris and Betty A. Dobratz. New Brunswick, N.J.: Transaction Books, 1977.

Garret, Charles. "La ligne Maginot et la dissuasion nucléaire: continuité de la pensée militaire française." Ph.D. diss., University of Nantes, 1985.

George, Alexander L. "The Causal Nexus between Cognitive Beliefs and Decision-Making Behavior: The 'Operational Code' Belief System." In *Psychological Models in International Politics*, edited by Laurence S. Falkowski. Boulder, Colo,: Westview, 1979.

Geyer, Michael. "German Strategy in the Age of Machine Warfare, 1914–1945." In *Makers of Modern Strategy from Machiavelli to the Nuclear Age*, edited by Peter Paret. Princeton, N.J.: Princeton University Press, 1986.

Gibbs, Norman Henry. "British Strategic Doctrine, 1918–1938." In *The Theory and Practice of War*, edited by Michael Howard. New York: Praeger, 1966.

———. *Grand Strategy: Rearmament Policy*. Vol. 1, *History of the Second World War*. United Kingdom Military Series, edited by J.R.M. Butler. London: Her Majesty's Stationery Office, 1976.

Gibson, Irving M. "The Maginot Line." *Journal of Modern History* 2 (June 1945).

Girardet, Raoul. "Opinion et politique de défense depuis un siècle." *Défense nationale* (August–September 1977).

Goffman, Erving. *Asylums: Essays on the Social Situation of Mental Patients and Other Inmates*. Chicago, Ill.: Aldine, 1961.

Goguel, François. *La politique des partis sous la troisième République*. Paris: Editions du Seuil, 1958.

Gorce, Paul-Marie de la. *The French Army: A Military-Political History*. London: Weidenfeld and Nicolson, 1963.

Gordon-Dean, Wing Commander H. "The Development of Leadership and Morale in the RAF." *Royal Air Force Quarterly* 3, no. 1 (1932).

Goyet, Colonel P. le. "Evolution de la doctrine d'emploi de l'aviation française entre 1919 et 1939." *Revue d'histoire de la deuxième guerre mondiale* 19 (January 1969).

Granville, Wilfred. *A Dictionary of Sailors' Slang*. London: Andre Deutsch, 1962.

Grazin, Captain Fernand-Charles. "Essai d'emploi d'autos mitrailleuses sur chenilles aux manoeuvres de la Sarre." *Revue de Cavalerie* 3, no. 6 (1923).

Gunsburg, Jeffrey A. "Coupable où non? Le rôle du Général Gamelin dans la défaite de 1940." *Revue historique des armées*, no. 4 (1979).

Guttsman, W. L., ed. *The English Ruling Class*. London: Weidenfeld and Nicolson, 1969.

Guyot, Raymond. *Les problèmes de la défense nationale et de l'armée*. Paris: Editions par le Parti communiste français, 1951.

Hacker, Barton C. "The United States Army as a National Police Force: The Federal Policing of Labor Disputes, 1877–1898." *Military Affairs* 33, no. 1 (1969).

Hacker, Brian. "The Military and the Machine: An Analysis of the Controversy over Mechanization in the British Army." Ph.D. diss., University of Chicago, 1968.

Hall, Peter. "Conclusion: The Politics of Keynesian Ideas." In *The Political Power of Economic Ideas: Keynesianism across Nations*, edited by Peter Hall. Princeton, N.J.: Princeton University Press, 1989.

———. "Introduction." In *The Political Power of Economic Ideas: Keynesianism across Nations*, edited by Peter Hall. Princeton, N.J.: Princeton University Press, 1989.

Hall, Peter, ed. *The Political Power of Economic Ideas: Keynesianism across Nations*. Princeton, N.J.: Princeton University Press, 1989.

Halperin, Morton H. *Bureaucratic Politics and Foreign Policy*. Washington, D.C.: Brookings Institution, 1974.

Hamilton, Alexander. *The Federalist Papers*, edited by Clinton Rossiter. New York: New American Library, 1961.

Hamilton, Major G. D. Baillie. "The Re-forming Army: Some Suggestions." *Journal of the Royal United Service Institution* 65, no. 557 (1920).

Harries-Jenkins, Gwyn. *The Army in Victorian Society*. London: Routledge and Kegan Paul, 1977.

Harrison, Richard J. "Keeping the Faith: A Model of Cultural Transmission in Formal Organizations." *Administrative Science Quarterly* 36, no. 4 (1991).

Hartcup, Guy. *The Challenge of War: Britain's Scientific and Engineering Contributions to World War Two*. New York: Taplinger, 1970.

Harvey, Donald J. "French Concepts of Military Strategy, 1919–1939." Ph.D. diss., Columbia University, 1953.

Head, Richard G. "Doctrinal Innovation and the A-7 Attack Aircraft Decisions." In *American Defense Policy*, 4th ed., edited by John E. Endicott and Roy W. Stafford, Jr.. Baltimore, Md.: Johns Hopkins University Press, 1977.

Hébrard, Jean. *Vingt-cinq années d'aviation militaire, 1920–1945*. Paris: Editions Albin Michel, 1946.

Hedberg, Bo L. T. "How Organizations Learn and Unlearn." In *Handbook of Organizational Design*, Vol. 1, edited by Paul C. Nystrom and William H. Starbuck. New York: Oxford University Press, 1981.

Hellman, Judith Adler. *Journeys among Women: Feminism in Five Italian Cities*. New York: Oxford University Press, 1987.

Henderson, Darryl. *Cohesion: The Human Element in Combat*. Washington, D.C.: National Defense University Press, 1985.

Hermann, Charles F. "Some Consequences of Crises Which Limit Viability of Organizations." *Administrative Science Quarterly* 8, no. 1 (1963).

Hernu, Charles. *Soldat-citoyen*. Paris: Flammarion, 1975.

Herwig, Holger H. *The German Naval Officer Corps: A Social and Political History, 1980–1918*. Oxford, Eng.: Clarendon, 1973.

Hoff, Pierre. *Les programmes d'armement de 1919 à 1938*. Vincennes: Service historique de l'armée de terre, 1982.

Hofstede, Geert H. *Culture's Consequences: International Differences in Work-Related Values*. Beverly Hills, Calif.: Sage, 1980.

Hogg, Ian V. *Forteresses: histoire illustrée des ouvrages défensifs*. London: Purnell, 1975.

Holloway, David. "Doctrine and Technology in Soviet Armaments Policy." In *Soviet Military Thinking*, edited by Derek Leebaert. Boston: George Allen and Unwin, 1984.

Hoop, J. M. d'. "La politique française du réarmement, 1933–1939." *Revue d'histoire de la deuxième guerre mondiale* 14 (April 1954).

Horne, Alistair. *To Lose a Battle: France, 1940*. London: Macmillan, 1969.

———. *The Price of Glory: Verdun 1916*. London: Macmillan, 1962.

"A Horse! A Horse! My Kingdom for a Horse!" *Army Quarterly* 28, no. 1 (1934).

Hovland, Carl I., Irving L. Janis, and Harold H. Kelley. *Communication and Persuasion*. New Haven, Conn.: Yale University Press, 1953.

Howard, Michael. *The Continental Commitment*. London: Temple Smith, 1972.

———. *The Franco-Prussian War*. New York: Macmillan, 1961.

———. "The Liddell Hart Memoirs." *Journal of the Royal United Service Institution* 3, no. 1 (1966).

———. "Military Science in an Age of Peace." *Journal of the Royal United Services Institute for Defence Studies* 119, no. 1 (1974).

———. "Soldiers in Politics." *Encounter* 108 (September 1962).

———. *War in European History*. Oxford, Eng.: Oxford University Press, 1976.

Howorth, Jolyon, and Patricia Chilton, eds. *Defence and Dissent in Contemporary France*. New York: Croom Helm, 1984.

Hughes, Judith M. *To the Maginot Line: The Politics of French Military Preparations in the 1920s*. Cambridge, Mass.: Harvard University Press, 1971.

Huntington, Samuel. *The Soldier and the State: The Theory and Politics of Civil-Military Relations*. Cambridge, Mass.: Belknap, 1957.

Hyde, Harford Montgomery. *British Air Policy between the Wars, 1918–1939*. London: Heinemann, 1976.

"Infantry Reorganization: A Reply." *Journal of the Royal United Service Institution* 77, no. 507 (1932).

Ingraud, Louis. *Le chemin de croix de l'aviation française*. Lyon: La nouvelle édition, 1943.

Ironside, Major General W. E. "The Modern Staff Officer." *Journal of the Royal United Service Institution* 73, no. 491 (1928).

Jackson, Robert. *Before the Storm: The Story of Royal Air Force Bomber Command, 1939–42*. London: Arthur Barker, 1972.

Janowitz, Morris. *The Professional Soldier: A Social and Political Portrait*. New York: Free Press, 1960.

———. *Sociology and the Military Establishment*. Beverly Hills, Calif.: Sage, 1974.

Jauffret, Jean-Charles. "L'image de l'armée britannique devant le parlement français et le conseil supérieur de la guerre de 1871 à 1900." In *Forces armées et systèmes d'alliances*. Montpellier: Fondation pour les études de défense nationale, 1981.

———. "L'officier français 1871–1919." In *L'officier français des origines à nos jours*, edited by Claude Croubois. St-Jean-d'Angely: Editions Bordessoules, 1987.

Jauneaud, Jean-Henri. *De Verdun à Dien Bien Phu*. Paris: Les Editions du Scorpion, 1959.

Jaurès, Jean. *L'armée nouvelle*. Paris: Editions sociales, 1977.

Jeffery, Keith. "The Post-War Army." In *A Nation in Arms: A Social Study of the British Army in the First World War*, edited by Ian F. W. Beckett and Keith Simpson. Manchester, Eng.: Manchester University Press, 1985.

Jepperson, Ronald L., and Ann Swidler. "What Properties of Culture Should We Measure?" *Poetics* 22, no. 4 (1994).

Jervis, Robert. "Cooperation under the Security Dilemma." *World Politics* 30, no. 2 (1978).

Joffre, Marshal Joseph. *Mémoires de Maréchal Joffre, 1910–1917*. Vol. 1. Paris: Librairie Plon, 1932.

Johnson, Franklyn Arthur. *Defence by Committee: The British Committee of Imperial Defence, 1885–1959*. London: Oxford University Press, 1960.

Johnston, Alastair Iain. *Cultural Realism: Strategic Culture and Grand Strategy in Ming China*. Princeton, N.J.: Princeton University Press, 1995.

———. "Thinking about Strategic Culture." *International Security* 19, no. 4 (1995).

Jones, Neville. *The Origins of Strategic Bombing: A Study of the Development of British Air Strategic Thought and Practice Up to 1918*. London: Kimber, 1973.

Journal officiel de la République française, débats parlementaires, Chambre des députés. Paris: Imprimerie des journaux officiels, 1870–1940.

Jouvenel, Bertrand de. "Le service militaire obligatoire . . . est-il une institution de gauche?" *La voix* 9 (February 1930).

Kaempffert, Waldemer. "War and Technology." *American Journal of Sociology* 46 (January 1941).

Karsten, Peter, ed. *The Military in America: From the Colonial Era to the Present*. New York: Free Press, 1980.

Katzenbach, Edward L., Jr. "The Horse Cavalry in the Twentieth Century." In *American Defense Policy*, 4th ed., edited by John E. Endicott and Roy W. Stafford, Jr. Baltimore, Md.: Johns Hopkins University Press, 1977.

———. "Political Parties and the French Army since Liberation." In *Modern France*, edited by Edward Mead Earle. Princeton, N.J.: Princeton University Press, 1951.

Katzenstein, Peter, ed. *The Culture of National Security: Norms and Identity in World Politics*. New York: Columbia University Press, 1996.

———. *Small States in World Markets*. Ithaca, N.Y.: Cornell University Press, 1985.

Keegan, John. "Regimental Ideology." In *War, Economy and the Military Mind*, edited by Geoffrey Best and Andrew Wheatcroft. London: Croom Helm, 1976.

Kelleher, Catherine McArdle. "Mass Armies in the 1970s: The Debate in Western Europe." *Armed Forces and Society* 5, no. 1 (1978).

Keller, Maryann. *Rude Awakening: The Rise, Fall, and Struggle for Recovery of General Motors*. New York: William Morrow, 1990.

Kennedy, Paul. "Great Britain before 1914." In *Knowing One's Enemies: Intelligence Assessment before the Two World Wars*, edited by Ernest R. May. Princeton, N.J.: Princeton University Press, 1986.

———. *The Realities behind Diplomacy: Background Influences on British External Policy, 1865–1980*. London: Fontana, 1981.

———. *The Rise and Fall of British Naval Mastery*. London: Allen Lane, 1976.

Keohane, Robert O. *After Hegemony: Cooperation and Discord in the World Political Economy*. Princeton, N.J.: Princeton University Press, 1984.

Kets de Vries, Manfred F. R., and Danny Miller. "Personality, Culture, and Organization." *Academy of Management Review* 11 (April 1986).

Khandwalla, Pradip N. "Environment and Its Impact on the Organization." *International Studies of Management and Organization* 2, no. 3 (1972).

Kiesling, Eugenia C. *Arming against Hitler: France and the Limits of Military Planning*. Lawrence: University Press of Kansas, 1996.

Kirkland, Faris R. "Anti-Military Group Fantasies and the Destruction of the French Air Force, 1928–1940." *Journal of Psychohistory* 14, no. 1 (1986).

———. "Combat Leadership Styles: Empowerment versus Authoritarianism." *Parameters* 20 (December 1990).

———. "Governmental Policy and Combat Effectiveness: France, 1920–1940." *Armed Forces and Society* 18, no. 2 (1992).

———. "Professionalism and the Defense of Corporate Interests in the French Air Force, 1933–1940." Paper presented at the Northeast Regional Conference of the Inter-University Seminar on Armed Forces and Society, State University of New York at Albany, April 12–13, 1985.

Kirshner, Jonathan. *Currency and Coercion: The Political Economy of International Monetary Power*. Princeton, N.J.: Princeton University Press, 1995.

Kraehe, Enno. "The Motives behind the Maginot Line." *Military Affairs* 8, no. 2 (1944).

Kratochwil, Friedrich, and John Gerard Ruggie. "International Organization: A State of the Art on an Art of the State." *International Organization* 40, no. 4 (1986).

Krauskopf, Robert W. "French Air Power Policy, 1919–1939." Ph.D. diss., Georgetown University, 1965.

Krepinevich, Andrew F. *The Army and Vietnam*. Baltimore, Md.: Johns Hopkins University Press, 1986.

Kupchan, Charles A. *The Vulnerability of Empire*. Ithaca, N.Y.: Cornell University Press, 1994.

Lacouture, Jean. *Léon Blum*. Paris: Editions du Seuil, 1977.

Laffargue, General André. *Justice pour ceux de 1940*. Limoges: Charles Lavauzelle, 1952.

Laitin, David. *Hegemony and Culture: Politics and Religious Change among the Yoruba*. Chicago, Ill.: University of Chicago Press, 1986.

Lammers, Cornelis J., and David J. Hickson. "A Cross-National and Cross-Institutional Typology of Organizations." In *Organizations Alike and Unlike: International and Inter-institutional Studies in the Sociology of Organizations*, edited by Cornelis J. Lammers and David J. Hickson. London: Routledge and Kegan Paul, 1979.

Lamy, Etienne. "L'armée et la démocratie." *Revue des deux mondes*, June 15, 1885.

Langeron, Lieutenant Colonel André. *Misère et grandeur de notre aviation.* Paris: Editions Baudinière, 1942.

Langlois, Lieutenant Colonel Pierre-Louis-Guillaume. "Cheval et chenille." *Revue de cavalerie* 3, no. 2 (1923).

Larson, Robert H. *The British Army and the Theory of Armored Warfare, 1918–1940.* Newark, Del.: University of Delaware Press, 1984.

Laure, General Auguste. *Pétain.* Paris: Editions Berger-Levrault, 1941.

Laurent, André. "The Cultural Diversity of Western Conceptions of Management." *International Studies of Management and Organization* 13, no. 1–2 (1983).

Lawrence, T. E. *The Mint.* London: Jonathan Cape, 1955.

Lee, Bradford A. "Strategy, Arms, and the Collapse of France, 1930–1940." In *Diplomacy and Intelligence during the Second World War: Essays in Honor of F. H. Hinsley*, edited by Richard Langhoren. Cambridge, Eng.: Cambridge University Press, 1985.

Lefranc, Georges. *Histoire du front populaire, 1934–1938.* Paris: Payot, 1974.

———. *Le mouvement socialiste sous la troisième République.* Paris: Payot, 1963.

Lefranc, Jacques, and Léo Moulin. "Dialogue sur l'armée de la classe 15 à la classe 25." *Esprit* 32 (May 1935).

Legro, Jeffrey W. *Cooperation under Fire: Anglo-German Restraint during World War II.* Ithaca, N.Y.: Cornell University Press, 1995.

Levite, Ariel. *Offense and Defense in Israeli Military Doctrine.* Boulder, Colo.: Westview, 1989.

Levy, Jack S. "The Offensive/Defensive Balance of Military Technology: A Theoretical and Historical Analysis." *International Studies Quarterly* 28, no. 2 (1984).

Lewal, General Jules-Louis. *Contre le service de deux ans.* Paris: Librairie Militaire de Baudoin, 1895.

———. *Le danger des milices.* Paris: Librairie Militaire de Baudoin, 1898.

Liddell Hart, Basil H. "The Army Exercise of 1930." *Journal of the Royal United Service Institution* 75, no. 500 (1930).

———. *The British Way in Warfare.* New York: Macmillan, 1933.

———. *The Memoirs of Captain Liddell Hart.* Vols. 1 and 2. London: Cassell, 1965.

Lodge, George C., and Ezra F. Vogel. *Ideology and National Competitiveness: An Analysis of Nine Countries.* Boston: Harvard Business School Press, 1987.

Loge maçonnique, les enfants de Gergovie. *L'armée cléricale.* Clermont-Ferrand: La Laborieuse, 1903.

———. *Démocratisation des cadres de l'armée.* Clermont-Ferrand: La Laborieuse, 1903.

Loustaunau-Lacau, Colonel Georges. *Mémoires d'un Français rebelle, 1914–1948.* Paris: Laffont, 1948.

Lundberg, Craig C. "On the Feasibility of Cultural Intervention in Organizations." In *Organizational Culture*, edited by Peter L. Frost, Larry Moore,

Meryl Reis Louis, Craig C. Lundberg, and Joanne Martin. Beverly Hills, Calif.: Sage, 1985.

Luttwak, Edward, and Dan Horowitz. *The Israeli Army*. New York: Harper and Row, 1975.

Luvass, Jay. *The Education of an Army: British Military Thought, 1815–1940*. London: Cassell, 1964.

[Lyautey, Hubert]. "Le rôle social de l'officier." *Revue des deux mondes*, March 15, 1891.

MacCearney, James. *Les lois de recrutement de 1905, 1928, et 1970: analyse thématique des débats à la chambre des députés et à l'assemblée nationale*. Paris: Centre de sociologie de la défense nationale, 1976.

McEntree, Girard Lindsley. *Military History of the World War: A Complete Account of the Campaigns on all Fronts*. New York: Charles Scribner's, 1937.

Mackenzie, Major General J.J.G., and Brian Holden Reid, eds. *The British Army and the Operational Level of War*. London: Tri Service, 1989.

Macksey, Major Kenneth. *Armoured Crusader: A Biography of Major General Sir Percy Hobart*. London: Hutchinson, 1967.

————. *A History of the Royal Armoured Corps and Its Predecessors, 1914–1975*. Beaminster, Eng.: Newtown, 1983.

Maclean, Wing Commander L. L. "The Royal Air Force Training Year at Home." *Journal of the Royal United Service Institution* 80, no. 517 (1935).

McMillan, Charles, David Hickson, Christopher R. Hinings, and Rodney Schneck. "The Structure of Work Organizations Across Societies." *Academy of Management Journal* 16 (1973).

Macmillan, David T. "Technology: The Catalyst for Doctrinal Change." *Air University Review* 29 (November–December 1977).

McNair, Major J. K. "The Study of War by Junior Officers." *The Journal of the Royal United Service Institution* 77, no. 506 (1932).

McNeill, William H. *The Pursuit of Power*. Oxford: Basil Blackwell, 1982.

Mahony, Captain E. R. "A Junior School of Tactics and Leadership." *Journal of the Royal United Service Institution* 81, no. 522 (1936).

Mandelbaum, Michael. *The Fate of Nations: The Search for National Security in the Nineteenth and Twentieth Centuries*. Cambridge, Eng.: Cambridge University Press, 1988.

Marder, Arthur J. *From the Dreadnought to Scapa Flow: The Royal Navy in the Fisher Era, 1904–1919*. Vol. 1, *The Road to War, 1904–1914*. London: Oxford University Press, 1961.

Marmour, Peter J. *The French Radical Party in the 1930s*. Stanford, Calif.: Stanford University Press, 1964.

Maroselli, André. *Le sabotage de notre aviation: cause principale de notre défaite*. Paris: Librairie Gedalge, 1941.

Marrane, Jean. "Intérêt national, militarisme, et anti-militarisme." *Cahiers du communisme* 4 (April 1979).

Martel, Lieutenant General Sir Giffard le Q. *Our Armoured Forces*. London: Faber and Faber, 1945.

Martin, André. "La doctrine française de contre offensive à l'épreuve de la deuxième guerre mondiale." *Relations internationales* 35 (autumn 1983).

Mason, Timothy W. "The Primacy of Politics—Politics and Economics in National Socialist Germany." In *Nazism and the Third Reich*, edited by Henry Turner. New York: Quadrangle, 1972.

Masson, Philippe. "De Douhet et de quelques marins." *Revue historique des armées* 172 (September 1988).

Masters, John. *Bugles and a Tiger: A Volume of Autobiography*. New York: Viking, 1956.

Maurice, Marc, Arndt Sorge, and Malcolm Warner. "Societal Differences in Organizing Manufacturing Units: A Comparison of France, West Germany, and Great Britain." *Organizational Studies of Management and Organization* 10, no. 4 (1980).

Mayeur, Jean-Marie. *La vie politique sous la troisième République, 1870–1940*. Paris: Editions du Seuil, 1984.

Mearsheimer, John J. *Conventional Deterrence*. Ithaca, N.Y.: Cornell University Press, 1983.

———. *Liddell Hart and the Weight of History*. Ithaca, N.Y.: Cornell University Press, 1988.

Meyer, Alan D. "Adapting to Environmental Jolts." *Administrative Science Quarterly* 27, no. 4 (1982).

Michel, Henri. *Le procès de Riom*. Paris: Albin Michel, 1979.

Milling, Major J. M. "The Training of the Army Officer." *Journal of the Royal United Service Institution* 73, no. 491 (1928).

Milward, Alan S. *The German Economy at War*. London: University of London, Athlone Press, 1965.

Ministère de la guerre, Etat-major de l'armée. *L'instruction provisoire sur l'emploi des chars de combat*. Paris: Charles Lavauzelle, 1920.

———. *L'instruction provisoire sur l'emploi tactique des grandes unités*. Paris: Charles Lavauzelle, 1921.

———. *L'instruction sur l'emploi des chars de combat*. Paris: Charles Lavauzelle, 1929.

———. *L'instruction sur l'emploi tactique des grandes unités*. Paris: Charles Lavauzelle, 1936.

———. *Règlement des unités de chars légers*. Paris: Charles Lavauzelle, 1929–30.

Miquel, Pierre. *La paix de Versailles et l'opinion publique française*. Paris: Flammarion, 1972.

Mitroff, Ian I., and Ralph H. Kilmann. "Corporate Taboos as the Key to Unlocking Culture." In *Gaining Control of the Corporate Culture*, edited by Ralph H. Kilmann, Mary J. Saxton, Roy Serpa, and Associates. San Francisco, Calif.: Jossey-Bass, 1985.

———. *Corporate Tragedies: Product Tampering, Sabotage, and Other Catastrophes*. New York: Praeger, 1984.

Monteilhet, Joseph. "L'avènement de la nation armée." *Revue des études Napoléoniennes*, September–October 1918.

———. *Les institutions militaires de la France*. Paris: Felix Alcan, 1932.

Mordacq, General Henri. *La défense nationale en danger*. Paris: Editions de France, 1938.

Morison, Elting E. *Men, Machines, and Modern Times*. Cambridge, Mass.: MIT Press, 1966.

Moskos, Charles C. *The American Enlisted Man: The Rank and File in Today's Military*. New York: Russell Sage, 1970.

Murray, Williamson. *The Change in the European Balance of Power, 1938–1939*. Princeton, N.J.: Princeton University Press, 1984.

———. "Force Strategy, Blitzkrieg Strategy, and the Economic Difficulties: Nazi Grand Strategy in the 1930s." *Journal of the Royal United Service Institute for Defence Studies* 128, no. 1 (1983).

———. "German Army Doctrine, 1918–1939, and the Post-1945 Theory of 'Blitzkrieg Strategy.'" In *German Nationalism and the European Response, 1890–1945*, edited by Carole Fink, Isabel V. Hull, and MacGregor Knox. Norman: University of Oklahoma Press, 1985.

———. "The German Response to Victory in Poland: A Case Study in Professionalism." *Armed Forces and Society* 7, no. 2 (1981).

Mysyrowicz, Ladislas. *Anatomie d'une défaite: origines de l'effondrement militaire français*. Lausanne: Editions de l'age d'homme, 1973.

Nachin, L. *Charles de Gaulle: Général de France*. Paris: Editions Colbert, 1944.

Nardain, Bertrand. *Vers l'armée de la République*. Paris: Editions France d'Abord, 1945.

Neame, Philip. *German Strategy in the Great War*. London: Edward Arnold, 1923.

Neufeld, Mark. "Interpretation and the 'Science' of International Relations." *Review of International Studies* 19, no. 1 (1993).

Nicholson, Nigel, and Gary Johns. "The Absence Culture and the Psychological Contract—Who's in Control of Absence?" *Academy of Management Review* 10, no. 3 (1985).

Niessel, General Henri. "Chars, antichars, et motorisation dans la guerre d'Espagne." *Revue militaire générale*, December 1938.

Nobecourt, Jacques. *Une histoire politique de l'armée*. Paris: Editions du Seuil, 1967.

Normann, Richard. "Developing Capabilities for Organizational Learning." In *Organizational Strategy and Change*, edited by Johannes M. Pennings and Associates. San Francisco: Jossey-Bass, 1985.

O'Neill, Robert J. "Doctrine and Training in the German Army, 1919–1939." In *The Theory and Practice of War*, edited by B. H. Liddell Hart. New York: Praeger, 1965.

Ogorkiewicz, Richard M. *Armour: The Development of Mechanized Forces and Their Equipment*. London: Stevens, 1960.

Ott, J. Steven. *The Organizational Culture Perspective*. Chicago, Ill.: Dorsey, 1989.

Ouchi, W. G. *The M-form Society*. Reading, Mass.: Addison-Wesley, 1984.

Overy, Richard. "Hitler's War and the German Economy: A Reinterpretation." *Economic History Review* 35 (May 1982).

Padfield, Peter. *The Great Naval Race: The Anglo-German Rivalry, 1900–1914*. London: Hart-Davis, MacGibbon, 1974.

Paillat, Claude. *Dossiers secrets de la France contemporaine.* Vol. 3, *La guerre à l'horizon, 1930–1938.* Paris: Editions Robert Laffont, 1981.

Paoli, François André. *L'armée française de 1919 à 1939.* 4 vols. Vincennes: Service historique de l'armée de terre, 1974.

Paret, Peter. *French Revolutionary Warfare from Indochina to Algeria: The Analysis of a Political and Military Doctrine.* London: Pall Mall, 1964.

———. *Innovation and Reform in Warfare: The Harmon Memorial Lectures in Military History.* Colorado Springs, Colo.: U.S. Air Force Academy, 1966.

Payne, Roy, and Derke S. Pugh. "Organizational Structure and Climate." In *Handbook of Industrial and Organizational Psychology*, edited by Marvin D. Dunnette. Chicago, Ill.: Rand McNally College Publishing, 1976.

Peden, G. C. *British Rearmament and the Treasury, 1932–39.* Edinburgh: Scottish Academic Press, 1979.

———. "The Burden of Imperial Defense and the Continental Commitment Reconsidered." *Historical Journal* 27, no. 2 (1984).

Percin, General. *La guerre et la nation armée.* Paris: Ligue des droits de l'homme et du citoyen, n.d. (before 1914).

Perré, Jean. "La refonte de la réglementation relative aux chars de combat." *Revue de l'infanterie* 75 (October 1929).

Pettigrew, Andrew M. "Examining Change in the Long-Term Context of Culture and Politics." In *Organizational Strategy and Change*, edited by Johannes M. Pennings and Associates. San Francisco: Jossey-Bass, 1985.

———. "On Studying Organizational Cultures." *Administrative Science Quarterly* 24, no. 4 (1979).

Pile, General Sir Frederick. "Liddell Hart and the British Army, 1919–1939." In *The Theory and Practice of War: Essays Presented to Captain B. H. Liddell Hart*, edited by Michael Howard. New York: Praeger, 1966.

Planchais, Jean. "Crise de modernisme dans l'armée." *Revue française de sociologie* 2, no. 2 (1961).

Poe, Bryce. "British Army Reforms: 1902–1914." *Military Affairs* 31, no. 3 (1967).

Pognon, Edmond. *De Gaulle et l'armée.* Paris: Librarie Plon, 1976.

Porch, Douglas. *Army and Revolution: France, 1815–1848.* London: Routledge and Kegan Paul, 1974.

———. *The March to the Marne: The French Army, 1871–1914.* New York: Cambridge University Press, 1981.

Posen, Barry R. "Inadvertent Nuclear War? Escalation and NATO's Northern Flank." *International Security* 7, no. 2 (1982).

———. *The Sources of Military Doctrine: France, Britain, and Germany between the World Wars.* Ithaca, N.Y.: Cornell University Press, 1984.

Possony, Stefan T. "Organized Intelligence: The Problem of the French General Staff." *Social Research* 8, no. 2 (1941).

Post, Gaines. "Mad Dogs and Englishmen: British Rearmament, Deterrence, and Appeasement, 1934–35." *Armed Forces and Society* 14, no. 3 (1988).

Postan, Michael Moissey, D. Hay Postan, and J. D. Scott. *Design and Develop-*

ment of Weapons: Studies in Government and Industrial Organisation. London: Her Majesty's Stationery Office, 1964.

Powers, Barry D. "The Development of British Air Defense: Concepts in the Theory and in Practice, 1914–1931." Ph.D. diss., University of Delaware, 1973.

———. *Strategy without Slide-rule: British Air Strategy, 1914–1939*. Cambridge: Cambridge University Press, 1975.

Preston, Adrian, and Peter Dennis, eds. *Soldiers as Statesmen*. London: Croom Helm, 1976.

Price, Alfred. *Blitz on Britain, 1939–1945*. London: Ian Allan, 1977.

Prochasson, Christophe. "Les grandes dates de l'histoire de la conscription: de la milice au service national." *Revue historique des armées* 2, no. 147 (1982).

Pugens, Lieutenant Colonel. "La guerre de 1870 et ses répercussions sur les débuts de 1914." *Revue historique des armées* 3, no. 172 (1988).

Pye, Lucien W., and Sidney Verba, eds. *Political Culture and Political Development*. Princeton, N.J.: Princeton University Press, 1965.

Quandt, William B. *Revolution and Political Leadership: Algeria, 1954–1968*. Cambridge, Mass.: MIT Press, 1969.

Quester, George C. *Offense and Defense in the International System*. New York: John Wiley, 1977.

Racine, Nicole, and Louis Bodin. *Le Parti communiste français pendant l'entre deux guerres*. Paris: Armand Colin, 1972.

Raleigh, Walter. *The War in the Air*. Oxford: Clarendon, 1922.

Ralston, David B. *The Army of the Republic: The Place of the Military in the Political Evolution of France, 1871–1914*. Cambridge, Mass.: MIT Press, 1967.

Ramspacher, E. *Le général Estienne: "père des chars."* Paris: Charles Lavauzelle, 1983.

Raven, Simon. *The English Gentleman: An Essay in Attitudes*. London: Anthony Blond, 1961.

Reader, William Joseph. *Professional Men: The Rise of the Professional Classes in Nineteenth-Century England*. London: Weidenfeld and Nicolson, 1966.

Rémond, René. *La droite en France de 1815 à nos jours*. Paris: Aubier, 1954.

Réquin, General Edouard. *D'une guerre à l'autre, 1919–1931*. Paris: Charles Lauvazelle, 1949.

Reussner, André. "La réorganisation du haut-commandement au mois de mai 1940." *Revue d'histoire de la deuxième guerre mondiale* 3, nos. 10 and 11 (June 1953).

Reynaud, Paul. *Mémoires: envers et contre tous*. Paris: Flammarion, 1963.

———. *Le problème militaire français*. Paris: Flammarion, 1937.

Rikhye, Ravi. *The War That Never Was: The Story of India's Strategic Failures*. Delhi: Chanakya, 1988.

Risse-Kappen, Thomas. *Cooperation among Democracies: The European Influence on U.S. Foreign Policy*. Princeton, N.J.: Princeton University Press, 1995.

Ritter, Gerhard. *The European Powers and the Wilhelminian Empire, 1890–1914*. Vol. 2, *The Sword and the Scepter: The Problem of Militarism in Germany*. Trans. Heinz Norden. London: Penguin, 1972.

Rochlin, Gene I., Todd R. La Porte, and Karlene H. Roberts. "The Self-Designing High-Reliability Organization: Aircraft Carrier Flight Operations at Sea." *Naval War College Review* 40, no. 4 (1987).

Rolbant, Samuel. *The Israeli Soldier: Profile of an Army*. London: Thomas Yoseloff, 1970.

Romain, Colonel Charles-Armand. "La réorganisation de l'armée: les chars de combat." *Revue de Paris* 29, no. 5 (1922).

Romjue, John L. *From Active Defense to Airland Battle: The Development of Army Doctrine, 1973–1982*. Ft. Monroe, Va.: U.S. Army Training and Doctrine Command, 1984.

Rose, Arnold. "The Social Structure of the Army." *American Journal of Sociology* 51, no. 5 (1946).

Rosen, Stephen Peter. *Societies and Military Power: India and her Armies*. Ithaca, N.Y.: Cornell University Press, 1996.

———. *Winning the Next War: Innovation and the Modern Military*. Ithaca, N.Y.: Cornell University Press, 1991.

Roskill, Stephen W. *The Strategy of Sea Power*. London: Collins Clear-Type, 1962.

Rothenberg, Gunther E. *The Anatomy of the Israeli Army*. London: B. T. Batsford, 1979.

Rouquie, Alain. "Les processus politiques au sein des partis militaires: définitions et dynamiques." In *La politique de mars*, edited by Alain Rouquie. Paris: Le Sycomore, 1981.

Roux, Lieutenant-Colonel Adrien. *Gardons le service de deux ans*. Paris: Librairie positiviste, 1912.

Rowlinson, Michael, and John Hassard. "The Invention of Corporate Culture: A History of the Histories of Cadbury." *Human Relations* 46, no. 3 (1993).

"The Royal Horse Artillery with Cavalry." *Cavalry Journal*, July 1922.

Sackmann, Sonja A. "Culture and Subcultures: An Analysis of Organizational Knowledge." *Administrative Science Quarterly* 37, no. 1 (1992).

———. "Uncovering Culture in Organizations." *Journal of Applied Behavioral Science* 27, no. 3 (1991).

Sagan, Scott D. "1914 Revisited: Allies, Offense, and Instability." *International Security* 11, no. 2 (1986).

Sanders, Charles W. *No Other Law: The French Army and the Doctrine of the Offensive*. Santa Monica, Calif.: Rand Corporation, 1987.

Sathe, Vijay. "How to Decipher and Change Corporate Culture." In *Gaining Control of the Corporate Culture*, edited by Ralph H. Kilmann, Mary J. Saxton, Roy Serpa, and Associates. San Francisco, Calif.: Jossey-Bass, 1985.

Schein, Edgar H. "Coming to a New Awareness of Organizational Culture." *Sloan Management Review* 25, no. 2 (1984).

———. *Organizational Culture and Leadership: A Dynamic View*. San Francisco, Calif.: Jossey-Bass, 1985.

Schelling, Thomas C. *The Strategy of Conflict*. Cambridge, Mass.: Harvard Univ. Press, 1960.

Schmidt, Gustav. *The Politics and Economics of Appeasement: British Foreign Policy in the 1930s*. New York: St. Martin's, 1986.

Schuker, Stephen A. "France and the Remilitarization of the Rhineland." *French Historical Studies* 14, no. 3 (1986).

Schumacher, Alois. *La politique de sécurité française face à l'Allemagne: les controverses de l'opinion française entre 1932 et 1935.* Frankfurt: Peter Lang, 1978.

Schwoerer, Lois G. *"No Standing Armies!" The Antiarmy Ideology in Seventeenth-century England.* Baltimore, Md.: Johns Hopkins University Press, 1974.

Selznick, Philip. *Leadership in Administration: A Sociological Interpretation.* New York: Row, Peterson, 1957.

Semmel, Bernard. *Liberalism and Naval Strategy: Ideology, Interest, and Sea Power during the Pax Britannica.* Boston: Allen and Unwin, 1986.

Sénéchal, Michel. *Droits politiques et liberté d'expression des officiers des forces armées.* Paris: Librairie générale de droit et de jurisprudence, 1964.

Sergiovanni, Thomas J. "Cultural and Competing Perspectives in Administrative Theory and Practice." In *Leadership and Organizational Culture: New Perspectives on Administrative Theory and Practice,* edited by Thomas J. Sergiovanni and John E. Corbally. Urbana, Ill.: University of Illinois Press, 1984.

Serre, Charles. *Les événements survenus en France de 1933 à 1945.* Rapport fait au nom de la commission chargée d'enquêter sur les événements survenus en France de 1933 à 1945, Commission d'enquête parlementaire. Paris: Presses Universitaires de France, 1947.

Service historique de l'armée de l'air (SHAA), Vincennes. Files of Conseil supérieur de la défense nationale, Conseil supérieur de l'air.

Service historique de l'armée de terre (SHAT), Vincennes. Files of Conseil supérieur de la guerre, Conseil supérieur de la défense nationale, Etat-major de l'armée.

Setear, John K., Carl H. Builder, M. D. Baccus, and Wayne Madewell. *The Army in a Changing World: The Role of Organizational Visions.* Santa Monica, Calif.: Rand Corporation, R-3882-A, 1990.

Setzen, Joel A. "The Doctrine of the Offensive in the French Army on the Eve of World War I." Ph.D. diss., University of Chicago, 1972.

Shay, Robert Paul, Jr. *British Rearmament in the Thirties: Politics and Profits.* Princeton, N.J.: Princeton University Press, 1977.

Sheppard, Eric William. *A Short History of the British Army.* London: Constable, 1950.

Sherbrooke-Walker, Colonel Ronald. *Khaki and Blue.* London: Saint Catherine, 1952.

Sherman, Serge William. "Le corps des officiers français sous la deuxième République et le second Empire." Ph.D. diss., University of Paris, 4, 1976.

Shirer, William L. *The Collapse of the Third Republic: An Inquiry in the Fall of France, 1940.* New York: Simon and Schuster, 1969.

Silverman, Peter. "The Ten Year Rule." *Journal of the Royal United Service Institution* 116, no. 661 (1971).

Simpkin, Richard E. *Race to the Swift: Thoughts on Twenty-first Century Warfare.* London: Brassey's Defence, 1985.

Singh, Gurdial. "Let Us Reorganize Our Logistical Services." *Journal of the United Service Institution of India* 111, no. 463 (1981).

Skowronek, Stephen. *Building a New American State: The Expansion of National Administrative Capacities, 1877–1920*. Cambridge, Eng.: Cambridge University Press, 1982.

Slessor, Sir John. *The Central Blue*. London: Cassell, 1956.

Smith, Malcolm. *British Air Strategy between the Wars*. Oxford: Clarendon, 1984.

———. "The RAF and Counter-force Strategy before World War II." *Journal of the Royal United Service Institute for Defence Studies*, June 1976.

———. "The Royal Air Force, Air Power, and British Foreign Policy." *Journal of Contemporary History*, vol. 12, no. 1 (1977).

Smith, Perry M. "The Role of Doctrine." In *American Defense Policy*, edited by John Endicott and Roy Stafford, Jr. 4th ed. Baltimore, Md.: Johns Hopkins University Press, 1977.

Snyder, Jack. *The Ideology of the Offensive: Military Decision Making and the Disasters of 1914*. Ithaca, N.Y.: Cornell University Press, 1984.

———. *Myths of Empire: Domestic Politics and International Ambition*. Ithaca, N.Y.: Cornell University Press, 1991.

———. "The Origins of Offense and the Consequences of Counterforce." *International Security* 11, no. 3 (1986–87).

Solomon, Charlene Marmer. "Transplanting Corporate Cultures Globally." *Personnel Journal*, October 1993.

Sorb, Captain [Charles Cormier]. *La doctrine de défense nationale*. Paris: Librairie Militaire Berger-Levrault, 1912.

Souchon, Captain Lucien. *Feue l'armée française*. Paris: Fayard, 1929.

Spiers, Edward M. *The Army and Society, 1815–1914*. London: Longman, 1980.

Stanhope, Henry. *The Soldiers: An Anatomy of the British Army*. London: Hamish Hamilton, 1979.

Starbuck, William, Arent Greve, and Bo L. T. Heberg. "Responding to Crisis." *Journal of Business Administration* 9, no. 2 (1978).

Staw, Barry M., Lance E. Sandelands, and Jane E. Dutton. "Threat-Rigidity Effects in Organizational Behavior: A Multilevel Analysis." *Administrative Science Quarterly* 26, no. 4 (1981).

Steiner, Zara. "Review of Gustav Schmidt, *The Politics and Economics of Appeasement: British Foreign Policy in the 1930s*." *American Historical Review* 93, no. 5 (1988).

Stepan, Alfred. *The Military in Politics: Changing Patterns in Brazil*. Princeton, N.J.: Princeton University Press, 1971.

Stewart, Nora Kinzer. *Mates and Muchachos: Unit Cohesion in the Falklands/Malvinas War*. Washington, D.C.: Brassey's, 1991.

Stinchcombe, Arthur L. *Constructing Social Theories*. New York: Harcourt, Brace, 1968.

———. "Social Structure and Organizations." In *Handbook of Organizations*, edited by James G. March. Chicago, Ill.: Rand McNally, 1965.

Stockton, Paul N. "Organizations and Military Doctrine: U.S. Institutional

Adaptation to the Rise and Fall of the Soviet Threat." Paper presented at the Annual Meeting of the American Political Science Association, Chicago, Ill., September 1995.

Stolfi, Russell H. S. "Equipment for Victory in France in 1940." *History* 55, no. 183 (1970).

Strachan, Hew. "The British Way in Warfare." In *The Oxford Illustrated History of the British Army*, edited by David Chandler. Oxford, Eng.: Oxford Univ. Press, 1994.

Swidler, Ann. "Culture in Action: Symbols and Strategies." *American Sociological Review* 51 (April 1986).

Tagiuri, Renato, and George H. Litwin, *Organizational Climate: Explorations of a Concept*. Cambridge, Mass.: Harvard University Press, 1968.

Tanenbaum, Jan Karl. "French Estimates of Germany's Operational War Plans." In *Knowing One's Enemies: Intelligence Assessment before the Two World Wars*, edited by Ernest R. May. Princeton, N.J.: Princeton University Press, 1986.

"The Tank Corps." *Cavalry Journal*, July 1922.

Targe, General Antoine. *La garde de nos frontières: constitution et organisation des forces de couverture*. Paris: Charles Lavauzelle, 1930.

Taylor, A.J.P. *English History, 1914–1945*. New York: Oxford University Press, 1965.

Temperley, H.W.V. *The Settlement with Germany*. Vol. 2, *A History of the Peace Conference of Paris*. London: Oxford University Press, 1920.

Teyssier, Arnaud. "L'appui aux forces de surface: l'armée de l'air à la recherche d'une doctrine, 1933–1939." In *Histoire de la guerre aérienne*. Vincennes: Service historique de l'armée de l'air, 1987.

Tint, Herbert. *The Decline of French Patriotism*. London: Weidenfeld and Nicolson, 1964.

Tournoux, General Paul-Emile. *Haut commandement, gouvernement et défense des frontières du nord et de l'est, 1919–1939*. Paris: Nouvelles éditions latines, 1960.

———. "Les origines de la ligne Maginot." *Revue d'histoire de la deuxième guerre mondiale* 33 (January 1959).

Trachtenberg, Marc. "The Meaning of Mobilization." *International Security* 15, no. 3 (1990/91).

Travers, Tim. *The Killing Ground: the British Army, the Western Front, and the Emergence of Modern Warfare, 1900–1918*. London: Allen and Unwin, 1987.

———. "The Offensive and the Problem of Innovation in British Military Thought, 1870–1915." *Journal of Contemporary History* 13, no. 3 (1978).

Trice, Harrison M., and Janice M. Beyer. "Studying Organizational Cultures through Rites and Ceremonials." *Academy of Management Review* 9, no. 4 (1984).

Truelle, General Jean. "La production aéronautique militaire française jusqu'en juin 1940." *Revue d'histoire de la deuxième guerre mondiale* 19, no. 73 (1969).

Turner, Barry A. "The Organizational and Interorganizational Development of Disasters." *Administrative Science Quarterly* 21, no. 3 (1976).

Turner, Major C. C. "British and Foreign Air Exercises of 1931." *Journal of the Royal United Service Institution* 76, no. 504 (1931).

Turner, Ernst Sackville. *Gallant Gentlemen: A Portrait of the British Officer, 1600–1956*. London: Michael Joseph, 1956.

Turner, Jonathan H., and Alexandra Maryanski. *Functionalism*. Menlo Park, Calif.: Benjamin-Cummings, 1979.

Upham, Frank K. *Law and Social Change in Post-War Japan*. Cambridge, Mass.: Harvard University Press, 1987.

Vagts, Alfred. *A History of Militarism: Civilian and Military*. London: Hallis and Carter, 1959.

Vaisse, Maurice. "Les militaires français et l'alliance franco-soviétique au cours des années 1930." In *Forces armées et systèmes d'alliances*. Montpellier: Fondation pour les études de défense nationale, 1981.

———. "Le pacifisme français dans les années trente." *Relations internationales* 53 (spring 1988).

———. *Sécurité d'abord: la politique française en matière de désarmement*. Paris: Pédone, 1981.

van Creveld, Martin. *Fighting Power: German and U.S. Army Performance, 1939–1945*. Westport, Conn.: Greenwood, 1982.

van Doorn, Jacques. "The Officer Corps: A Fusion of Profession and Organization." *Archives européennes de sociologie* 6, no. 2 (1965).

Van Evera, Stephen. "Causes of War." Ph.D. diss., University of California, Berkeley, 1984.

———. "The Cult of the Offensive and the Origins of the First World War." *International Security* 9, no. 1 (1984).

Vennesson, Pascal. "La fabrication de l'armée de l'air en France: innovation institutionnelle et compromis socio-technique." *Genèses* 15 (March 1994).

———. *L'institutionalisation de l'armée de l'air en France, 1890–1934*. Paris: Presses de la fondation nationale des sciences politiques, 1996.

Vial, General Robert. "La défense nationale: son organisation entre les deux guerres." *Revue d'histoire de la deuxième guerre mondiale* 18 (April 1955).

———. "Les doctrines militaires françaises et allemandes au lendemain de la première guerre mondiale." In *L'influence de l'école supérieure de guerre sur la pensée militaire française de 1876 à nos jours*. Paris: Ecole militaire, 1976.

Vidéo [pseud.], *L'armée et la politique*. Paris: Librairie d'action française, 1937.

Vigny, Alfred de. *Servitude et grandeur militaire*. Paris: Livres de Poche, 1988.

Vlahos, Michael E. "Military Reform in Historical Perspective." *Orbis* 27, no. 2 (1983).

Waltz, Kenneth N. *Theory of International Politics*. Reading, Mass.: Addison-Wesley, 1979.

War Office. *Cavalry Training*. Vol. 1, *Training*. London: His Majesty's Stationery Office, 1924.

———. *Cavalry Training, Mechanized*, Pamphlet No. 1, *Armoured Cars*. London: His Majesty's Stationery Office, 1937.

———. *Field Service Regulations*. Vol. 2, *Operations*. London: His Majesty's Stationery Office, 1920.

War Office. *Field Service Regulations, Provisional.* Vol. 2, *Operations.* London: His Majesty's Stationery Office, 1920.

——. *Infantry Training.* Vol. 1, *Training.* London: His Majesty's Stationery Office, 1926.

——. *Infantry Training.* Vol. 2, *War.* London: His Majesty's Stationery Office, 1926.

——. *Infantry Training: Training and War.* London: His Majesty's Stationery Office, 1937.

——. *Mobile Division, Training Pamphlet No. l: Notes on the Tactical Employment of a Cavalry Light Tank Regiment.* Unpublished, 1938.

——. *Operations: Military Training Pamphlet No. 23: Part I—General Principles, Fighting Troops and Their Characteristics.* London: His Majesty's Stationery Office, 1939.

——. *Report on War Office Exercises No. 2.* London: His Majesty's Stationery Office, 1927.

——. *Training Manual, Royal Flying Corps, Provisional.* Part 1. London: His Majesty's Stationery Office, 1914.

Wark, Wesley K. *The Ultimate Enemy: British Intelligence and Nazi Germany, 1933–1939.* London: Oxford University Press, 1986.

Watson, Thomas J., Jr. *A Business and Its Beliefs: The Ideas That Helped Build IBM.* New York: McGraw-Hill, 1963.

Watson-Watt, Sir Robert. *Three Steps to Victory.* London: Odhams, 1957.

Watt, Donald Cameron. "British Intelligence and the Coming of the Second World War in Europe." In *Knowing One's Enemies: Intelligence Assessment Before the Two World Wars,* edited by Ernest R. May. Princeton, N.J.: Princeton University Press, 1986.

——. *Too Serious a Business: European Armed Forces and the Approach to the Second World War.* Berkeley: University of California Press, 1975.

Watteville, Lieutenant Colonel H. G. de. "A Hundred Years of the British Army: Personnel and Administration." *Journal of the Royal United Service Institution* 76, no. 502 (1931).

Wavell, Brigadier Archibald Percival. "The Training of the Army for War." *Journal of the Royal United Service Institution* 78, no. 510 (1933).

Wavell, Major General Archibald Percival. "The Higher Commander." *Journal of the Royal United Service Institution* 81, no. 521 (1936).

Weber, Eugen. *Action Française: Royalism and Reaction in Twentieth-Century France.* Stanford, Calif.: Stanford University Press, 1962.

Weigold, Marilyn E. "National Security versus Collective Security: The Role of the 'Couverture' in Shaping French Military and Foreign Policy, 1905–1934." Ph.D. diss., St. John's University, 1970.

Weinberg, Gerhard L. *The Foreign Policy of Hitler's Germany: Starting World War II, 1937–1939.* Chicago, Ill.: University of Chicago Press, 1980.

Weir, Margaret. "Ideas and Politics: The Acceptance of Keynesianism in Britain and the United States." In *The Political Power of Economic Ideas: Keynesianism across Nations,* edited by Peter A. Hall. Princeton, N.J.: Princeton University Press, 1989.

Wendt, Alexander. "Anarchy Is What States Make of It." *International Organization* 46, no. 2 (1992).

Westmorland, Captain H. C. "The Training of the Army Officer." *Journal of the Royal United Service Institution* 75, no. 499 (1930).

Weygand, General Maxime. *La France est-elle défendue?* Paris, 1937.

———. *Histoire de l'armée française.* Paris: Flammarion, 1938.

———. "L'unité de l'armée." *Revue militaire générale,* January 1937.

Whiteclay, John. *To Raise an Army: The Draft Comes to Modern America.* New York: Free Press, 1987.

Wilkins, Alan L., and William G. Ouchi. "Efficient Cultures: Exploring the Relationship between Culture and Organizational Performance." *Administrative Science Quarterly* 28, no. 3 (1983).

Willcocks, Brigadier M. A. "Air Mobility and the Armoured Experience." In *British Army Operational Level War,* edited by Major General J.J.G. Mackenzie and Brian Holden Reid. London: Tri Service, 1989.

Wilms, Wellford W., Alan J. Hardcastle, and Deone M. Zell. "Cultural Transformation at NUMMI." *Sloan Management Review* 36 (fall 1994).

Winton, Harold R. *To Change an Army: General Sir John Burnett-Stuart and British Armored Doctrine, 1927–1938.* Lawrence: University of Kansas Press, 1988.

Wolfers, Arnold. *Britain and France between Two Wars: Conflicting Strategies of Peace from Versailles to World War II.* New York: Harcourt, Brace, 1940.

Wolsely, General Viscount. "The Army." In *The Reign of Queen Victoria,* vol. 1, edited by Thomas Humphry Ward. London: Smith, Elder, 1887.

Wood, Derek, and Derek Dempster. *The Narrow Margin: The Battle of Britain and the Rise of Air Power, 1930–1940.* London: Arrow Books, 1961.

Wright, Robert. *Dowding and the Battle of Britain.* London: Macdonald, 1969.

Wykeham, Peter. *Fighter Command: A Study of Air Defence, 1914–1960.* London: Putnam, 1960.

Young, Robert J. "L'attaque brusquée and Its Use as Myth in Interwar France." *Historical Reflections* 8, no. 1 (1981).

———. "French Military Intelligence and Nazi Germany, 1938–1939." In *Knowing One's Enemies: Intelligence Assessment before the Two World Wars,* edited by Ernest R. May. Princeton, N.J.: Princeton University Press, 1986.

———. "Le haut commandement français au moment de Munich." *Revue d'histoire moderne et contemporaine* 24 (January–March 1977).

Zimbardo, Philip, and Ebbe B. Ebbesen. *Influencing Attitudes and Changing Behavior.* Reading, Mass.: Addison-Wesley, 1970.

Zisk, Kimberly Marten. *Engaging the Enemy: Organization Theory and Soviet Military Innovations, 1955–1991.* Princeton, N.J.: Princeton University Press, 1993.

Index

About the Author

Elizabeth Kier is Assistant Professor of Political Science at the
University of California, Berkeley.

PRINCETON STUDIES IN INTERNATIONAL

HISTORY AND POLITICS

Series Editors
Jack L. Snyder and Richard H. Ullman

———————————

History and Strategy by Marc Trachtenberg (1991)

George F. Kennan and the Making of American Foreign Policy, 1947–1950
by Wilson D. Miscamble, C.S.C (1992)

*Economic Discrimination and Political Exchange: World Political Economy in
the 1930s and 1980s* by Kenneth A. Oye (1992)

Whirlpool: U.S. Foreign Policy Toward Latin America and the Caribbean
by Robert A. Pastor (1992)

Germany Divided: From the Wall to Reunification by A. James McAdams (1993)

A Certain Idea of France: French Security Policy and the Gaulist Legacy
by Philip H. Gordon (1993)

The Limits of Safety: Organizations, Accidents, and Nuclear Weapons
by Scott D. Sagan (1993)

*Mercenaries, Pirates, and Sovereigns: State-Building and Extraterritorial Violence
in Early Modern Europe* by Janice E. Thomson (1994)

We All Lost the Cold War by Richard Ned Lebow and Janice Gross Stein (1994)

*Who Adjusts? Domestic Sources of Foreign Economic Policy during the
Interwar Years* by Beth A. Simmons (1994)

*America's Mission: The United States and the Worldwide Struggle for Democracy
in the Twentieth Century* by Tony Smith (1994)

The Sovereign State and Its Competitors: An Analysis of Systems Change
by Hendrik Spruyt (1994)

*Cooperation among Democracies: The European Influence on U.S. Foreign
Policy* by Thomas Risse-Kappen (1995)

The Korean War: An International History by William Stueck (1995)

Cultural Realism: Strategic Culture and Grand Strategy in Chinese History
by Alastair Iain Johnston (1995)

Does Conquest Pay? The Exploitation of Occupied Industrial Societies
by Peter Liberman (1996)